The Republican War on America:
Dangers of Trump and Trumpism

THE BOOK

Donald J. Trump and his followers are bad for America. They want Trump to occupy the White House again and to preside as autocrat, ignoring any laws or traditions that constrain his whims and wishes. They do not recognize the outcome of the 2020 election or, indeed, any election that goes against Trump. To create his one-man rule, they resort to mob rule.

How is this a war on America? Trump and Trumpism attack trust in democracy and its institutions. Having investigated the January 6 attack on the Capitol, Mississippi representative Bennie Thompson concluded that Trump was at the center of a "sprawling, multi-step conspiracy to subvert American democracy." Trumpists include not only the armed militias who tried to stop Joe Biden's election. They include the many Republican politicians who continue to deny the legitimacy of the 2020 presidential election.

What happened to the "Grand Old Party?" The GOP has become the instrument of a war by Donald Trump and Trumpists against America—against its institutions and highest values. The Republican virus as well as the coronavirus has weakened America's body politic. The disease is due not only to the former president but also to Republican politicians who have wrapped themselves inside his cloak of racism, religiosity, and the Big Lie.

As president, "the Donald" created a kakistocracy—rule by the incompetent, the morally depraved, and grifters determined to profit by pillaging the common good. If they get their way, our flawed democracy could become an autocracy—the absolute rule of one wicked individual and his entourage of blind believers and true cynics.

The United States has improved since Trump exited the White House, but Trumpism and the Republican virus continue to threaten America. The virus has undermined the nation's health, education, economy, and justice system, as well as America's place in the world. Other nations may fear the United States, but many have ceased to admire the land once symbolized by the Statue of Liberty with its welcome to the "huddled masses yearning to breathe free.".

The violence on January 6 was not an outlier. A parade of Republicans in October 2022 thought it funny that an unhinged, hammer-wielding right-wing fanatic put Nancy Pelosi's husband into the intensive care unit of a San Francisco hospital. As Tom Nichols observed in *The Atlantic,* their response showed that GOP had completed its transition from a political party to a brutal mob for whom "cruelty is the point."

This book explains what has gone wrong, and what needs to be done to reboot America. Transforming a way of life based on "me-first" to a quest for mutual gain is a job for every individual and institution. Americans need to replace leaders who think only of themselves with others who are both farsighted and compassionate- -problem-solvers who look and plan ahead, girded with knowledge and mindful of global realities

WHAT EXPERTS SAY ABOUT THIS BOOK

"Walter Clemens has produced a devastating indictment of Republican politics alongside an appeal for a human-centered 'reboot' of American society, economy, and values."

~ **Mel Gurtov, Professor Emeritus of Political Science, Portland State University and Senior Editor,** *Asian Perspective*

"Walter Clemens presents a vivid and clearly written analysis of America's current state of affairs and suggests both innovative and commonsense approaches to 'rebooting' the nation. This is not just another journalistic Jeremiad but a well-researched and thoughtful analysis of social inequities, declining public health, a twisted justice system, and the political virus shaped by the Republican Party's embrace of a psychopathic president. This is the sort of analysis that Americans need to ingest before going to the polls." ~ **Christopher Miller, Professor of History, University of Texas, Rio Grande Valley and Co-editor,** *NETSOL*

"You may think you know all about Trump's presidency and the impact it has had on the U.S. and the world. Yet this powerful book will show you that the devastation is worse, considerably worse. Combing his analytical skills with deep understanding of history, Clemens

has mapped out the present catastrophe but also outlined a solution. I can't recommend it highly enough."

~ Igor Lukes, University Professor, Pardee School of Global Studies, Boston University

"Clemens provides an encyclopedic review of the damage inflicted on American democratic processes, institutions, and values by Donald Trump, his enablers, and those bent on using our government to empower and enrich themselves. At the same time, a call to undertake the daunting task of taking action to fulfill our promises to all of ourselves." **~ Ronald H. Linden, Professor Emeritus of Political Science, University of Pittsburgh**

KIRKUS REVIEW

As a professor emeritus at Boston University and an associate at Harvard's Davis Center for Russian and Eurasian Studies, much of Clemens' prodigious scholarship has focused on complexity theory and international relations. In this book, he offers an impassioned and personal case against Trump not just as an academic, but also as an ex-Republican. Clemens argues that "what was the Grand Old Party now ignores many of the principles championed" by GOP luminary Ayn Rand, from an emphasis on personal character to sound government. Clemens implores both conservatives and progressives to reject the "Trump-Republican virus" that "has sickened America's body politic" and threatens to turn the nation into an autocracy. Refusing to pull his punches, the author devotes an entire chapter, for example, to examining the "parallels" between Hitler and Trump, who follows the "Nazi model" by deploying "colorful language to people who felt left behind," exploiting racism, and skirting the law to solidify power. Yet the administration's political machinations were limited by its ineptitude, as Clemens describes Trump's regime as a "kakistocracy" ruled by the "ignorant, incompetent, and venal." Blending a polemic with a scholarly analysis (and ample footnotes), other chapters look at Trump's ability to unite the alt-right and evangelical Christians behind a rhetoric that blends faith and nationalism, which provides legitimacy to extrem-

ists and an excuse for religious fundamentalists to ignore the president's own salacious history. Both groups are unified through their "hostility to liberal democracy," which celebrates racial, religious, and cultural diversity.

Additional chapters skillfully showcase Trump's hypocrisy of "imposing Law and Order with Storm Troopers" on Black protesters while filling his cabinet with criminal "Dirty Old Men," like Paul Manafort and Roger Stone, who brazenly defy the law. Indeed, the book's most compelling chapters are those that systematically detail case after case of corruption inside Republican administrations since the 1980s. While Trump and the modern GOP are the villains of his narrative, Clemens sees the president as the culmination of a Republican strategy since the late 20th century. Tellingly, Republicans have allowed Trump to supplant traditional conservative ideas, such as family values, fiscal responsibility, and a foreign policy that promotes freedom, with a new "Amoral Code" that justifies criminal behavior and ignores the national debt in favor of a tax system that rewards political donors. This code turned the nation away from alliances with liberal democracies, embracing under Trump authoritarian partners in Saudi Arabia and Russia. The volume concludes with a pragmatic and comprehensive plan to "reboot America" that includes a massive federal investment in science and technology and a host of voter empowerment initiatives. Overall, this is a searing indictment not just of Trump and his cronies, but also of insincere Republican politicians who have for nearly a generation supplanted President Ronald Reagan's idealized "city on a hill" with "a model of venal greed mocked and despised by people of good will." Though some may dismiss Clemens' comparisons between Trump and Hitler as hyperbolic, the author's scholarly bona fides and Republican background lend credibility to a book that is both erudite and accessible.

THE REPUBLICAN WAR ON AMERICA

Dangers of Trump and Trumpism

WALTER C. CLEMENS, JR.

Westphalia Press
An Imprint of the Policy Studies Organization
Washington, DC
2023

THE REPUBLICAN WAR ON AMERICA:
DANGERS OF TRUMP AND TRUMPISM

All Rights Reserved © 2023 by Policy Studies Organization

Westphalia Press
An imprint of Policy Studies Organization
1367 Connecticut Avenue NW
Washington, D.C. 20036
info@ipsonet.org

ISBN: 978-1-63723-612-3

Daniel Gutierrez-Sandoval, Executive Director
PSO and Westphalia Press

Updated material and comments on this edition
can be found at the Westphalia Press website:
www.westphaliapress.org

For

Anna Sophia, Lani, Rose, Julian, Ben, and Julia

CONTENTS

PROLOGUE

The former Grand Old Party now sickens the American body politic at every level. Republican stalwarts such as Liz Cheney and Mitt Romney have reached the same conclusion. Another generation of progressive Republicans may wait in the wings, but today's GOP leaders must retire or be voted out of office. Some—including Donald J. Trump—should be jailed.

"You are the light of the world," Jesus told his followers. "A city on a hill cannot be hidden" (Matthew 5:14). Using similar language, John Winthrop cautioned his fellow Puritans in 1630 that their new community would be "as a city upon a hill, the eyes of all people are upon us." John F. Kennedy, Barack Obama, and other U.S. leaders have called on U.S. citizens of all colors and faiths to contribute to a light-filled city upon a hill. Of course, there would be huge risks. "You are the salt of the earth," Jesus warned, "But if the salt loses its savor, how can it be made salty again? It is no longer good for anything, except to be thrown out and trampled by men." If we do wrong, Winthrop warned those sailing to America, "we shall be made a story and a byword through the world." Such is America's destiny as shaped by Trump and Trumpists.

For more than half a century, most Republican leaders have been bad for the United States. Presidents Richard M. Nixon, Ronald Reagan, and George W. Bush broke U.S. as well as international laws. They set poor models for personal and public morality; undermined the country's health, education, and economic well-being; exploited white hostility toward blacks for their own partisan advantage; and eroded the nation's trust in the legitimacy and efficiency of its political system. The last decent Republican president, George H. W. Bush, avoided most of these abuses,[1] but the presidency of Donald J. Trump pushed them to new extremes. Gone was any ideal of a city on the hill inspiring Americans and people everywhere. In its place, the image of a still powerful juggernaut led by a self-centered bully

---

1 Even he sold his integrity, if not his soul, by speaking at Unification Church ("Moonie") events in Argentina, Uruguay, and Japan for millions of dollars after his one term as president. See James Ridgeway, "Bush Sr. To Celebrate Rev. Sun Myung Moon—Again," *Mother Jones*, April 29, 2007.

breaking every rule, defying science, and lacking a "decent respect for the opinions of mankind," as demanded by the Declaration of Independence in 1776.

Trump and many Republican Party politicians have become like a virus infecting the body politic.[2] Their MAGA virus ("Make America Great Again") poses a triple threat to America's body politic. The first danger has been from Trump's own whims and actions; the second comes from the Republican Party politicians who have linked their stars to Trump's wagon; the third is from Trump's base—the many voters who, like lemmings, have willingly followed their Pied Piper into the abyss. The former president and most Republican politicians are far wealthier than average Americans, but they keep popular hopes alive that Trump and his party will miraculously make those who feel left out richer, healthier, and happier.

The health of the body politic has declined in recent years. America's electorate is more deeply split than at any time since the years before the Civil War. As president, Trump never obtained a "favorable" rating by more than half the electorate, This was a man so desperate for approval that he lied several times every day—so desperate that his minions destroyed mail boxes to make it harder for Democrats to vote.

Many of those who voted for Trump in 2016 continue to back him—even when his policies hurt them. Most of the Republicans running in the 2022 midterm elections were deniers. They denied that Trump lost the 2020 election to Joe Biden. On the other hand, most of the candidates strongly endorsed by Trump lost in 2022. Instead of a Red Wave, as many observers predicted, there was only a Purple Ripple. Democrats increased their hold on the Senate and almost kept their control of the House. Republicans gained a small majority in the House but were split between Trumpists and others attempting a return to GOP traditions.

The tasks ahead for those seeking to repair the damage caused by Trump Republicans are enormous. Deep and far-reaching,

---

2   A virus is an infective agent that can multiply only within the living cells of a host. In society, it connotes a harmful or corrupting influence. As in the world of computers, the virus of Trump/Republicans is capable of copying itself and corrupting the system and destroying data as well as honesty and hope.

within and beyond U.S. borders, the harm will not be easy to undo. Democrats and traditionalist Republicans must try not only to fix the harm done but rebuild the foundations of a healthier society.

How did things get this way?

OVERVIEW

Chapter 1: Trump, like Hitler, has engaged his supporters with colorful language and promises to raise all those left behind. Like Hitler and other Republicans since Richard Nixon, Trump has played the race card. Trump and the alt-right have exploited each other, leaving many Americans confused and beguiled by conspiracy theories such as Q'Anon.

Chapter 2: Trump poses as a defender of Christian religion—especially its evangelical currents and their political goals. Mike Pompeo and other Trump disciples flaunt their evangelical convictions. Like Hitler, Trump and his affianced news media have mobilized the power of the Big Lie. Trumpists sought a government *of* the upper classes, *for* the upper classes, and *by* the upper classes. To be sure, most of Trump's base is from the lower and middle classes—individuals and groups who hope that Trumpism will benefit them and make America great again.

Chapter 3: Top Republicans have followed Trump in adopting a no-holds-barred approach to ethics. There is no rule they won't break. These practices have forged a Trumpist code of higher immorality.

Chapter 4: Top Republicans celebrated injustice in high places. If people object to police brutality, Trump and his Attorney General sent in federal forces to break up peaceful protests. The president tried and dismissed several top law officers until he landed on William Barr, a former teenage bully who—as AG—twisted every law to justify a president who could do no wrong. Trump and his lieutenants repressed peaceful demonstrations for causes such as "Black Lives Matter." Together Trump and Barr freed from prison allies of the president who were convicted of serious crimes threatening national security. After Joe Biden's election, however, Barr said that stories of voting fraud were "B.S." Having lied for Trump by distorting the Mueller Report, Barr opted to tell the truth.

Chapter 5, The U.S. government under Trump became a kakistocracy—rule by the incompetent and evil--as well as a kleptocracy--rule by thieves. Incompetence and ignorance go along with immorality and injustice. Trump nominated and a Republican Senate approved cabinet officials, many of whom were unqualified to do their jobs. Trump and the GOP crawled through every possible loophole to abort the checks and balances of the Constitution and push the United States toward autocracy. Many indicators show that the United States has become a deeply flawed democracy and could be maneuvered into authoritarian tyranny,

Chapter 6: Trump threw away America's lives, treasure, honor, and friends. U.S. hard power remained, while its soft power—the ability to persuade and coopt—evaporated. Smart power—the ability to use assets wisely—nearly disappeared. America-firsters added to chaos in the world and weakened America's prestige and influence everywhere. Trumpists sabotage efforts to cope with climate change and the dangers posed by Vladimir Putin and Xi Jinping. Trumpists have spurned arms controls at home as well as abroad. The 400 million privately owned weapons in the United States wreak havoc at home and generate disdain and disbelief overseas.

Chapter 7: Did the Trump presidency make life better for most Americans? No, by all measures of human development, the quality of life worsened. Health, education, and material well-being deteriorated. Millions died deaths of despair. Americans came to trust each other less and the government, not at all. The Biden administration made some progress in reversing these trends, but Republicans in Congress and in state governments thwart enlightened policies whenever and however they can.

Chapter 8: Ex-president Trump in 2021 and 2022 continued to assert that he won the 2020 election and called on supporters to "stop the steal." He urged them to invade the Capitol and stop Vice President Pence from approving the Electoral College vote for Joe Biden. The House Committee investigating the January 6, 2021, events found that Trump knowingly violated his constitutional obligations.

Having authorized the FBI to remove boxes of documents from Trump's estate in Florida, the Justice Department began to investigate whether Trump violated the Espionage Act and other laws by taking huge quantities of classified documents to Mar-a-Lago. Continuing to deny the validity if the 2020 election, Trump and Trumpists put the GOP on a track to chaos as they attacked non-Trumpist Republicans as well as Democrats.

Chapter 9: Rebooting America requires effectively coping with complex challenges on many fronts—economic, educational, social, political, and moral. These issues were addressed by five laws enacted in 2021-2022: the Infrastructure Investment and Jobs Act, the Inflation Reduction Act, the CHIPS and Science Act, and the Promise to Address Comprehensive Toxics Act. A legislative compromise tightened background checks for gun buyers under the age of 21.

The American Academy of Arts and Sciences laid out a set of political reforms to bolster democracy, for example, by ending voter suppression and gerrymandering.

To reboot America, the country's political culture must be reoriented from a quest for individual profit to a shared quest for mutual gain.

Traditional conservatives as well as liberals and independents should work to cleanse the country of the Trumpist Republican virus.

Please read on to appreciate what has gone wrong, and how some, if not all, of the country's problems can be addressed. To close, our Shih-Tzu Eddie offers some advice that could benefit not just Trumpists but all politicians.

1

HITLER AND TRUMP: RACE, RELIGION, AND THE BIG LIE

THE AUTHORITARIAN NIGHTMARE

How did these two mediocrities, Adolf Hitler and Donald J. Trump, rise to supreme power in one of the world's most influential countries—each country a leader in science and industry—and push their countrymen in new and basically crazy directions?

The parallels between the rise of Hitler and Trump are striking. Each was a gifted speaker who could enthrall and mobilize crowds. Each spoke in colorful language to people who felt left behind.[1] Each exploited racism, religion, and the Big Lie to win popular support. Each rose lawfully to the pinnacle of a democratic system and then skirted, ignored, or rewrote the laws supposed to limit the nature and scope of government.

Hitler led Germany into wars that proved catastrophic; Trump's actions harmed America in many ways, but they stopped short of disaster thanks to the 2020 election, which Trump denounced as "stolen."

DOMINATORS AND FOLLOWERS

The authoritarian nightmare has been spearheaded by would-be leaders who strive to dominate and are sustained by a social base that is comfortable following charismatic leaders.[2] This framework of dominators and followers simplifies but helps us make sense of a puzzling reality.[3]

---

1   Germany was nominally a democratic republic from 1918 to 1933, its constitution written in the city of Weimar. Benjamin Carter Hett, *Death of Democracy: Hitler's Rise to Power and the Death of the Weimar Republic* (New York: St. Martin's, 2018).

2   Bob Altemeyer and John Dean *Authoritarian Nightmare: The Ongoing Threat of Trump's Followers* (Brooklyn: Melville House, 2020). Altemeyer taught social science in Canada for decades; Dean, an attorney for Richard Nixon, helped expose the former president's wrong-doing.

3   The model does not account for the conservatives attracted to the dictator's

Would-be dominators tend to be pitiless; intimidating and bullying; dishonest, amoral, and manipulative; hungry for personal power and against real equality; prejudiced, racist, and homophobic, vengeful, nationalistic and militant; and—last but not least—ostensibly religious.

Followers of authoritarian dominators, on the other hand, show a high degree of submissiveness to what they see as rightful authority. They tend to be aggressive in the name of their authorities and highly conventional, insisting everyone follow the norms set out by their authorities, such as Trump's advice on how to deal with Covid-19. Social followers are given to compartmentalized thinking and double-standard judgments; they have difficulty evaluating evidence. They tend to be ethnocentric, prejudiced, and dogmatic. They have a deep, life-long tendency to submit and are terrified what will happen if they stop believing what their authorities preach.

Would-be dominators like Hitler and Trump are personally insecure but compensate by aspiring to dominate others and obtain their support. Many followers of people like Hitler and Trump are themselves aspiring dominators but—having failed to reach the top—take pride and pleasure in acting as adjutants to *der Führer*. But the largest fraction of the authoritarian's base are followers—coiled like a tightly wound spring with sufficient energy to drive a dictator through all barriers. In the United States they needed only a demagogue to lead them while they chanted "make America great again" and "lock (Hillary Clinton) up." As it happened, in 2016 Clinton got 48.2 percent of the popular vote and Trump just 46.1 percent. He prevailed in the Electoral College by winning some key states albeit with small margins. Trump won the votes not only of social followers but of independents who disliked him, but disliked Clinton or Blacks even more.

This combination of social dominators and social followers transformed the GOP of Dwight D. Eisenhower, Jacob Javitz, and Nelson Rockefeller into one that—goaded by Barry Goldwater, Newt Gingrich, and the Tea Party—weaponized "cultural" issues to

---

support for traditional values or the non-conservatives who want change—any change.

unify its diverse membership and kow-tow to the mob that stormed the Capitol on January 6, 2021.

The Führer and "The Donald": Similar but Different

Hitler's family, headed by a failed farmer turned Austrian customs official, was not rich, while Trump was born with a silver spoon. Hitler's father kept him in trade schools though the boy wanted to study art and music. Twice rejected by Vienna's Academy of Fine Arts, Hitler sold his not-so-bad paintings on the streets of Vienna. Early on a racist, Hitler despised the multiethnic Austro-Hungarian empire where he grew up. Rejected by the Austrian army for physical reasons, he eventually served in the German army throughout World War I. Twice wounded and still hospitalized, he was infuriated to learn that Germany had surrendered. His anger boiled again when some German leaders felt compelled to sign the Versailles Treaty. Hitler and other right-wingers called this "a stab in the back," because, they said, the German Army was never really defeated.

On the other side of the Atlantic, Donald's father, Fred Trump (1905-1999), became wealthy selling and renting real estate in the New York boroughs of Queens and Brooklyn. The Donald Trump virus of self-centered toughness may have originated with his father, said to have demanded that his sons be strong and aggressive—cheating and lying as needed. Fred and his sickly wife Mary had three sons and two daughters. All the children wanted their father's approval, but he usually remained aloof. The oldest son, Fred Jr. did not embody his father's expectations and suffered humiliation and shame. Fred Jr.'s daughter, Mary L. Trump (a Ph.D. in clinical psychology) has recorded the family history and how it impacted her father, who died an alcoholic at age 43.[4] The senior Fred Trump

---

4 Mary L. Trump, *Too Much and Never Enough: How My Family Created the World's Most Dangerous Man* (New York: Simon & Schuster, 2020), pp. 51-59, 88. In college, Fred Jr. joined an historically Jewish fraternity, a possible rebuke of his father, who used to complain someone tried to "Jew me down." When Fred Jr. told his father that he was leaving Trump Management to become a commercial pilot, Fred saw it as a betrayal and never let his son forget it. At age 25, however, Fred Jr. became a pilot flying Boeing 707 planes for TWA. Youngest son Robert attended Boston University and later created a business that as we shall see later, got preferential treatment from President Trump. He was

ignored his two daughters and youngest son, Robert, but came to see Donald, his second son, as his successor. Donald chose "to ingratiate himself with their father by smashing through every barrier his older brother never dared test .... He took what he wanted without asking permission ..." The combative rigid persona Donald developed to shield himself from the terror of his early abandonment "cut him off from real human connection."

A bully in school and often in trouble, Donald lacked discipline and so was sent off to the New York Military Academy at age thirteen—a sort of exile. However, Donald's father recognized that Donald felt abandoned at the academy and drove sixty miles to visit his son most weekends for four years.

Mary Trump writes that the senior Fred Trump was a narcissist with, quite possibly, an "antisocial personality disorder." Fred kept his son Donald from feeling or expressing tenderness. "By limiting Donald's access to his own feelings and rendering many of them unacceptable, Fred perverted his son's perception of the world and damaged his ability to live in it."[5]

Fred could see that Donald was too impetuous and flighty to be competent as a businessman, but he believed he could leverage Donald's skills "as a savant of self-promotion, shameless liar, marketeer, and builder of brands" to achieve the level of fame that matched his own ego. By the late 1980s, when Donald's businesses turned south, the father had no choice but to stay invested. His monster had been set free. All Fred could do was to "mitigate the damage, keep the cash flowing, and find somebody else to blame."[6]

Mary Trump believes the United States "is now suffering from

---

also an officer in the Trump Organization. At age 71 Robert died in 2020 and was honored with a funeral service at the White House. Afterwards, according to the *New York Post* (August 22, 2020), one of Robert's mourners struck a restaurant employee who said the eatery could not accommodate his large group because of coronavirus restrictions.

5   What has been the role of fathers? Obama's father retreated to Kenya and died in a car crash. Bill Clinton's died in an auto accident before he was born. Ronald Reagan at age 11 found his father drunk in the snow and pulled him inside. See Karen Tumulty, "The Trump father-son psychodrama," *The Washington Post*, July 7, 2020.

6   Mary Trump, *Too Much*, p. 103.

the same toxic positivity that [her] grandfather deployed specifically to drown out his ailing wife, torment his dying son, and damage past healing the psyche of his favorite child, Donald J. Trump."[7] The inability of the "court jester from Queens," as Mary calls Donald, to succeed without being heavily subsidized by his father created a tension where he knew he was inadequate but could never admit it. "At a very deep level," Mary writes, "his bragging and false bravado are not directed at the audience in front of him but at his audience of one: his long-dead father."[8]

The opinions of Donald's sister, Maryanne Trump Barry, are equally sharp. "All he wants to do is appeal to his base. He has no principles. None. And his base ... if you were a religious person, you want to help people. Not do this." She was aghast as his tweets, lying, and lack of preparation.[9]

Unlike Hitler, Trump was exposed to an elite education, but academic learning was not his forte, His sister Maryanne often did his homework.[10] Maryanne recalled that she drove him around New York looking for a college. He got into Fordham University and stayed for two years. Maryanne recalled that Donald hired a substitute to pass the SAT in his name and so cheated his way into the Wharton School at the University of Pennsylvania, helped by brother Fred Jr. who intervened with a friend on the school's admissions board. Trump got into Wharton and graduated with a B.S. in economics in 1968.[11] Trump and his lawyers have kept these schools from releasing his transcripts.

Unlike Hitler, Trump eschewed military duty. Trump got four

---

7   Ibid., p. 211.

8   Ibid., p. 202.

9   Michael Kramish, "In secretly recorded audio, President Trump's sister says he has 'no principles' and 'you can't trust him,'" *The Washington Post*, August 22, 2020, with excerpts from the audio.

10 The academic in the family, Maryanne Trump Barry, became a lawyer and an appellate judge. Her recollections, as recorded by her niece Mary L. Trump, helped to substantiate *Too Much*. Maryanne grants that Donald helped her become a judge by having his lawyer Roy Cohn recommend her to President Reagan. Donald often reminded Maryanne of this help. But she believed she merited the job and was later elevated to higher judgeships on her own.

11 Mary Trump, *Too Much,* p. 72.

student deferments in college. After graduation, his father engaged a podiatrist to find that Donald had a bone spur so troublesome that it warranted exemption from the draft.[12] Trump's fixer lawyer Michael Cohen on February 26, 2019, testified to the Senate Intelligence Committee that the president acknowledged to advisers that he made up a fake injury to avoid military service, because "I wasn't going to Vietnam."[13]

The Donald is said to have regarded the Marines who died at Belleau Wood in 1918 as "losers"; ditto George W. H. Bush, shot down by Japanese guns over the Pacific; ditto John McCain, captured and imprisoned for five years by North Vietnamese; ditto the Americans killed in the Middle East. Visiting Arlington National Cemetery, Trump asked Homeland Security John Kelly, whose 29-year-old son, once an Army captain, lies there, "What was in it for them?" Besides disparaging the intelligence of service members, Trump has tried to keep wounded veterans out of military parades. A retired four-star general commented that Trump "just thinks that anyone who does anything when there's no direct personal gain ... is a sucker. There's no money in serving the nation." A friend of Kelly said that "Trump can't imagine anyone else's pain."[14] Since Trump's grandfather was banished from Bavaria for avoiding military service, by Donald's logic, he was no "sucker."[15]

In public, Hitler kept his distance from any kind of sex, while Trump plunged right in, boasting in public of his lascivious ways. As Stephen Greenblatt describes Macbeth, so Trump also seems to have been driven by "sexual anxieties: a compulsive need to

---

12 The podiatrist who provided the diagnosis did so as a favor to Donald's father, who was his landlord in Queens, according to two daughters of the doctor (*The New York Times*, December 26, 2018, which also carries a photo of Trump looking very athletic sitting with his military academy basketball team.).

13 https://www.militarytimes.com/news/pentagon-congress/2019/02/27/tru mps-lawyer-no-basis-for-presidents-medical-deferment-from-vietnam/ (accessed 3/15/19).

14 Jeffrey Goldberg, "Trump: Americans Who Died In War Are 'Losers' and 'Suckers,'" *The Atlantic*, September 3, 2020.

15 Bavarian authorities accused Donald's grandfather, Friedrich, of having moved to the United States (at age 16) to avoid conscription, only later to return. A royal decree ordered Friedrich to leave Bavaria and never return. So he and his family moved back to the United States, where he was naturalized in 1892.

prove his manhood, dread of impotence, a nagging apprehension that he will not be found sufficiently attractive or powerful, a fear of failure. Hence the penchant for bullying, the vicious misogyny, and the explosive violence. Hence, too, the vulnerability to taunts. Especially those bearing a latent or explicit sexual charge." Maureen Dowd suggests that "Trump's fear of emasculation led to his de-mask-ulation . . . Like Macbeth, the president made tragic errors of judgment and plunged his country into a nightmare."[16]

Both Hitler and Trump could mesmerize crowds. The insightful American journalist Dorothy Thompson interviewed Hitler in the early 1930s and described him as an "agitator of genius ... the most golden tongued of demagogues." She advised her readers: "Don't bother about the fact that what he says, read the next day in cold newsprint, is usually plain nonsense." To understand what was happening, 'You must imagine the crowds he addresses: Little people. Weighted with a feeling of inferiority." Hitler himself, she wrote, is "inconsequent and voluble, ill poised and insecure"—the "very prototype of the little man."[17] In 1934, Thompson became the first American journalist expelled from Hitler's Germany.

Hitler blamed the Jews as well as the Treaty of Versailles for Germany's ills. Hitler's appeals to racial pride became a form of self-exaltation. If one was burdened with debt, if one had not made a success in life, there was still the consolation that one belonged to the Master Race. Across Europe in the 1920s and 1930s, people "searched for a leader, a savior, a dictator to rescue them from their economic and political woes. Hitler believed he was that man." The aspiring Führer proved himself "a chameleon able to articulate the unspoken emotional language of his listeners."[18]

Wealthy industrialists secretly financed Hitler's rise to power after 1924. For unemployed workers, he promised full employment; for the neglected German, he pledged respect. Hitler

---

16 "Double, Double, Trump's Toil, Our Trouble," *The New York Times*, August 2, 2020.

17 Dorothy Thompson, *I Saw Hitler* (New York: Farrar and Rinehart, 1932) and *"Goodbye to Germany," Harper's Magazine (December 1934)*. In 1939, *Time Magazine* ranked Thompson as equal in influence to Eleanor Roosevelt.

18 James M. Longo, *Hitler and the Habsburgs: The Führer's Vendetta Against the Austrian Royals* (Diversion Books, 2018).

won financial support and many followers, but he craved legitimacy and political power to make his vision a reality. In public, Hitler met with enthusiastic crowds. Behind closed doors, he beguiled wealthy monarchists. One-third of German's ancient nobility joined his Nazi Party, while many others supported him through their silence. As noted in the next chapter, there was a current of despair in German culture that provide a welcoming context for Nazism.

Though he disliked heights, Hitler entertained Nazi leaders at his Eagle's Nest chalet overlooking the town of Berchtesgaden. Trump often retreated to his Mar-a-Lago resort in Palm Beach (bringing family and a huge security detail at taxpayer expense), where he golfed and hosted not only donors and government officials but foreign dignitaries such as Xi Jinping.

Germany in the 1930s was a far more troubled country than the United States when Trump entered politics. Still, economic and political troubles clouded the judgment of many Americans in the early 21st century, as they did many Germans in the 1920s and 1930s. Trump did not lay out his plans in a book like *Mein Kampf,* but his *Art of the Deal*, written largely by Tony Schwartz, bragged of his business skills and revealed his self-centered transactionalism. Trump explained: "I play it very loose. I don't carry a briefcase. I try not to schedule too many meetings. I leave my door open .... I prefer to come to work each day and just see what develops."[19]

Hitler bragged that he was the greatest German of all time; Trump, more modestly, claimed only to be one of the greatest U.S. presidents. At least five times, however, Trump claimed that he is "a very stable genius." Like Hitler, Trump was deeply insecure and appealed to the "little man." But he was physically large and full of braggadocio. Like Hitler, Trump also craved symbols of legitimacy. As president, he worked to destroy any sign that he was not duly and freely elected. This anxiety showed in his efforts to challenge intelligence reports that Russians helped his 2016 election and to uncover evidence that it was Ukraine—not Russia—that influenced the 2016 elections, and his claims that his inauguration crowd filled the mall when photos showed it was quite modest.

---

19 *Art of the Deal* (New York: Random House, 1987).

Michael Cohen, close to Trump for many years, gave this appraisal: "I bore witness to the real man, in strip clubs, shady business meetings, and in the unguarded moments when he revealed who he really was, a cheat, a liar, a fraud, a bully, a racist, a predator, a con man."[20]

The Base: Race, Religion, and the Big Lie

How could the same country that leads the world in science and technology and twice elected a black man president opt to make Donald Trump its president? How did someone with a racist, anti-intellectual, anti-science orientation win the White House in 2016? How could roughly four in ten voters vote for him and then applaud his tweets and policy choices?

Reading a draft of this book, Connecticut social psychologist Stephen Advocate sent me an e-mail on May 25, 2020. "You need to shift your focus from Trump as eyeball-magnet to the 'you-couldn't-make-this-up' phenomenon of his yahoo power base. Let your fingers take a trip through Trump Country. What you see will not look pretty. Rallies scarier than Hitler's. And the people! Beyond belief. What is it beneath the hate, stupidity, maliciousness, and thug-level posturing that drives them? How did this richest of lands create such moral and cultural impoverishment? Forty goddamn percent behind the president! It's they who've created Trump—not the other way around. Trump is the clapper to their bell—sleeper cells waiting for the call. Your focus should be on the people who make it all possible."

Stephen continued: "Trump himself is as easy to unpack as any con man with his tricks. His bluster and flagrant self-displays are the smokescreen behind which hides a more disturbing phenomenon: the people who thrive on this man, people who may even *need* a Trump for their psychic survival." If not for Trump, "might there be even more suicides in Trump Country? America has to figure out how the horde of Trump-addicts was produced. Until we understand and thwart the conditions of their manufacture, new

20 Michael Cohen, *Disloyal: A Memoir: The True Story of the Former Personal Attorney to President Donald J. Trump* (2020).

Trumps will come forward to satisfy their deepest needs."

Stephen's portrait of Trump's base may be too broad. No doubt many of Trump's backers do not fit this picture. Some are highly educated and ultra rich with manicured nails. Still, the portrait probably fits many of those who voted for and supported Trump for four years and more.

Peggy Noonan, the primary speechwriter for President Ronald Reagan in 1984-1986, describes the Trump base in ways that recall Dorothy Thompson's picture of the "little men" enraptured by Hitler. Trump ascended politically thanks to "the growing realization of on-the-ground Americans that neither party seemed to feel any particular affiliation with or loyalty to them." Both parties "considered them lumpen bases to be managed and manipulated." Trump emerged in the social and cultural distance between the national GOP and the party's base. Many GOP movers and shakers believed that to keep their jobs and its benefits all they had to do was talk—not legislate. Legislating involves compromise and, "compromise is for quislings."

Noonan wrote that Trump rode to power on "a spirit of frustration among a sizable segment of the electorate--something like a spirit of nihilism." Here, in this perfect storm, was Mr. Trump's simple genius. "He declared for president as a branding exercise and went out and said applause lines, and when the crowd cheered, he decided 'This is my program,' and when it didn't cheer, he thought, 'Huh, that is not my program.'" They cheered, but they were not for "cutting entitlement benefits. They were still suffering from the effects of 2008 and other things. They weren't for open borders or for more foreign fighting. They were for the guy who said he hated the elites as much as they did."[21]

Many of the people Noonan portrays have been the white men without college degrees who are dying of despair. After four years of Trump's policies, however, most are no better off than when they voted him president.

---

21 Peggy Noonan, "Burn the Republican Party Down?" *The Wall Street Journal,* July 30, 2020.

But Trump's base is not just down-trodden whites, whose condition could leave them listless. His base includes an "alt-right" congeries of racists, gun lovers, anarchists, and religious fanatics intolerant of others' outlooks.

Trump, like Hitler, used populist language to justify the authoritarian values driving his kind of government.[22] Earlier populists emphasized sharing of power and wealth among the people--Chartists in Victorian England, the People's Party that nominated William Jennings Bryan for president in 1896, Huey Long's "Share the Wealth" movement in the mid-1930s.

Unlike these movements, Trump's message was a meatless abstraction: "Leave it to me and your lives will get better." Like Senator Joe McCarthy's claim that Communists infected the U.S, State Department, Trump's rhetoric appealed to the emotions of worried citizens but lacked a foundation in facts.

Race and Racism

Trump became president by exploiting the race card—the Republican Party's basic sin since the time of Richard N, Nixon. Instead of calling blacks "Niggers," the party for more than 50 years has employed code words such as "invading the suburbs" to show that it aligns with champions of white power. This is the considered verdict of a political strategist who helped three Republicans campaign for the White House. [23]

Race is the visible agent of caste. "Caste is the bones, race the skin," writes Isabella Wilkerson. A caste system is an artificial "ranking of human value that sets the presumed supremacy of one group against the presumed inferiority of other groups on the basis of ancestry." A caste ranking determines respect, authority, and assumptions of competence. Nazi Germany and the United States,

---

22 Pippa Norris and   Ronald Inglehart, *Cultural Backlash: Trump, Brexit, and Authoritarian Populism* (Cambridge, UK: Cambridge University Press, 2019).

23 Stuart Stevens, *It Was All a Lie: How the Republican Party Became Donald Trump* (New York: A. A. Knopf, 2020). Satirist Andy Borowitz reported in *The New Yorker*, October 22, 2012, that New Hampshire Governor John Sununu worried that the Republican Party's emphasis on misogyny was threatening to drown out its "winning message of racism."

like India, have "relied on stigmatizing those deemed inferior to justify the dehumanization necessary to keep the lowest-ranked people at the bottom and to rationalize the protocols of enforcement."[24] Hitler was explicit that Germans are a superior race ordained to conquer the earth. His policies led to the extermination of millions of Jews along with many Roma and homosexuals. A Polish lawyer, Rafal Lemkin, who lost many relatives in Nazi death camps, devised the word "genocide"—murder of a particular group of people—and inspired the United Nations in 1948 to create a treaty outlawing genocide.

Trump's political impulses are autocratic and his rhetoric divisive. When demonstrators protested police brutality after the murder of George Floyd in June 2020, the president demanded a tough response: "When the looting starts, the shooting starts." Trump's racism went back decades. In the 1970s, he and his father were fined for racial discrimination in their real estate business. In 1989, he supported the campaign against the Central Park Five and refused to apologize even after they served long prison sentences but were then found innocent.[25] Trump exploited birtherism as a political launchpad ("Isn't Obama a crypto Muslim? Was he really born in the United States?"). Trump raised the same questions in August 2020 about Kamala Harris after Joe Biden selected her to be his running mate.

Trump's way of speaking, according to Columbia University linguistics professor James McWhorter, is "oddly adolescent"—

---

24 Isabel Wilkerson, *Caste: The Origins of Our Discontents* (New York: Random House, 2020).

25 Five teenagers, three blacks and two Latinos, were convicted of raping a white woman in 1989. During their trial Trump spent $85,000 to place full-page ads in *The New York Times, The Daily News, The New York Post,* and *New York Newsday* demanding "Bring Back the Death Penalty. Bring Back the Police." After the five had spent years in prison, a serial rapist confessed to the crime in 2002. The city awarded the men $41 million in 2014, a decade after some of the men sued the city for how it handled the case. When asked about the wrongly convicted defendants in 2019, Trump refused to apologize for invoking the death penalty. "You have people on both sides of that," the president said—a remark that recalled the president's comment about a white nationalist rally in Charlottesville in 2017 when a woman was killed by a driver who crashed his vehicle into counter-protesters. The president observed: "There was blame on both sides."

full of "believe me" and "people don't know," referring to topics most newspaper readers should know.[26] While not up to Ivy League standards, this way of speaking connects with many in Trump's base.

Trump does not openly glorify his own race, but he hints at its superiority and the need to keep down non-whites and expel aliens from the United States. Trump denies he is a racist but gives his followers every reason to despise people of color—from the Obama family to the Latinos walking northward to Muslims seeking refuge from war and ideological fanaticism. Trump was elected by tens of millions of Americans who either endorsed his bigotry or were willing to tolerate it. That base of support has not contracted to any significant degree.[27]

Hostility to the "other" is built into many white Americans—particularly White Anglo-Saxon Protestants—and extends back many centuries. WASPs chose to exterminate Native Americans and enslave Africans.[28] They tried to limit immigration by "Orientals" and Catholics from southern Europe. In the 1850s, some proudly called themselves "Know-Nothings." In the 1930s, Henry Ford, Charles Lindbergh, and the "Radio Priest," Father Charles E. Caughlin, joined in the anti-Semitic and pro-Fascist rhetoric of America Firsters.

Richard M. Nixon developed a "Southern Strategy" to turn

---

26 Interview on "The Eleventh Hour," MSNBC, September 16, 2017.

27 David Remnick, "An American Uprising." *The New Yorker*, May 31, 2020.

28 No longer a threat, Native Americans became mascots—the Cleveland Indians, Boston Braves, Washington Redskins. The Town of Sudbury, Massachusetts, where I live, has a King Philip's Conservation Land—named for a Wampanoag sachem who sought good relations with Puritans but then, when whites kept encroaching, led armed resistance. Assassinated by a "praying" Indian in 1676, Philip's head was mounted on a pike at the entrance to Plymouth, Massachusetts, where it remained for more than two decades. His body was cut into quarters and hung in trees. After his death, his wife and nine-year-old son were captured and sold as slaves in Bermuda. Nonetheless more than thirty sites honor his name in Massachusetts and Rhode Island. For the background, see Jill Lapore, *The Name of War: King Philip's War and the Origins of American Identity* (New York: Alfred A. Knopf, 1998). For Native American perspectives, see Lisa Brooks, *Our Native Kin: A New History of King Philip's* War (New Haven: Yale University Press, 2018).

southern voters away from Democrats to the Republican camp. Ronald Reagan, George H. W. Bush, and George W. Bush exploited elements of this strategy to win the White House. Donald J. Trump continued to back various forms of white power and directed white resentments not just against blacks, but all people of color plus the LGBTQ community, as well as strong women such as Kamala Harris.

Sensing wide resentment of foreign workers, candidate Trump promised he would build a huge wall to keep them out. As president, he tried to divert money from the Defense budget for a wall that most observers thought impractical and harmful. Courts ruled against some of Trump's efforts to ban immigrants, but he managed to prohibit travel from seven Muslim-majority countries. When white supremacists and their opponents gathered in Charlottesville in 2017, the president averred there were good people on each side. Later he questioned the intelligence of basketball star LeBron James and numerous other African American figures; attacked the national anthem protests of black football players; and demanded that four Democratic congresswomen of color "go back" to the "crime infested places" from which they came.

One support for this orientation came from the "alt-right" — the hate-filled, sometimes violent, paranoid, and racist radical right. The alt-right has no *Communist Manifesto* or *Mein Kampf*. It has no hierarchy in which leaders give orders with followers to carry them out. Its members have diverse agendas, but their common demand is for a white ethno-state in North America.[29]

The alt-right exerted only a marginal influence on U.S. politics in the Clinton, Bush, and Obama years, but it played an important role in 2016 and later. Its reach embraced and continues to contain many ultra-conservative sub-groups—"Patriots," Tea Party supporters, Oath Keepers, xenophobes, Klansmen, skinheads, Christian Identity adherents, and neo-Nazis. What glues them together is racism— hatred of all blacks including Barack Obama and anything he represents or champions—coupled with white supremacy as tribal identity. A second unifier is their virulent hostility to any kind of gun

---

29 George Hawley, *Making Sense of the Alt-Right* (New York: Columbia University Press, 2017).

control.[30] As time went on, alt-righters displayed their image with armed militias in public spaces.

Oath Keepers

The Oath Keepers movement was founded in March 2009 by Elmer Stewart Rhodes—Yale Law School graduate, former U.S. Army paratrooper, and former staffer for Republican Texas Congressman Ron Paul. So, Rhodes was not part of a neglected and exploited underclass. In 2009, Barack Obama was just beginning his first term and Donald Trump some of his first political gestures. On April 19, 2009, "Patriots' Day" in Massachusetts, my family watched the parade in Lexington (recalling the first shots in 1775 in the War for Independence). That afternoon we saw Rhodes and his Oath Keepers use the Lexington Green to enlist members and commit them to a ten-point pledge. Several hundred active-duty and retired military, policemen, and firemen swore they would never "disarm" their compatriots. These events took place in "blue state" Massachusetts, ranked third in anti-Semitic acts a few years later.

Rhodes assured his followers that a full-blown dictatorship "cannot happen here if the majority of police and soldiers obey their oaths to defend the Constitution and refuse to enforce the unconstitutional edicts of the 'Leader.'" Oath Keepers claimed just 30,000 members nationwide in 2015, but they have been active in many places where they regarded law and order to be either too weak or too oppressive—Ferguson 2014, Bundy Ranch 2014, Kim Davis in Kentucky 2015, and Parkland 2018. When the Oregon State Senate pressed all Senators to be present and vote on gas emissions, Oath Keepers on June 20, 2019, addressed the governor: "Gov. Brown, you want a civil war, because this is how you get a civil war." On June 22, 2019, a session of the Oregon Senate was cancelled and the state capitol closed when the state police warned of a "possible militia threat."

The Oath Keepers claim not to be racist, but when their heavily armed white members appear at demonstrations against police violence, as in Ferguson, they appear to champion white power.

---

30 David Neiwert, *Alt-America: The Rise of the Radical Right in the Age of Trump* (New York: Verso, 2017).

Perhaps they oppose all forms of liberalism. Their website on April 14, 2016, opined that if Hillary Clinton had won the 2016 U.S. presidential election, "the result would probably be outright civil war in the U.S." Stewart Rhodes called on members to visit polling places incognito to "hunt down" and document suspected voter fraud.[31] Armed Oath Keepers helped to spearhead the January 6, 2021 attack on the U.S. Capitol.

The Alt-Right in Germany

A somewhat similar movement has taken shape in Germany in recent years.[32] Members of a group known as North Cross (*Nordkreutz*) have agreed to round up political enemies who defend migrants and refugees, put them on trucks, drive them to a secret location, and kill them. They have bought 30 body bags and ordered more, along with quicklime, used to decompose organic material. North Cross members are not lumpen proletariat—downtrodden and passive. They include a lawyer, a doctor, an engineer, a decorator, a gym owner, a local fisherman, two active army reservists, and two police officers, including Marko Gross, a police sniper and former parachutist who has acted as unofficial leader. The group grew out of a nationwide chat network for soldiers and others with far-right sympathies set up by a member of Germany's elite special forces, the KSK. Some members of these groups pilgrimage to the Thule Seminar in Kassel, Germany, where portraits of Hitler adorn the wall and leaders preach white supremacy. An emerging far-right party, Alternative for Germany (AfD), has become the third largest force in the German parliament.

Like the alt-right in the United States, its German counterpart is xenophobic—angered by the removal of borders within the European Union and the arrival of hundreds of thousands of asylum seekers from Syria, Iraq, Afghanistan, and elsewhere in 2015-2016.

---

31 On December 8, 2015, Rhodes was disbarred by the Montana Supreme Court for conduct violating the Montana Rules of Professional Conduct after refusing to respond to two bar grievances filed against him in the federal district court in Arizona. For more details, see the heavily referenced article at https://en.wikipedia.org/wiki/Oath_Keepers (accessed 8/2/20).

32 Katrin Bennhold, "Body Bags and Enemy Lists: How Far-Right Police Officers and Ex-Soldiers Planned for 'Day X,'" *The New York Times*, August 2, 2020.

Many of the newcomers are Muslim. Some have assaulted German women, and some have conducted armed attacks across Europe.

Like some American evangelicals who expect an Apocalypse, some of Germany's neo-Nazi groups look forward to a Day X–moment when Germany's social order collapses, requiring committed far-right extremists to save themselves and rescue the nation. Day X preppers are drawing in serious people with serious skills and ambition. German authorities consider the scenario a pretext for domestic terrorism by far-right plotters or even for a takeover of the government.[33]

Many neo-Nazis live in the former East Germany. Some seem both to hate and to like the old ways. One says he recalls the chaos when the Communist regime collapsed. Another compares state-media coverage of coronavirus to the censored state broadcasts during Communism. But the same individual subscribes to YouTube to access RT, noted for following the Kremlin line, and other alternative media. In this parallel universe of disinformation, he learns that the German government secretly flies in refugees after midnight; that coronavirus is a ploy to deprive citizens of their rights; that Chancellor Merkel works for the "deep state."

The online magazine *Compact* has become a mouthpiece for the AfD party—something like Fox News for Trumpists. Reviewing a few years of *Compact*, we see that no single theme dominates. *Compact* opposes the "coronavirus dictatorship" that requires facemasks; it condemned Angela Merkel for pledging huge sums to a corona-recovery fund; it assails the Greens and their energy programs; it blames asylum and multicultural programs (*Multikulti Politik*) for deaths and moves to abolish Germany's way of life. It features anti-Semitic and anti-Israel as well as anti-U.S. and anti-EU themes.

---

33 *The Jerusalem Post* (August 3, 2020) reported that a rally supported by neo-Nazi groups drew more than 20,000 protesters in Berlin on August 1 to demand an end to coronavirus restrictions. The rally celebrated a "Day of Freedom," referring to a 1935 documentary about the Nazi army by Adolf Hitler's pet filmmaker, Leni Riefenstahl. Some attendees displayed anti-Semitic slogans, while others compared today's rules meant to stop the spread of the coronavirus to Nazi regulations.

Some of the magazine's pet themes resonate with many Germans, but they also coincide with the goals of Vladimir Putin's foreign policies.[34] *Compact* is against a united and Green Europe; against face masks to contain the coronavirus; for chaos (e.g., an article entitled "Asylum, How Civil War Comes to Us"); against the United States ("Ami Go Home! How the NSA, CIA, and Army Occupy Germany"); against NATO ("War Against Russia: How NATO Marches East"). An issue with Obama's face on the cover denounced "War Lies of the USA—Propaganda for a New World Order, 1991 to the Present." With Hillary Clinton's face on the cover, *Compact* cried out "Heil Hillary! The candidate of U.S.– Fascism." But another issue displayed then President Trump's face on the cover, with a selection of the president's speeches, translated, is inside. "I like Trump," Herr Gross told an interviewer.

The Kremlin (led by an expert on Germany) must welcome if not subsidize this force, weakening the kind of U.S.-led world order championed by presidents George H.W. Bush and Barack Obama, and Joe Biden. As we know from many sources, Russia's social media, RT, and hackers have labored to foment chaos across Europe and in the United States.

How Trump and the Alt-Right Use Each Other

President Trump inspired and legitimized what before his election in 2016 was a demoralized and divided movement. The Alt-Right seized this opportunity to come boldly out of the shadows—their ranks fortified with fresh recruits. They soon saw themselves as a decisive constituency in Republican primaries. Both Trump and alt-right organizers exploited right-leaning websites, Fox News, and Twitter to promote their messages. The business-establishment right joined with the extremist right to oppose a president who was not only black but also liberal.

The Southern Poverty Law Center tracks the numbers and nature of far-right groups. At the end of the Clinton presidency in 2000, the number of hate groups was 599. It rose to 986 in 2008 when Obama

---

34 For references, see https://de.wikipedia.org/wiki/Compact_%28Magazin%29 (accessed 8/3/20).

became president; climbed to 1,018 in 2012; but then fell to 892 in 2015, Obama's last year in office. It rose to 917 in 2016 when Trump entered the White House and climbed to 1,020 in 2018, declining to 940 in 2019.[35] The numbers of anti-gay organizations moved in tandem with other hate groups. Of nearly 1,100 "bias incidents," the SPLC reported, "37 percent of them directly referenced either President-elect Trump, his campaign slogans, or his infamous remarks about sexual assault."

The numbers of anti-Muslim coalitions rose sharply in the Trump era. From 2015 to 2017 the number of explicitly anti-Muslim groups nearly tripled to over 100 nationwide. There was also a spike in reported incidents of "hate" violence against Muslims including harassment, physical assault, and bullying in schools.

The evidence suggested that Trump-era radicals were shifting their activity from organizations to online media. Here are two samples showing what they broadcast:

> "These people [migrants approaching the U.S.-Mexican border] are being paid to come here and crash the system. Why? Because that's the only way the deep state can still win. These people [the migrants] don't care about the American people. They're here because they want to kill ...."[36]

> Talking about the "caravans" of migrants, another self-styled patriot stated: "If these people make it to here, it's going to be a war in our own country and it's coming. We're going to have a war on the border."[37]

Is there any limit to the extremist views that win elections in the United States? On August 11, 2020, Marjorie Taylor Greene won a Republican primary runoff in Georgia's 14th Congressional District. She endorsed Q'Anon, the viral conspiracy theory among

---

35 Southern Poverty Law Center at https://www.splcenter.org/hate-map

36 Chuck Davis on the "United Constitutional Patriots Radio Live Stream," YouTube, March 29, 2019.

37 Larry Hopkins (Johnny Horton Jr.) on the "United Constitutional Patriots Radio Live Stream," YouTube, April 1, 2019.

people who believe the president is secretly battling a criminal band of sex traffickers. Endorsing the Q'Anon conspiracy theory, Greene sees herself as fighting a global cabal of Satan-worshiping pedophiles. She has also made hostile comments about Jews, blacks, and Muslims. After her victory, President Trump immediately hailed Greene as a "future Republican Star," tweeting that she is "strong on everything and never gives up—a real WINNER!"

President Trump on August 19, 2020, offered encouragement to proponents of QAnon, suggesting that its proponents were patriots upset with unrest in Democratic cities. "I've heard these are people that love our country. So I don't know really anything about it other than they do supposedly like me."

THE GOP AND POLITICAL VIOLENCE

Far from reducing violence, the 2020 election and its aftermath heralded a step-change in the mainstream acceptance of violence as a political tool. In the past violence took place sporadically as a political tool. By 2021-2022, it had spread and become partially mainstreamed. Proud Boys and Oath Keepers militias helped lead the Trump-inspired effort to nullify the 2020 election on January 6, 2021. A report by Dr. Rachel Kleinfeld at the Carnegie Endowment for International Peace details how armed militias have been embraced by GOP leaders at the national, state, and local levels.[38] The AfD backed Russia in Ukraine.

The FBI arrested Michigan gubernatorial candidate Ryan Kelley after he egged on the January 6 crowd in Washington D.C. with cries of "Come on, let's go. This is it! This is – this is war, baby." Kelley met with poll workers in Michigan alongside Michigan State Senate candidate Mike Detmer, who suggested in response to concerns about future election fraud: "Be prepared to lock and load .... If you ask what we can do, show up armed." Senate candidate Eric Greitens, already facing domestic violence and sexual assault allegations from different women, has a video showing the former

---

38 Rachel Kleinfeld, "The GOP's Militia Problem: Proud Boys, Oath Keepers and Lessons from Abroad," July 6, 2022 at https://www.justsecurity.org/81898/the-gops-militia-problem-proud-boys-oath-keepers-and-lessons-from-abroad (accessed 7/21/22).

Navy Seal armed and hunting "RINOS" (Republicans in Name Only). He encouraged his supporters to do the same, given that there is "no bag or tag limit" to killing other human beings. In Texas, Allen West, then-Chair of the Republican Party, offered an oath to "swear in" militia members at a "Stop the Steal" rally in November 2020. Just days after the January 6 riot Chairman West posed with armed militia members. In March, he appeared alongside other Republican state politicians at a rally with the leader of the Oath Kepers militia, while the latter was being investigated for his involvement in the January 6th attack.

Why would a faction of Republicans still in power or running for office at the federal, state, and local level make common cause with violent criminals? Because violence and intimidation are already bolstering their power. Intimidation is being used to silence opposition. Anthony E. Gonzalez, House Representative from Cleveland, Ohio was one of ten Republicans who voted to impeach Trump. After threats to his wife and young children, he decided not to run for reelection.

As Trump fumed in Mar-a-Lago, Trumpists increased their threats—not only against politicians in Washington but also against state officials and volunteer election workers attempting to process votes accurately.

Do Black Lives Matter?

Responding to police and vigilante killings, a Black Lives Matter movement took shape in the United States, Canada, and Australia. Two of the most notorious murders took place after Obama became president—that of Trayvon Martin in 2012 in Sanford, Florida, followed by the acquittal of Martin's killer, and the murder of Mike Brown in Ferguson, Missouri, in 2014. Other murders and more protests followed, but the "I can't breathe" death of George Floyd in Minneapolis in May 2020 galvanized many whites and Hispanics to join blacks in large scale protests against police bruta*lity*. *Investigators found that, over the past decade, at least 70 people died in law enforcement* custody after saying "I can't breathe." The dead ranged in age from 19 to 65. The majority of them had been stopped or held due to nonviolent infractions, 911 calls about suspicious behavior, or concerns about their mental health. More than half were black.[39]

The *Black Lives Matter* website claims that the Ferguson case "helped to catalyze a movement to which we've all helped give life. Organizers ... have ousted anti-Black politicians, won critical legislation to benefit Black lives, and changed the terms of the debate on Blackness around the world. Through movement and relationship building, we have also helped catalyze other movements and shifted culture with an eye toward the dangerous impacts of anti-Blackness."

Trump and much of his base became alarmed by the Black Lives Matter demonstrations. Trump said the movement's slogan would be "a symbol of hate" if painted on Fifth Avenue in New York. He called racial justice demonstrators "thugs." Trump celebrated Independence Day 2020 in South Dakota's Black Hills, sacred to Lakota Sioux, with a dystopian speech excoriating racial justice protesters as "evil" representatives of a "new far-left fascism" whose ultimate goal is "the end of America."

How the president and attorney general used armed forces against protestors outside the White House is detailed below in the chapter "Injustice in High Places." But in summer 2020, President Trump showed that he sees himself not only as the Republican standard-bearer but as a leader of a modern grievance movement animated by civic strife and marked by calls for "white power."[40] To be sure, the president also claimed that he had done more for black Americans than any president with the exception of Abraham Lincoln, who freed slaves and ended the Civil War —though Trump added to Fox News Channel anchor Harris Faulkner that Lincoln "did good, although it's always questionable."

Trump attacked efforts to take down Confederate statues as an assault on "our heritage." In an ominous hypothetical scenario, he described a "very tough hombre" breaking into a young woman's home while her husband was away.

---

39 Mike Baker and others, "Three Words. 70 Cases. The Tragic History of 'I Can't Breathe,'" *The New York Times,* June 29, 2020.

40 Robert Costa and Philip Rucker, "Trump's push to amplify racism unnerves Republicans who have long enabled him," *The Washington Post,* July 4, 2020.

Not to omit China from his racist litany, the president referred to the disease caused by the novel coronavirus as the "Chinese flu" or the "Kung flu."

But Trump's repeated championing of monuments, memorials, and military bases honoring Confederate leaders began to run up against the tide of social consciousness that, polls show, began to favor removing racist icons. Some Republicans fretted—mostly privately, to avoid Trump's wrath—that the president's fixation on racial and other cultural issues left their party running against the currents of change.[41]

Former Ohio governor John Kasich said in 2020 that his fellow Republicans "coddled this guy the whole time and now it's like some rats are jumping off of the sinking ship. It's just a little late." Kasich added: "It's left this nation with a crescendo of hate not only between politicians but between citizens .... It started with Charlottesville and people remained silent then, and we find ourselves in this position now."[42]

Hoping to mobilize the xenophobes in his base, Trump tried in July 2020 to cancel residence visas for any foreign students who did not attend in-person classes. With one blow the administration could kill two birds at once—the spread of knowledge and the presence of foreigners. If non-U.S. citizens did not attend in-person classes, the Immigration and Customs Enforcement agency said, they must stay away or depart. After protests from universities and businesses, the order was withdrawn.

Some business leaders agreed that xenophobia is myopic. On July 21, 2020, the National Association of Manufacturers, the U.S. Chamber of Commerce, National Retail Federation, TechNet, and Intrax asked a federal court to stop the Department of Homeland Security and the State Department from implementing President Trump's suspension of new nonimmigrant visas.[43] The CEO of the U.S. Chamber of Commerce explained: "If you want businesses to

---

41 Ibid.

42 Cole Behrens in *The Cincinnati Enquirer*, July 7, 2020.

43 National Association of Manufacturers press release: "NAM Files Suit Against Administration's 'Unlawful Restrictions' to Visas."

grow and the economy to rebound, you allow skilled workers to come here legally to work and contribute to the well-being of our nation; you don't lock them out. If you want the next revolutionary start-up to be founded in America, you welcome foreign students; you don't threaten to upend their lives and send them home during the middle of a pandemic. And if you want children to grow up to reach their potential and live their American dream, you give them the tools and certainty to succeed; you don't kick them out of the only country they've ever known."[44]

PSYCHOPATH AT THE HELM?

Beside the roles played by social dominators and social followers noted earlier in this chapter, a comparison of Hitler and Donald Trump must include a discussion of the antisocial personality disorder known as psychopathology—a term based on the Greek words for "soul" and "suffering." Walter Langer (cited in the next chapter) and other scholars have depicted Hitler as a psychopath. From his teenage years to his seventies, Donald Trump has also shared many traits of a psychopath. How strong each trait is in a particular individual and when each will emerge is a complicated challenge for science, but the list of relevant traits studied looks like a description of Trump the casino builder, the TV personality, and U.S. president.[45] Here is the list:

- glib and superficial charm
- grandiose estimation of self
- need for stimulation

---

44 Thomas J. Donohue, "Why the U.S. Chamber of Commerce Is Suing the Trump Administration," *The New York Times*, July 23, 2020.

45 R. D. Hare, *The Hare Psychopathy Checklist Revised*, 2nd edition (Toronto, ON: Multi-Health Systems, 2003); also http://www.minddisorders.com/Flu-Inv/Ha re-Psychopathy-Checklist.html#ixzz2VY2BrSPx (accessed 9/1/20); Hale's list updates that of Hervey M. Cleckley, *The Mask of Sanity: An Attempt to Clarify Some Issues About the So-Called Psychopathic Personality* (St. Louis: Mosby, 1941). His term "mask of sanity" referred to the tendency of psychopaths to appear confident, personable, and well-adjusted. For a literature review and discussion of explanatory variables, see Meagan Docherty et al., "Exploring Primary and Secondary Variants of Psychopathy in Adolescents in Detention and in the Community," *Journal of Clinical Child and Adolescent Psychology* 45, 5 (September-October 2016: 564-578).

- pathological lying
- cunning and manipulativeness
- lack of remorse or guilt
- shallow affect (superficial emotional responsiveness)
- callousness and lack of empathy
- parasitic lifestyle
- poor behavioral controls
- sexual promiscuity
- early behavior problems
- lack of realistic long-term goals
- impulsivity
- irresponsibility
- failure to accept responsibility for own actions
- many short-term marital relationships.

These traits overlap with the markers of a social dominator. Sooner or later—and probably sooner—a leader with such traits is a danger to society. After a dozen years, Hitler's Reich ended in flames. Trump's realm entered a steep decline in less than four. Still, Trumpism lingered inside the Republican virus, sickening America's body politic.

Why Have the Big Lies Stuck?

Trump made his Big Lies appear more plausible by attaching them to a truth. The gaps between people in red and in blue states are widening. Between 2008 and 2018, median household income in Democratic congressional districts rose from $54,000 to $61,000 while incomes in Republican districts fell from $55,000 to $53,000. There is also a health gap. White men living in Republican counties die years earlier than in Democratic counties. This gap increased sixfold from 2001 to 2019. These gaps feed an outlook gap. Poor rural whites are less optimistic about the future than equally poor black or Hispanic people.[46]

---

46 The ideas and data summarized here are from Arlie Russell Hochschild,

Many in Appalachia feel they are ignored by a more prosperous blue-state America: A 40-year old man an in Kentucky told a visitor: Outsiders "blame us for our problems. We're drawing government checks. We have drug problems. But they don't see all the things we've lost—good jobs, closeness to family, community trust, a debt-free life, pride.

From "loss" Trump moved the emotional needle to "stolen." For Trump followers, the right to work and remain maskless during a pandemic--stolen. The story of heroic America--stolen. White power--stolen. Real manhood--stolen. Election--stolen. It is easier to assign blame with "stolen" than with mere "loss.". For stolen white livelihoods: for example, blame China, immigrants, minorities. Many MAGA enthusiasts believe that Democrats are stealing Trump from them. So he called out to his backers, "Steal me back."

Breaking with moderate Republicans, Trump aligned with far-right activists who painted Antifa as a far greater threat than anything on the right. The reality was that over the past 25 years, right-wing extremists in the United States killed 320 people while Antifa (left-wing antifascists) killed one. Since Trump's inauguration, right-wing terrorists have carried out 140 violent attacks; left-wingers, a dozen.[47]

The storm arrived in threats of public violence and at the ballot box. It did so because a loss for too long was not recognized, and because a lie that tied itself to this loss felt more compelling to some than a truth that ignored it.

"Turbulence Ahead," a review of Luke Morgelson, *The Storm Is Here: An American Crucible* (New York: Penguin, 2022), in *The New York Times Book Review,* October 16, 2022.

47 See also Rachel Kleinfeld, "Rise in Political Violence in the United States and Damage to Our Democracy," Testimony before the Select Committee to Investigate the January 6th Attack on the United States Capitol, March 31, 2022 at https://carne gieendowment.org/2022/03/31/rise-in-political-violence-in-united-states-and-damage-to-our-democracy-pub-87584 (accessed 10/15/22).

2

TRUMP UNITES THE ALT-RIGHT
AND CHRISTIAN RIGHT

As Republicans convened in August 2020 to honor President Trump as a living god destined to reign forever, one of his most important supporters from the Christian Right fell from grace. Jerry Falwell, Jr. was brought down in a sex scandal. Jerry Jr. is the son of the man, Jerry Sr., who helped turn white Evangelicals into a potent political force. Jerry Jr. was also one of Trump's most fervent advocates on the Christian Right. In late August 2020, however, he resigned as the president of Liberty University after a social media post showed him with pants half unzipped and his arm around a young woman. It emerged that Jerry Jr. had sometimes watched as his own wife had sex with a certain "pool boy." Former Trump fixer Michael Cohen had helped the Falwells put the lid on other racy photos. Also, Cohen used an IT expert from Liberty University to rig online polls for Trump in 2015.[1]

NO SHAME POLITICS

Is it an embarrassment to Trump that one of his closest allies on the Christian Right is publicly shamed? No, his evangelical base supports him no matter what. he does or their leaders say. The initial hesitancy of evangelical leaders to endorse a man so morally depraved was not shared by the grassroots. "The base didn't like Trump because Jerry Falwell endorsed him. They already liked Trump," says historian Sarah Posner. The leaders just follow the followers.

Whether Trump cheated on all of his many wives is irrelevant. What matters is that Trump hates whom Evangelicals hate and will fight crudely and viciously on their behalf. Posner states that they

---

1 Paul Waldman, "Why the Jerry Falwell scandal won't weaken Trump's evangelical support," *Washington Post*, August 25, 2020. Waldman interviewed Sarah Posner, author of *Unholy: Why White Evangelicals Worship at the Altar of Donald Trump* (New York: Penguin Random House, 2020).

"have chosen to see him not as a sinner but as a strongman, not as a con man but as a king who is courageously unshackling them from what they portray as liberal oppression."

Evangelicals see Trump as their champion. From Trump, they have gotten far-right judges committed to undermining abortion rights and expanding "religious liberty" for conservative Christians. So it doesn't matter if Trump cannot cite a Bible verse. "Sometimes, God picks an unlikely leader to carry out His will."[2]

While Ronald Reagan and the two Bush presidents usually tried to be subtle about their close ties to the religious right, Trump is forthright. He has made conservative Christians central to the ceremonial, public-facing aspects of his administration and its policies.

Trump is not himself religious, but he often brings evangelical pastors to the Oval Office because they tell him how great he is, how God's hand is on him, and how he was chosen by God to save the country. At the Republican convention, in 2020 there were plenty of mentions of God along with descriptions of Trump as a near-deity himself.

Why don't people on the Christian Right worry about Trump's mishandling of the Covid-19 pandemic? Sarah Posner's answer: "They are not reading or listening to or absorbing the same kind of information about the pandemic that the rest of America is." Their leaders have told them "not to listen to the fake news media or ... the deep state because the deep state is actually trying to take down Donald Trump ... So the distrust of the media and of science and of the government has been baked in. It's hard to convey how intense this alternative universe is."

Trump has managed to appeal both to the non-religious Alt-Right and the Christian Right.[3] The unifying force is their shared hostility to liberal democracy with a free press, civil rights for

2   Sarah Posner interviewed by Terry Gross on *Fresh Air*, July 8, 2020 at https://www.npr.org/2020/07/08/888906337/unholy-examines-the-alliance-between-white-evangelicals-and-trump (accessed 8 /1/2020).

3   Starting in 2015, Trump used Christian televangelism to coalesce the racist, nativist strand of the 1970s-1980s New Right with the Christian Right. He brought the Moral Majority into Republican politics.

everyone, accountable government, and an independent judiciary.[4] Trump speaks to both of these constituencies simultaneously when he articulates the grievances of white America. Both the Alt-Right and Christian Right fear that white America is being threatened by Blacks, Muslims, and Mexicans. Attacking "Black Lives Matter" Trump energizes the Alt-Right and evangelicals at the same time.

How did America's political culture become so sick? Let us review the background. What triggered the Christian Right's entry into politics was the 1954 Supreme Court decision requiring schools to desegregate. It led them to set up segregation academies—private schools to avoid desegregation.[5]

TRUMP'S PROMISE TO EVANGELICALS

Like Hitler and Vladimir Putin, "the Donald" kowtowed to organized religion. Trump claimed in 2015 to attend the Marble Collegiate Church in Manhattan, which his parents joined in the 1970s, but the church publicly stated he "is not an active member."[6] Nonetheless, "Christianity will have power," Trump promised evangelicals at a Christian college church in Sioux Center, Iowa in January 2016.[7] "If I'm there, you're going to have plenty of power, you don't need anybody else. You're going to have somebody representing you very, very well. Remember that." This was the same speech in which Trump said "I have the most loyal people. I could stand in the middle of Fifth Avenue and shoot somebody and I wouldn't lose any voters. OK?"[8] The public response to Trump's behavior as president

---

4   There are evangelical ministers like Russell Johnson, who exhorted a few hundred people at an Ohio voter-registration rally in front of a banner that commingled the Christian cross and the American flag: "We're on the beaches of Normandy, and we can see the pillbox entrenchments of academic and media liberalism. We'll take back our country for Christ."

5   Posner interviewed by Terry Gross.f course, there are Christians who would never go to a rally where people raise Hitler salutes. And many on the Alt-Right scoff at religious moralizing.

6   https://edition.cnn.com/2015/08/28/politics/donald-trump-church-member/index.html (accessed 6/13/20).

7   Ambitious whites pushed the "Sioux" westward long ago, but their reputed name still had some appeal. They called themselves Dakota and Lakota.

8   Elizabeth Dias, "Christianity Will Have Power." *The New York Times*, August

and former president confirms the validity of this strange claim.

In November 2016, some 81 percent of white evangelicals voted for Trump nationwide. As Elizabeth Dias explains; "Evangelicals did not support Mr. Trump in spite of who he is. They supported him because of who he is, and because of who they are. He is their protector, the bully who is on their side, the one who offered safety amid their fears that their country as they know it, and their place in it, is changing, and changing quickly." Evangelicals worry that their entire way of life, "one in which their values were dominant, could be headed for extinction. And Mr. Trump offered to restore them to power, as though they have not been in power all along."[9]

The Trump era has revealed the complete fusion of evangelical Christianity and conservative politics. There are some signs of fraying at the edges of the coalition, among some women and young people. If even a small fraction turns away from Mr. Trump, it could make the difference to re-election prospects. Trump's support among white evangelicals dropped in spring 2020, but the Pew Research Center found that, as of June 2020, some 82% of evangelicals said they intended to vote for him—essentially unchanged since 2016.[10]

CHRISTIAN DOMINION THEOLOGY

There are major differences and overlaps among Protestant supporters of conservative politics. Many, including evangelicals, have been influenced by what some observers call Christian

---

9, 2020. One evangelical woman told Dias that, after Obama's election, "It was dangerous to voice your Christianity, because we were viewed as bigots, as racists — we were labeled as the haters and the ones who are causing all the derision and all of the problems in America ... If you are a hard-working Caucasian-American, your rights are being limited because you are seen as against all the races or against women. Or there are people who think that because we have conservative values and we value the family and I value submitting to my husband, I must be against women's rights."

9 Ibid.

10 Which groups approved of Trump? All Protestants, 52%; white evangelicals, 72%; black Protestants, 12%; white Catholics, 54%; black Catholics, 23%; agnostics and atheists, 15%. Details at https://www.pewresearch.org/fact-tank/2020/07/01/white-evangelical-approval-of-trump-slips-but-eight-in-ten-say-they-would-vote-for-him/ (accessed 8/25/20).

dominion theology. Several versions of Christian dominion theology have shaped American politics for decades.[11]

This outlook, like Republicans' use of the race card, had antecedents in Germany. In the late 19th and early 20th centuries, some German thinkers regretted the passing of old ways and traditional old values. They expressed a kind of cultural despair that provided a receptive context for Nazism. They blamed external agents— Jews, the press, and liberals—for disrupting the ancient unity of the German *Volk*. They despised intellectuals who put reason and science above feeling and intuition. Some Protestant academics fused Christianity with German idealisms to form a *Kulturreligion*.[12] This fusion retained a religious tone even after the basics of religion disappeared–a trait we see also in "Christian" elements within America's Alt-Right. Hitler's personal life and his policies, like those of Donald Trump, should have repelled serious Christians. But Hitler tried to silence his critics and unite his followers by fusing independent Lutheran churches in a "Protestant Reich Church." An ardent Nazi, Ludwig Müller, became its presiding bishop. Müller vetted Lutheran clergy to ensure they were "politically reliable," that is, accepted the superiority of the Aryan race.

The starting point for dominion theology is *Genesis* 1-28, the passage in which God grants humanity "dominion over the fish of the sea, and over the fowl of the air, and over every living thing that moveth upon the earth." Some Christians interpret this to mean that they—white Protestants—should rule over not just the fish and fowl but over all persons who do not share their religious faith. This privileged few should rule not just in religious matters but in political, economic, and social. They should govern and do so in

---

11 Sara Diamond, *Not by Politics Alone: The Enduring Influence of the Christian Right (New York: Guilford Press, 1998);* Michelle Goldberg, *Kingdom Coming: The Rise of Christian Nationalism* (New York: W.W. Norton, 2006); also John W. Whitehead, "The Rise of Dominionism and the Christian Right," *Liberty Magazine* July/August 2006 http://libertymagazine.org/article/the-rise-of-dominionism-and-the-christian-right (accessed 8/20/20).

12 Germany's "ideologists of the conservative revolution superimposed a vision of national redemption upon their dissatisfaction with liberal culture and with the loss of authoritative faith." Fritz Stern, *The Politics of Cultural Despair: A Study in the Rise of the Germanic Ideology* (Berkeley: University of California Press, 1961), pp. xxi, xxv.

accordance with God's law as interpreted by them. That Christians are Biblically mandated to "occupy" all secular institutions has become the *central unifying ideology* for the Christian Right. They see it as their Christian duty to take "control of a sinful secular society."

Dominionists deny the Enlightenment roots of American democracy. They believe that the United States once was, and should again be, a Christian nation. They seek a theocracy in which biblical law, as interpreted by them, governs, and other religions have no standing. They seek dominion—not just a voice. Their Christian politics seeks "conquest of the land—of men, families, institutions, bureaucracies, courts, and governments for the Kingdom of Christ."[13]

Some Christian nationalists say they are simply responding to anti-Christian persecution. They say that secularism is itself a religion, one unfairly imposed on them. They say they're the victims in the culture wars. On the other hand, Christian nationalist ideologues do not want mere equality. They want dominance. One vows: "World conquest. That's what Christ has commissioned us to accomplish. We must win the world with the power of the Gospel. And we must never settle for anything less." A "softer" version of dominion theology seeks merely to make the United States a Christian nation with no separation of church and state.

One researcher concludes that "dominionism is more a political phenomenon than a theological one. It cuts across Christian denominations, from stern, austere sects to the signs-and-wonders culture of modern megachurches. Think of it like political Islamism, which shapes the activism of a number of antagonistic fundamentalist movements, from Sunni Wahabis in the Arab world to Shiite fundamentalists in Iran."[14]

Against dominionism in any form, Christian libertarians maintain that state intervention to promote piety or generosity can

---

13 George Grant, *The Changing of the Guard: Biblical Principles for Political Action* (1987) quoted in Goldberg, *Kingdom Coming.*

14 Michelle Goldberg, "Dominionism: Michele Bachmann and Rick Perry's Dangerous Religious Bond,". *Daily Beast,* August 14, 2011 updated July 13, 2017 at https://www.thedailybeast.com/dominionism-michele-bachmann-and-rick-perrys-dangerous-religious-bond (accessed 8/20/20).

be unethical and counterproductive. Coercion by threat of violence robs otherwise moral acts of their virtue, inspires resentment and disrespect—even for just laws—and has a spiritually deleterious effect upon the coercers. Going further, anarchists believe that all government is bad. Thus, Leo Tolstoy in his later years argued that even if a government wants to support some higher law, it inevitably gives in to expediency: "Not only does the action of governments not deter men from crimes; on the contrary, it increases crime by always disturbing and lowering the moral standard of society."

THE CHRISTIAN RIGHT IN HIGH PLACES

By the early 1980s the Christian Right formed a powerful voting bloc. It helped to usher Ronald Reagan, George H. W. Bush, and George W. Bush into the presidency. It moved from the fringes of society to the floor of Congress. Christian fundamentalists held a majority of seats in eighteen Republican Party state committees. Forty-five Senators and 186 House members earned between 80 and 100% approval ratings from advocacy groups such as the Christian Coalition and Family Resource Council. Representatives of the Christian Right boasted of representing 30 million voters and having a direct line to the "W" White House.[15]

Regardless of Donald Trump's beliefs or non-beliefs, white evangelical Christians are a powerful force within the Republican Party.[16] George W. Bush claimed to be evangelical, as does Vice

---

15 Chris Hedges, *The Christian Right and the Rise of American Fascism* (New York: Free Press, 2006).

16 Following Martin Luther, all evangelicals claim to follow Holy Writ. A series of evangelical revivals known as the Great Awakening swept Britain and its North American colonies in the 1730s and 1740s. There were two more great awakenings in the 19th century and, some analysts say, a fourth in the 1960s-1970s. The upshot was that mainline Protestant denominations lost members, while conservative denominations such as Southern Baptists and Missouri Synod Lutherans grew rapidly. It was these denominations that becamepolitically powerful. Evangelicalism is now a worldwide, trans-denominational movement within Protestant Christianity, but there are many varieties of the faith. Former president Jimmy Carter, a Democrat and a preacher at a Baptist church, has claimed to be a "born again" evangelical. Martin Luther King, Jr. and other Baptists were civil rights leaders. Still, to the contemporary politician, "evangelical" means white Christian Republican. One student of religion concludes that it is not

President Mike Pence. Trump's first attorney general, Jeff Sessions, another evangelical, helped craft the blend of faith and patriotism that became a hallmark of Trump rhetoric. It probably appealed to the 81% of evangelicals who voted for Trump.[17] In 2018, A.G. Sessions announced creation of a "Religious Liberty Task Force" to enforce a 2017 Department of Justice memo ordering federal agencies to follow the broadest possible interpretation of "religious liberty." That memo prohibits the IRS from threatening the tax-exempt status of any religious organization that actively lobbies on behalf of a political candidate—an unlawful practice banned by the [Senator Lyndon] Johnson Amendment forbidding nonprofit organizations, including churches, from taking explicit stances on political candidates. Sessions called the task force a necessary step in facing down the prevailing forces of secularism—a "dangerous movement … eroding our great tradition of religious freedom." Here was one of many instances in which Trump's Justice Department broke an explicit law.

Having forced Sessions to resign over his failure to stop the Mueller investigation, Trump appointed Matthew G. Whitaker to be Acting Attorney General in November 2018. A few years earlier, when Whitaker campaigned for the Senate, he courted the anti-abortion, evangelical movement, promising at one candidate's forum that he would scrutinize nominees for federal judge to ensure they had a "biblical view of justice."

Few U.S. officials have been so open about their evangelical convictions as Mike Pompeo. A graduate of West Point as well as Harvard Law School, Pompeo served as an Army officer and then as Director of the Central Intelligence Agency from January 2017 until

---

simply that the Evangelical movement resists easy definition. "It is, rather, that evangelicalism has been so buffeted by the waves of consumer trends, been so malleable and revisable for every cultural moment, that the movement cannot be meaningfully distinguished from a broader American religiosity. The disturbing conclusion might just be that evangelicalism does not exist." Kirsten Sanders, "The Evangelical Question in the History of American Religion," *Hedgehog Review* 24.2 (Summer 2022).

17 Tara Isabella Burton, "Jeff Sessions helped create Trump's brand of evangelical patriotism. It will outlast him," *Vox*, November 7, 2018 at https://www.vox.com/policy-and-politics/2018/11/7/18073016/jeff-sessions-resigns-christian-nationalism-trump (accessed 7/2/20).

April 2018 when he became Secretary of State.

Pompeo's religion is his own affair, but his religious beliefs actively shaped his policies.[18] Christian Zionists say that the gathering of Jews in Israel is foretold in the Biblical prophecy of the "rapture" —the ascent of Christians into the kingdom of God. Pompeo talked about the rapture in 2015. He urged a "God and Country Rally" in Kansas to be part of the "never-ending struggle" until "the rapture."[19] While Pompeo headed the CIA, the Trump administration in 2017 moved the U.S. Embassy from Tel Aviv to Jerusalem. After Pompeo became Secretary of State, the United States recognized the Golan Heights as part of Israel. The Trump administration's "peace plan" in 2020 authorized Israel to claim much of the West Bank and denied a possible Palestinian state many attributes of sovereignty. In a January 2020 speech in Cairo, Mr. Pompeo said his trip was "especially meaningful" for him "as an evangelical Christian, coming so soon after the Coptic Church's Christmas celebrations." He added, "In my office, I keep a Bible open on my desk to remind me of God and his word, and the truth." Pompeo articulated his version of evangelical Christianity in a capital of the Islamic world.

In August 2020, Pompeo became the first U.S. secretary of state to address a political party's convention, breaking both precedent and law (the Hatch Act, which prohibits federal employees from engaging in political activities while on the job), as well as State Department rules Pompeo had recently signed. The evangelical secretary sent a video to the multitude from Jerusalem. Referring to President Trump's earlier decision to move the U.S. embassy to the city, Pompeo called Jerusalem the "rightful capital of the Jewish homeland"—a cue to evangelical voters that Trump's policies were God's. On an earlier occasion, Pompeo told the Christian

---

18 Edward Wong, "The Rapture and the Real World," *The New York Times,* March 30, 2018.

19 How should Christians prepare for the Second Coming? There are two schools: pre-millennials want to form a global Christian empire for one thousand years before Christ comes again. Post-millennials expect Christ to arrive and then, with them, hold dominion over the globe. Alternatively, some millennials say that believers will rise with Him to the heavens, leaving non-believers to a painful fate.

Broadcasting Network that it is "possible" that Trump is like a modern-day Esther, a biblical character who persuaded the king of Persia not to destroy the Jews.[20]

The secretary's religiosity did not guarantee his professionalism. His lack of foreign policy achievements and failure to defend State Department officers denounced by the president led Thomas Friedman to call him the "worst Secretary of State ever" (*The New York Times*, May 27, 2020). Coupled with Pompeo's official failures were his grandiose efforts to attract backers for a possible presidential run--both in Kansas and in the State Department dining room—all paid for by all taxpayers. In May 2020 Pompeo persuaded Trump to fire the Inspector General who was investigating the secretary's role in promoting arms sales to Saudi Arabia against the express demands of Congress.

Outsiders cannot know whether self-styled evangelical politicians truly believe what they say. Talking to reporters, many GOP officials squirm to telegraph their great personal distaste for the "make-America-great" enterprise. If some Republicans support Trump for ulterior motives, however, Evangelical Jeff Sessions "was—is—a true believer." Even after being insulted and forced to resign by the president, he is "eager to hold forth on why he likes Trump, why his party—why the *country*—so desperately needs him."[21]

EVANGELICALS IN CONGRESS

The U.S. Congress elected in 2020 is mostly Christian (88%)—far more Christian than the general public (65%). Three politically active evangelical groups—Baptists, nondenominational Christians, and Pentecostals are underrepresented on Capitol Hill, while the "other" category continues to grow. The number of ostensibly faithful politicians has held steady even as the public moves away from religious participation. Just one member of Congress

---

20 Carol Morello, "Pompeo stirs up outrage among some diplomats over speech to RNC," *The Washington Post*, August 25, 2020.

21 Elaina Plott, "The Fall of Jeff Sessions, and What Came After," *New York Times Magazine* July 5, 2020.

considers herself unaffiliated, a group that now comprises more than a quarter of the country. As fewer members belong to mainline denominations, a growing number of lawmakers have adopted the more generic "unspecified/other" Protestant label rather than associating with particular evangelical traditions, even a group like "nondenominational." The "other Protestant" designation continues to be the fastest-growing faith label in Congress and the second most popular behind "Catholic." In 2021, 18 new members of Congress fell into the "other Protestant" camp—over a quarter of all freshman lawmakers—bringing the total to 96. While just 5 percent of Americans use this label, 18 percent of Congress does. In 2021 "unspecified/other" applied to "those who say they are Christian, evangelical Christian, evangelical Protestant, or Protestant, without specifying a denomination. Fewer members of Congress consider themselves Pentecostals (0.4% of Congress vs. 5% of the country), nondenominational (2% vs. 6%), or Baptist (12% vs. 15%) than the population as a whole, even though these groups are regularly involved in political discourse and political issues such as religious freedom and abortion. [22]

President Biden is Catholic as are six justices on the Supreme Court, five of the six nominated by Republican presidents. Contrary to church dogma, Biden and some justices favor legalized abortion; two justices are Protestant and one is Jewish. Justice Ketanji Brown Jackson says she is a nondenominational Protestant. Neil Gorsuch is Episcopalian, but was raised Catholic. Some 22% of American adults identify as Catholic compared to 67% on the Supreme Court.

"CHRISTIAN IDENTITY"

In many places around the globe, including the United States, autocrats such as Donald Trump exploit the synergies of populism, polarization, and post-truth ideologies.[23] Populist movements in

---

22 Pew Research Center, "Faith on the Hill,' January 4, 2021; Kate Shellnutt, "Evangelicals in Congress Prefer Generic Labels, *Christianity Today*, January 5, 2021 at https://www.christianitytoday.com/news/2021/january/evangelical-congress-baptist-pentecostal-nondenominational.html

23 Moisés Naím, *The Revenge of Power: How Autrocrats Are Reinventing Politics*

every Western country have native roots that contemporary activists help to mobilize. One element in the Alt-Right is the "Christian Identity" movement that emerged in the United States in the 1920s and 1930s as an offshoot of British "Israelism." Its leaders taught that all non-whites will either be exterminated or enslaved to serve the white race in the new Heavenly Kingdom on Earth under a returned Jesus Christ. Its doctrine states that only "Adamic" (white) people can achieve salvation and paradise. Many adherents are Millennialists who expect soon a Second Coming. Like slaveholders in the South, Christian Identity adherents see white supremacy as a Godly ideal. This ideology also colors the demands of Christian Dominionists— white Christians, and only white Christians, deserve to rule.

Like the Nazi worldview, Christian Identity is an anti-Semitic and racist theology. It is "Christian" in name only, asserting that white people, not Jews, are the true Israelites favored by God. The movement's relationship with evangelicals and fundamentalists has generally been hostile due to the latter's belief that the return of Jews to Israel is essential to the fulfillment of end-time prophecy.

Christian Identity adherents believe that whites of European descent can be traced back to the "Lost Tribes of Israel." Many consider Jews to be the Satanic offspring of Eve and the Serpent, while non-whites are "mud peoples" created before Adam and Eve. Its virulent racist and anti-Semitic beliefs are usually accompanied by extreme anti-government sentiments. According to the Southern Poverty Law Center, Christian Identity groups declined from seventeen to eleven in 2020, due to law enforcement and the non-replacement of key leaders. Although Christian Identity tenets are becoming more popular with members of neo-Confederate hate groups, there are not enough new churches being founded to slow the decay of organized congregations.

Despite its small size, Christian Identity influences virtually all white supremacist and extreme anti-government movements. It has also informed criminal behavior ranging from hate crimes to acts of terrorism. Christian Identity beliefs have been tied to dozens of white nationalist terrorist attacks over the past fifty years, including

---

in the 21st Century (New York: St. Martin's, 2022).

the 1968 bombing of a synagogue in Meridian, Mississippi, and the murder of Jewish radio personality Alan Berg in Denver in 1984. More recently it shaped the delusional thinking of the killer who murdered eleven congregants at the Tree of Life Synagogue in Pittsburgh in October 2018. Six months later, inspired by the Pittsburgh killing, a 19-year-old walked into a Chabad in Poway, California, and murdered 60-year-old Lori Gilbert-Kaye. As a writer for a Catholic magazine noted, the ideology of Christian Identity is a key conduit for violent anti-Semitism in America, but the problem is larger than one extremist faction.[24]

THE BIG LIE AND THE BODY POLITIC

Hostile to truth, both Hitler and Trump seemed to revel in delivery of what the German leader called the "Big Lie [*die grosse Lüge*]." Hitler's book *Mein Kampf* (1925) said that Jews used lies so "colossal" that no one would believe that someone "could have the impudence to distort the truth so infamously."[25] Hitler explained that "in the big lie there is always a certain force of credibility; because the broad masses … are always more easily corrupted in the deeper strata of their emotional nature than consciously or voluntarily. In the primitive simplicity of their minds, they more readily fall victims to the big lie than the small lie…" They could not imagine "that others could have the impudence to distort the truth so infamously. Even though the facts which prove this to be so may be brought clearly to their minds, they will still doubt and waver and will continue to think that there may be some other explanation." These realities are "known to all expert liars in this world and to all who conspire together in the art of lying."

Hitler and his propaganda apparatus made full use of *die grosse Lüge.* A psychological profile of Hitler said that his primary rules were: "never allow the public to cool off; never admit a fault or wrong; never concede that there may be some good in your "enemy"; never leave room for alternatives; never accept blame; concentrate

---

24 David Walsh, "The Bloody History of America's Christian Identity Movement," *The Tablet,* May 13, 2019.

25 Hitler said Jews used the big lie to blame Germany's loss in World War I on General Erich Ludendorff, a prominent nationalist and anti-Semite.

on one enemy at a time and blame him for everything that goes wrong."[26]

While Trump may not have studied Hitler, as if by instinct he adopted the Führer's techniques. Trying to catalog the president's falsehoods, the *Washington Post* found that President Trump lied several times each day—many thousands of times since taking over the White House. He even lied several times that his father was born—not in the Bronx (in 1905), but in Germany (birthplace of Donald's grandfather).

Here was a contradiction: Trump termed any reports critical of his administration "fake news." Because of fake news, the White House said it was canceling its subscriptions to the *The New York Times* and *The Washington Post*. On the other hand, Trump and his press people gushed out what they called "alternative facts"— deliberate distortions of reality.

An intelligence analyst at the Department of Homeland Security (DHS), Brian Murphy, told the House Intelligence Committee in September 2020 that his bosses demanded he downplay the threat of Russian interference in the November 2020 election because it "made the president look bad." In May 2020 he was told to "cease providing intelligence assessments on the threat of Russian interference . . . and instead start reporting on interference activities by China and Iran." He was demoted for refusing to alter reports on this and on threats from white supremacy groups. He was instructed to "modify intelligence assessments" on left-wing groups such as antifa "to ensure they matched up with the public comments by President Trump." Murphy wanted to be reinstated as principal deputy undersecretary in the Office of Intelligence and Analysis.

Murphy also said he was under pressure from the White House to exaggerate the number of migrants with links to terrorism at a time when the administration was implementing tougher measures to halt the flow of undocumented migrants reaching the U.S.-Mexico border and making the case for a wall. Murphy alleged that former

---

26 Walter C. Langer, *A Psychological Analysis of Adolph Hitler: His Life and Legend,* prepared for the Office of Strategic Services, available at the National Archives.

DHS Secretary Kirstjen Nielsen knowingly provided "false material information" about known or suspected terrorists apprehended at the border during testimony in December 2018 and March 2019. In March 2019 she inflated their number and "constituted a knowing and deliberate submission of false material information."

Indifference to truth is fatal for democracy, but it can be useful or bad for the social media business. Some liberals and conservatives hoped that social media would facilitate knowledge of the truth. But all kinds of groups learned how to twist reality on social media to fit their agendas. Facebook and other media companies pulled in millions in advertising revenues by turning a blind eye to falsehoods. Extremist propaganda in 2016 hurt Hillary Clinton's campaign for the presidency. Trump welcomed dirt on her from Wikileaks, even when it came from Russian sources.

In May 2020, Twitter began to portray the president himself as a purveyor of fake news, posting alongside his messages ways to find the real facts. An angry president replied on May 27 threatening to "strongly regulate" or even shut down social media platforms after Twitter applied a fact-check to two of his tweets. Trump did not elaborate on what actions he could take, but his threat showed his intent to use government power against his perceived political enemies in the private sector—businesses that already enjoyed wide latitude to moderate their platforms as they saw fit. And it raises the stakes for Twitter and Facebook as they grapple with Trump's misleading claims, for example, that cable TV news host Joe Scarborough had a hand in an aide's death nearly two decades earlier.

Trump tweeted: "Republicans feel that Social Media Platforms totally silence conservatives' voices. We will strongly regulate, or close them down, before we can ever allow this to happen,." He went on to accuse the tech industry of trying to interfere in the 2016 election. He then repeated his unfounded claim about voter fraud stemming from mail-in ballots. "We can't let large scale Mail-In Ballots take root in our Country," Trump tweeted. "It would be a free for all on cheating, forgery and the theft of Ballots. Whoever cheated the most would win. Likewise, Social Media. Clean up your act, NOW!!!!"

When Facebook banned Trump and refused to back down, he launched his own Twitter-like platform in May 2021 that allows followers to retweet, like, or post to Facebook his latest political missives. The site URL is donaldjtrump.com/desk. "In a time of silence and lies, a beacon of freedom arises," the flashy video states after an image of Earth from space zooms in on Mar-A-Lago in Florida. "A place to speak freely and safely straight from the desk of Donald J. Trump." The former president promptly used his new media platform to vilify his GOP critics Liz Cheney and Mitt Romney.

The Big Lie often worked in tandem with racism. Trump often used partial truths to distort the big picture. For example, the president complained that many Latino immigrants proved to be rapists and murderers when most are law-abiding and hard-working.[27]

Whether Trump attended church or not, a day after his acquittal of impeachment charges in February 2020, President Trump addressed the 68th annual National Prayer Breakfast (an institution founded by Rev. Abraham Vereide, founder of the secretive evangelical political movement, "The Fellowship," also known as "The Family")[28]. Speaking in the East Room of the White House, Trump made clear: "In America, we don't punish prayer. We don't tear down crosses. We don't ban symbols of faith. We don't muzzle preachers . . . In America, we celebrate faith, we cherish religion, we lift our voices in prayer, and we raise our sights to the Glory of God." He continued: "We are upholding the sanctity of life— sanctity of life. (Applause.) And we are doing that like nobody has ever done it before from this position."

---

27 For references, see Nicholas Kristof, "Now Is a Time to Learn From Hispanic Americans," *The New York Times*, June 27, 2020 and https://money.cnn.com/2018/06/22/news/economy/hispanic-social-mobility/index.html (accessed 7/27/20).

28 Douglas Coe, then co-director of The Fellowship, was tutoring Todd Tiahrt, a Republican congressman from Kansas, at the group's mansion in Arlington, Virginia. Coe told Tiahrt of men who had changed the world through the strength of the covenants they had forged with their "brothers." They were "like the Mafia," said Coe. "Look at Hitler," he said. "Lenin, Ho Chi Minh, Bin Laden." The Family, of course, possessed a weapon those leaders lacked: the "total Jesus" of a brotherhood in Christ. Jeff Sharlet, *The Family: The Secret Fundamentalism at the Heart of American Power* (New York: Harper, 2008), p. 30.

Critics found it odd that such a godless person, one accused of sexual aggressions by dozens of women and impeached for high crimes by the House of Representatives, could be idolized by huge numbers of believers including many GOP politicians. Did the evangelicals enter a Faustian bargain with a real live devil? Did they agree to put up with his slack morality on the condition that he back their anti-abortion and other causes? Or, as Elizabeth Dias suggests, do they simply see him as their savior?

Many Republicans shared both the president's racism and his indifference to truth. Former U.S. Attorney General Jeff Sessions, running in 2020 for his old Senate seat in Alabama, appeared to refer to a prominent black professor at Harvard as "some criminal," while disparaging former President Barack Obama's treatment of a police officer. The professor was Henry Louis Gates, who was apprehended while trying to enter his own residence close to the university. Sessions seemed to think that Obama shared a beer with Gates alone. The reality was quite different. On July 30, 2009, Obama and Vice President Biden sat with Gates and Cambridge police Sgt. James Crowley to discuss what went wrong and help them understand each other's perspectives. Was Sessions ignorant or just an agitator? This is what he said: "The police had been demoralized. There was all the Obama—there's a riot, and he has a beer at the White House with some criminal, to listen to him. Wasn't having a beer with the police officers. So we said, "'We're on your side. We've got your back; you got our thanks.'"[29]

Asked if he would support police reforms after the death of George Floyd in May 2020, Sessions replied: "I think you should probably have some money for actually training for riots. That's what really needs to be done. Not tell the police, 'If you were just more *sensitive*, riots wouldn't occur.'" This was not a new position for Sessions. As attorney general, he argued that officers were unfairly blamed for violence. His mantra was "Back the men and women in blue." The Evangelical faith of Sessions along with his racism, penchant for strong enforcement, sloppy thinking and way of speaking all fed on each other.

---

29 Plott, "The Fall of Jeff Sessions, and What Came After."

Floyd was murdered in the Minnesota district represented by Ilhan Omar, one of two female Muslims elected to the House of Representatives in 2018 (joining two Muslim men elected a decade earlier). Floyd's death became a catalyst for conversations about police brutality and structural racism. Omar told reporters: We are fighting to tear down systems of oppression not only in the criminal justice system but also in housing, in education, in health care, in employment, and in the very air we breathe. "As long as our economic and political systems prioritize profit, without considering who is profiting and who is being shut out, we will perpetuate this inequality." The Republican response to her comments was vicious.[30]

Ihan was one of the two Muslim women elected to Congress in 2018.[31] The 116th Congress was, as before, predominantly Christian—Protestant, 54.9% and Catholic, 30.5%. Some 6.4%. was Jewish. These numbers did not reveal how many Protestants were Evangelical or Dominionist, but Episcopalians, Presbyterians lost nine seats each and Catholics six. Some 16% of respondents did not specify their beliefs. Just one said she was unaffiliated.[32]

---

30 Omar reported that "The Republican National Committee clipped 27 seconds of my speech and added a false caption that said I had just called for getting rid of the entire U.S. economy and government. Instantly, Donald Trump Jr. and right-wing 'media outlets' were amplifying the false claim." She has received many death threats. See her op-ed in *The Washington Post*, July 15, 2020. In March 2020 a New York state resident who threatened to put a bullet in Omar's skull was jailed for one year and one day.

31 Omar and her father, escaping civil war in Somalia, obtained asylum in the United States in 1995. Omar became a U.S. citizen in 2000 at age 17. When she was bullied in school, her father told her: "They are doing something to you because they feel threatened in some way by your existence." In June 2020 he died of Covid-19 at age 67.

32 https://www.pewforum.org/2019/01/03/faith-on-the-hill-116/(accessed 8/25/20). Research by Roger Finke and Rodney Stark shows that when theology becomes too logical or too secular, it loses people. Religious organizations can thrive only when they comfort souls and demand sacrifice. Finke and Stark portray the religious environment as a free market where churches compete for souls. In the early 21st century six out of ten Americans belonged to some church (far more than in 1776 when just one in five were active in church affairs). Mainline churches such as Methodists have lost ground while Baptists and upstart sects have gained members. Ecumenical movements such as the post-Vatican II Catholic church have lost members. Roger Finke and Rodney Stark, *The Churching of America, 1776-1990: Winners and Losers in Our Religious Economy*, 2nd. Ed. (New

THE BIG LIE AND COVID-19

Like Hitler, Trump deftly employs the Big Lie. But big lies can and do harm the body politic—also its mind and soul. President Trump and some Republican governors told the public in 2020 not to worry much about Covid-19. Their message: "It usually is no more serious than a cold and will soon blow over. Not much need for face masks or social distancing. Just go enjoy yourselves and reinvigorate the world's greatest economy."

Trump persisted with this big lie even though his top national security advisers told him on January 28, 2020, that this virus posed the "biggest national security threat" of his presidency, one that could be as lethal as the 1918 influenza pandemic. Despite what Trump said in public, he revealed to journalist Bob Woodward that he knew the situation was far more dire than he had been saying publicly. "I wanted to always play it down," the president told Woodward on March 18. "I still like playing it down, because I don't want to create a panic. And while he told the public that children are "almost immune" to the virus, he told Woodward; "It's not just old, older. Young people too—plenty of young people." In April, as he urged the country to reopen, Trump told Woodward, the virus is "so easily transmissible, you wouldn't believe it."

Woodward's book, *Rage* (released in September 2020 by Simon & Schuster) is based on eighteen interviews with Trump (many of them recorded) and many "deep conversations" with his associates. Why would Trump choose to admit that he had been deceiving the public? It is possible that he valued his claim to knowing everything more than his claim to honesty. In the interviews he often stressed his priority on being a law-and-order president. He expressed resentment that black voters gave him little support. "I've done a tremendous amount for the black community," he told Woodward. "And, honestly, I'm not feeling any love." He scoffed at Woodward's suggestion that privileged whites, like himself and Trump, needed to empathize with the pain and anger many blacks feel toward the country. "You really drank the Kool-Aid," he told Woodward.

Trump's public stance on Covid-19 became more somber in

Brunswick NJ: Rutgers University. Press, 2006).

summer 2020 when infection and death rates climbed again in the South and West. But he and many Republican governors continued to scoff at face masks and social distancing. The harm had been done. Had the United States taken preventive measures like Canada, *The New York Times* estimated on September 9, 2020, at least 100,000 Americans would not have died. Trumpian lies were often repeated on social media.[33] As more of Trump's followers see that their emperor has no clothes, a few will laugh and many will desert him. Many will feel deceived.. But most stuck with him even after his electoral defeat.

By July 2022 just over one million Americans died from Covid— about one-sixth of the world total for a small fraction (4.25%) of the global population.[34] If Trump's big lies and failure to take Covid as a serious menace to public health contributed even to a small fraction of those deaths, it must be regarded as a major crime—even as genocide, since people of color died disproportionally.

Putin's Kremlin also uses the Big Lie. In August 2020 social media and Russian RT showed images of Black Lives protesters in Portland burning stacks of Bibles, topping off the fire with American flags—multiple affronts to God-fearing, patriotic Republicans. There was even a video to prove it. The reality was that just a few protestors among thousands lit one or two Bibles to kindle a fire. Here was one of Russia's first public forays into the 2020 elections. The disinformation was then published in the *New York Post* and repeated by Donald Trump Jr. and by Senator Ted Cruz.[35]

---

33 Social media profited from the anti-science fanatics, conspiracy theorists, and purveyors of snake oil remedies who, seconding the optimistic spiel, warned not to take anti-virus vaccines. Big Tech profited from an anti-vaxx industry that grew to 58 million followers during the pandemic. In 2020 there were over 400 anti-vaxx accounts with 58 million followers—a total swelling by millions every month. In mid-2020, some 31% of British and 41% of U.S. respondents did not plan to get a coronavirus vaccine if offered. Center for Countering Digital Hate [London] at https://twitter.com/CCDHate (accessed 7/5/20).

34 *The New York Times*, July 18, 2022, at https://www.nytimes.com/interactive/2021/us/covid-cases.html

35 Matthew Rosenberg and Julian E. Barnes, "A Bible Burning, a Russian News Agency and a Story Too Good to Check Out," *The New York Times,* August 12, 2020. Not to be outdone, a network of fake Chinese accounts posted videos bashing President Trump, criticizing his recent closure of China's consulate

REPUBLICANS, MARTIN LUTHER, AND MACHIAVELLI

Today's ostensible defenders of religion would do well to review the lives of reformers such as John Wycliffe, Jan Hus, and Martin Luther—each of whom risked his life for what he saw as truth.[36]

"Here I stand!" With these words, Martin Luther defied a church establishment that wanted no challenge to papal authority. Interrogated first by the pope's representative, Cardinal Cajetan, and then, three years later, by the Holy Roman Emperor Charles V himself, Luther refused to recant. *"Unless I am convinced by Scripture and plain reason, I do not accept the authority of the popes and councils, for they have contradicted each other. My conscience is captive to the Word of God. I cannot and I will not recant anything. It is neither right nor safe to go against conscience. Here I stand."*[37]

Five centuries later, Republicans in Congress abandoned all principles to bolster their own party establishment and their personal interests. Following Trump wherever his whims push him, Republicans follow the advice of Luther's contemporary, Niccolò Machiavelli. A Prince, "old Nick" wrote, should avoid dreams of justice, mercy, and temperance. Instead, he should employ all the tools of coercion and cooptation—violence and deception—to maximize his power, an end justifying any means.

---

in Houston, his 1handling of the coronavirus pandemic, and his threats to ban the popular social media app TikTok. *The Washington Post*, August 12, 2020, reported that one video showed flattering images of Biden and predicted that Trump would lose in November.

36 Catholic leaders such Stefan Cardinal Wyszynskia in Poland risked imprisonment and possible execution as they stood up to Communist rule, but they were not trying to reform their own establishment, as Luther did. For a survey, see Paul Higginson, "The Vatican and Communism from '*Divini Redemptoris*' to Paul VI: Part 2." *New Blackfriars* 61, 720 (1980): 234-244.

37 Initially, Luther sought to save the Catholic church—not destroy it. The young monk (aged 24) warned that the papacy was abandoning God's word in Holy Scripture by selling indulgences to finance the art and architecture of Rome. The recently invented printing presses quickly spread his writings. A reformation if not a revolution was brewing. Mindful that the Council of Constance in 1415 had burned at the stake Jan Hus, Luther stood up to Cardinal Cajetan in 1518 but then escaped back to Wittenberg. In 1521, Luther was summoned to the Imperial Diet in Worms where he twice met and defied Charles V. Luther departed Worms just before Charles V issued a sort of fatwa authorizing anyone to kill the heretic Luther without fear of prosecution.

Unlike Luther, today's Republicans put personal and partisan political interests above patriotism and concern for the country's standing in the world. What happened to courage? Unlike Republicans in Congress, Luther stood up to the whole power structure of Europe. As Thomas Cahill wrote in *Heretics and Heroes*, Luther's courage to say "no" became a central factor in Western civilization.[38] It inspired another Lutheran prelate, Dietrich Bonhoeffer to oppose the Nazification of the Lutheran church in the 1930s. Fearing the impending Holocaust, Bonhoeffer implored Christians not only to bandage wounds of the injured but also to jam the wheels of oppression. He disdained "cheap grace"—the moral laxity of many German Christians–in favor of the "costly grace" that links Christian belief to social consequences. Hitler's agents arrested Bonhoeffer in 1943 and hanged him in 1945.[39]

Luther risked his life to honor what he believed to be God's truth. Most GOP politicians in 2021-2022 continued to stand by Trump—even the many who in private condemned him, his lies, and his actions. Susan Collins and other Republicans risk nothing more ominous than defeat in the next election if they spurn the party bandwagon.

Despite their pious incantations, most Republicans (including pious Christians) follow Machiavelli rather than Luther. They do not take a stand on issues of justice. Instead, they murmur: "We are determined to please our donors, our own pocketbooks, and our easily manipulated base. Our courage is manifest in our willingness to endure criticism by so-called experts in the elite media."

Neither a libertarian nor an anarchist, one graduate of the

---

38 *Heretics and Heroes: How Renaissance Artists and Reformation Priests Created Our World* (New York: Doubleday, 2013).

39 Pope Pius XII and many other Catholic leaders opposed Hitler but valued a strong Germany as a bulwark against atheistic Soviet Communism. Still, as many as one-third of Catholic priests in Germany faced reprisals from Nazi authorities. Thousands of priests and nuns were sent to concentration camps. Some 400 Germans were among the 2,579 Catholic priests imprisoned at Dachau. Bishop Clemens August Graf von Galen developed a Catholic critique of Nazism and led protests against Nazi "euthanasia" of invalids. For more on Pius XII, see David I. Kertzer, "The Pope, the Jews, and the Secrets in the Archives," *The Atlantic*, August 27, 2020 at https://www.theatlantic.com/ideas/archive/2020/08/the-popes-jews/615736/

Harvard Divinity School says that when he sees how people in the Christian Right manipulate "the Christian religion for personal empowerment and wealth" and undermine "the very values that I think are embodied in the teachings of Jesus Christ, I'm angry."[40]

In the same vein, the editor of a leading evangelical publication wrote: "In our founding documents, Billy Graham explains that *Christianity Today* will help evangelical Christians interpret the news in a manner that reflects their faith." President Trump "has dumbed down the idea of morality in his administration. He has hired and fired a number of people who are now convicted criminals. He himself has admitted to immoral actions in business and his relationship with women, about which he remains proud. His Twitter feed alone—with its habitual string of mischaracterizations, lies, and slanders—is a nearly perfect example of a human being who is morally lost and confused . . . None of the president's positives can balance the moral and political danger we face under a leader of such grossly immoral character."

The editorial continued: "To the many evangelicals who continue to support Mr. Trump in spite of his blackened moral record, we might say this: Remember who you are and whom you serve . . . If we don't reverse course now, will anyone take anything we say about justice and righteousness with any seriousness for decades to come?" If evangelicals do not call a spade a spade, the whole game "will crash down on the reputation of evangelical religion and the world's understanding of the gospel."[41]

By stating the obvious about Trump, that he is immoral and should be removed from office, *Christianity Today* suffered the Christian Right's vicious and hypocritical backlash. Nearly 200 evangelical leaders, including former Arkansas Gov. Mike Huckabee, former Rep. Michele Bachmann, Jerry Falwell Jr., and Ralph Reed, signed a joint letter denouncing the *Christianity Today* editorial. In late 2019, 90% of Republicans polled said they opposed impeachment and ouster of the president. Among Republicans who identify as white

---

40 Chris Hodges to Michelle Goldberg, "The holy blitz rolls on," *Salon*, January 8, 2007.

41 Mark Galli, "Trump Should Be Removed from Office," *Christianity Today*, December 19, 2019, editorial.

Evangelical Protestants, that number rose to 99%.[42]

How could this happen? Tens of millions of Americans live hermetically sealed inside the vast media and educational edifice controlled by what Hedges terms "Christian fascists." In this world, miracles are real. Satan, allied with secular humanists and Muslims, seeks to destroy America, and Trump is God's anointed vessel to build the Christian nation and cement into place a government that instills "biblical values." These "biblical values," which include turning the Ten Commandments into secular law, crushing "infidels," especially Muslims, indoctrinating children in schools with "biblical" teachings and thwarting sexual license.[43]

Having covered the Balkan wars, the Middle East, and Latin American dictatorships, Hedges (part of a *New York Times* team that won a Pulitzer prize) saw how the dominant religions of these nations were often distorted by totalitarian movements into civic religions in which the goals of the movement or the state became the goals of the divine.

The greatest moral failing of the *liberal* Christian church has been its refusal to denounce the Christian Right as heretics, says Hedges. "By tolerating the intolerant, it ceded religious legitimacy to an array of con artists, charlatans and demagogues, and their cultish supporters. It stood by as the core Gospel message—concern for the poor and the oppressed—was perverted into a magical world where God and Jesus showered believers with material wealth and power. The white race, especially in the United States, became God's chosen agent. Imperialism and war became divine instruments for purging the world of infidels and barbarians, evil itself. Capitalism, because God blessed the righteous with wealth and power and condemned the immoral to poverty and suffering, became shorn of its inherent cruelty and exploitation. The iconography and symbols of American nationalism became intertwined with the iconography and symbols of the Christian faith. The mega-pastors, narcissists who rule despotic, cult-like fiefdoms, make millions of dollars by using this heretical

---

42 Chris Hedges, "Onward, Christian Fascists," *Truthdig*, December 30, 2019, at https://www.truthdig.com/articles/onward-christian-fascists/ (accessed 8/27/20).

43 Hedges, "Onward, Christian Fascists."

belief system to prey on the mounting despair and desperation of their congregations, victims of <u>neoliberalism</u> and <u>deindustrialization</u>. These believers find in Donald Trump a reflection of themselves, a champion of the unfettered greed, cult of masculinity, lust for violence, white supremacy, bigotry, American chauvinism, religious intolerance, anger, racism, and conspiracy theories that define the central beliefs of the Christian Right."[44]

The Capitol Attack as Christian Anarchy

Fanatical, extreme religious faith was a central force driving the January 6, 2021 assault on the Capitol. Institutional religion is breaking apart in the United States, becoming more individualized and more disconnected from organized denominations with theological credentials and oversight. For Russell Moore, writing in *Christianity Today* (January 5, 2022), "The Capitol attack threatened not only American democracy but also evangelical witness. The attack signaled a post-Christian Church--not merely a post-Christian culture

In the days leading up to the insurrection, evangelical Christians gathered on the National Mall for a "Jericho March," repeating the same falsehoods--that the election had been stolen and therefore should be overturned. Trump's admonition, "If you don't fight ... you won't have a country anymore," is not new for large sectors of American evangelicalism. Some have sold literal or metaphorical bunker supplies for the imminent collapse of civilization sure to come because of Y2K or sharia law or critical race theory or a pandemic plot to shutter churches. Many sectors of evangelicalism have become apocalyptic about everything but the actual Apocalypse.

The angry crowd storming the Capitol lifted high a sign that read, "Jesus Saves," while nearby a makeshift gallows was erected to threaten the execution of Vice President Pence. That these two images could coexist in the same mob reflected a crisis within American evangelicalism. Many if not most white evangelicals believed the lie behind the attack--that the 2020 election was stolen by a left-wing conspiracy that included, quite incongruously,

---

44 Ibid.

the conservative Republican governors and election officials in Georgia and Arizona.

There is a growing overlap between white Americans who put a high value on individualism and libertarianism and those who embrace Christian nationalism, a cultural belief that America is defined by Christian identity, heritage and social order and that the government needs to protect it. Trump has united disparate groups, largely white, under the umbrella of Christian nationalism.[45]

In the midst of the invasion of the U.S. Capitol Jacob Chansley, the bare-chested man in Viking horns known as the QAnon Shaman, stopped his fellow marauders in the Senate chamber to pray. "Thank you Heavenly Father for gracing us with this opportunity … to send a message to all the tyrants, the communists and the globalists, that this is our nation, not theirs," he said. "Thank you for filling this chamber with patriots that love you and that love Christ. Thank you for allowing the United States of America to be reborn."

The prayer scene illustrated how the insurrection intertwined with Christian nationalism. Across the sea of protesters in and outside the building, t-shirt and ball-cap slogans proclaimed "Jesus is my savior, Trump is my president"; "God, Guns, Trump"; or, on the sweatshirt of a man helping construct the rough gallows erected on the Capitol lawn, "Faith, Family, Freedom." Some protesters carried gigantic portraits of Jesus or chanted about the blood of Jesus washing Congress clean. A Nebraska priest performed an exorcism on the Capitol building to banish the demon Baphomet. Rioter Leo Brent Bozell IV, came from a long line of Christian right activists: His father, L. Brent Bozell III, founded the right-wing Media Research Center and his grandfather, L. Brent Bozell Jr., wrote speeches for Joseph McCarthy and a manifesto for Barry Goldwater.[46]

The January 6 events and their aftershocks in 2021-2022 illustrated the synergies of Moisés Naím's three P's—populism, polarization, and post-truths.

---

45 Michelle Bornstein, "A horn-wearing 'shaman.' A cowboy evangelist. For some, the Capitol attack was a kind of Christian revolt," *The Washington Post*, July 6, 2021.

46 Kathryn Joyce, "How Christian nationalism drove the insurrection: A religious history of Jan. 6,' *Salon*, January 2022.

3

Dirty Old Men and Their Higher Amorality

Let Boys Be Boys and Let Criminals Go Free

Sexual Liberation?

"When you are a TV star or a president, you can do whatever you want—right? I dropped all rules a long time ago." This is the mindset of the man who became America's president in 2017. Rule and standards mean nothing for a draft dodger who pretends he is strong and seems to admire tough guys. Amazingly, over 40% of the electorate voted for Trump knowing that he believes his fame permits him to grab any female and do whatever he wants.

Many public figures try to mask their dirty deeds with a sanctimonious decorum. Not "the Donald," who bragged about his sexual conquests.[1] He has been accused of rape, sexual assault, and sexual harassment by at least twenty-five women since the 1970s. The accusations resulted in several lawsuits. Despite the chorus of victims who confirmed his boasts, many women voted for Trump in 2016. They preferred him to another woman, Hillary Clinton. Trump's personal attorney, the fixer Michael Cohen, bribed some of Trump's paid sex partners to keep quiet.

Males have lorded it over females for millennia. Men of every race, religion, and party have abused women. Starting with Alexander Hamilton and Thomas Jefferson, both conservatives and ostensible liberals have been accused of sexual misconduct. In the 21st century, we like to think that moral standards are better. We take it for granted that gender exploitation is a violation of basic human rights. But the problem endures. In 1998, only five of 205 House Democrats voted to impeach Bill Clinton for lying about

---

1   For a transcript of the Hollywood Access tape, *The New York Times*, December 8, 2016 at https://www.nytimes.com/2016/10/08/us/donald-trump-tape-transcript. html (accessed 12/15/16).

his White House affair. In recent years, however, Democrats have shown their opposition to male bullying. They pressured Senators John Conyers in 2017 and Al Franken in 2018 to resign under the shadow of gender-abuse scandals. House Democratic leader Nancy Pelosi demanded their resignations even though these actions could cost her party's representation in Congress.

However "Republican leaders can't seem to take the problem seriously."[2] When Clarence Thomas was considered to be a Supreme Court justice in 1991, Republicans insulted and disdained his accuser Anita Hill.[3] This pattern recurred before and *after* Brett M. Kavanaugh joined the court in 2018.[4] When more criticism emerged leading some critics to call for Kavanaugh to be impeached, Trump tweeted: "He is an innocent man who has been treated HORRIBLY .... Such lies about him. They want to scare him into turning Liberal!" In another tweet, the president suggested that the Justice Department should come to Kavanaugh's rescue.

Despite Roy Moore's reputation as a pedophile, his candidacy in Alabama for the Senate in 2017 was backed by Trump and the Republican National Committee. Moore's ambiguous denial of the charges ("I don't remember ... dating any girl without the permission of her mother") was supposed to exonerate him. Most Republicans in Congress demonstrated their readiness to jettison their vaunted principles to get one more yes vote in the Senate.[5]

Besides Roy Moore and Brett Kavanaugh, Trump defended others accused of sex crimes—the late CEO of Fox News Roger

---

2 Editorial, *The New York Times*, September 18, 2018.

3 Four female witnesses reportedly waited in the wings to support Anita Hill's credibility, but they were not called—due to what the *Los Angeles Times* (October 17, 1991) described as a private compromise deal between Republicans and the Senate Judiciary Committee Chair, Democrat Joe Biden.

4 Calls for his impeachment emerged after publication of *The Education of Brett Kavanaugh: An Investigation* (New York: Portfolio, 2019) by Robin Pogrebin and Kate Kelly, two reporters who had covered the earlier hearings. In their subsequent investigations that found that a lawyer for one accuser, Deborah Ramirez, gave the FBI the names of twenty-five persons who could corroborate her accusations, but the FBI interviewed *none* of them.

5 Moore lost the election to Democrat Doug Jones. They were contesting the Senate seat vacated when Trump named Jeff Sessions Attorney General.

Ailes, the Fox host Bill O'Reilly, Trump's former campaign manager Corey Lewandowski, his former staff secretary Rob Porter, his first choice as secretary of labor Andrew Puzder, Boston Red Sox owner Robert Kraft, and the boxer Mike Tyson. On the other hand, Trump had harsh words for the putative sexual lives of Democrats Bill Clinton, Al Franken, Eliot Spitzer, and Miramax founder Harvey Weinstein.

After Ghislaine Maxwell was arrested on charges of helping Jeffrey Epstein set up a child sex ring, the U.S. president on July 21, 2020, volunteered: "I just wish her well, frankly. I've met her numerous times over the years especially since I lived in Palm Beach, and I guess they lived in Palm Beach. But I wish her well, whatever it is." Not a word about the victims of Maxwell and Epstein.[6] On June 28, 2022, she was sentenced to 20 years in a U.S. prison for helping former financier Jeffrey Epstein abuse young girls.

Trump's good wishes for Maxwell brought to mind Trump's comment about Jeffrey Epstein in 2002: "I've known Jeff for 15 years. Terrific guy," Trump told a reporter: "He's a lot of fun to be with. It is even said that he likes beautiful women as much as I do, and many of them are on the younger side. No doubt about it—Jeffrey enjoys his social life."[7] There was also evidence that Trump (like Bill Clinton) had flown on the "Lolita Express," one of Epstein's planes. Another woman, Virginia Giuffre, alleged that while working as a towel girl at Mar-a-Lago in 1999, she was recruited by Ghislaine Maxwell to become one of Epstein's sex workers—when she was 16 years old.[8] Epstein died in a New York prison cell on August 10, 2019, as he awaited, without bail, his trial on sex trafficking charges.

---

6   Jennifer Rubin, "Trump wishes Ghislaine Maxwell well—and the media barely reacts," *The Washington Post*, July 22, 2020. Ghislaine Maxwell's father, Robert Maxell, a tabloid rival to Rupert Murdoch in England, drowned in 1991 in what some observers called a suicide.

7   Landon Thomas, Jr., "Jeffrey Epstein: International Moneyman of Mystery," *New York*, October 25, 2002.

8   On the involvements of Elon Musk and others in these affairs, *see* Ben Widdicombe, "Ghislaine Maxwell, Jeffrey Epstein's Alleged Madam, Has Spent Her Life in the Headlines," *Town & Country*, July 2, 2020.

Goodbye Law and Morality, Welcome Pretend Tough!

Who needs law, discipline, and morality? In 2019, Trump bragged that he lifted a court-martial on a Navy SEAL, Chief Petty Officer Edward Gallagher. He had been formally charged with more than a dozen criminal acts, including premeditated murder, which occurred during his eighth deployment overseas.[9] Other U.S. servicemen accused Gallagher of stabbing to death an Arab teenager who was under sedation because of a previous injury. The boy was so skinny that his watch slid easily off his wrist. In no way ashamed of his feat, Gallagher than posed for a triumphal photo holding his dead victim by the hair.

Before his most recent deployment, Gallagher asked a friend to make him a custom hunting knife and hatchet, vowing in a text, "I will try and dig that knife or hatchet on someone's skull." This was the same knife used against the sedated Iraqi teenager wearing a tank top. On previous deployments, Gallagher was said to have shot an Iraqi schoolgirl in a flower-print hijab and a man carrying a water jug. He was also accused in 2010 of shooting through an Afghan girl to hit the man carrying her and, in 2014, of trying to run over a Navy police officer. One SEAL told investigators he tried to damage the chief's sniper rifle to make it less accurate. These and similar incidents were either not reported or, if reported, elicited no charges.

Gallagher was tried in a military court and acquitted in July 2019 of all charges, except one count of wrongfully posing for photographs with the body of a dead Islamic State fighter. The jury sentenced him to four months, the maximum possible. Because he had served that amount of time waiting for trial, he was released. Despite this extremely modest punishment, President Trump intervened to make sure that Gallagher was not demoted when he retired and that he could keep his Trident medal, a SEAL badge of honor.

To view the former SEAL as a cruel sadist does not ignore that Gallagher, like many other U.S. soldiers and sailors, served in multiple combat deployments. His life experiences could harden

---

9   David Philipps, *Alpha: Eddie Gallagher and the War for the Soul of the Navy SEALs* (New York: Crown, 2022).

anyone, just to survive. But surely the military court that judged Gallagher was quite attuned to such realities and willing to make some allowance for them.

Encouraged by Fox News, the president boasted for his base that he upended the military code of justice to protect the petty officer from punishment. Trump seemed to assume that the voters who support him as president are also indifferent to law, discipline, and basic morality. Perhaps he thinks that they may go to church on Sunday but behave as they please the rest of the week.

The highest ranks in the Navy insisted that Gallagher be held responsible for his action, seen by professionals as a war crime. But the president commanded his Secretary of Defense to fire the Secretary of the Navy for resisting his (Trump's) interventions. As the lead article in *The New York Times* put it on December 1: "The case pits a Pentagon hierarchy committed to enforcing long-standing rules of combat against a commander-in-chief with no military experience but [with] a finely honed sense of grievance against authority."

If President Trump were asked to evaluate the Nazi Jew killer Adolf Eichmann, he would probably praise him for duly "following orders" and ignoring global standards of "political correctness." Trump claimed to back a strong military establishment, but often expressed distrust in the generals and admirals who run it. As *The New York Times* put it: "Rather than accept information from his own government, he responds to television reports that grab his interest . . . . He bulldozes past precedent and norms." He sees the top military brass as part of the "deep state" opposing him, along with the intelligence community, law enforcement agencies, and diplomatic corps. Pentagon officials as well as their civilian colleagues worried that Trump's intervention in the Gallagher case "emboldens war criminals and erodes the order of a professional military."

After he was fired for his handling of the Gallagher case, former Navy Secretary Richard V. Spencer called the president's actions "a shocking and unprecedented intervention" and "a reminder that the president has very little understanding of what it means to be in the military, to fight ethically or to be governed by a uniform set of rules and practices." Spencer wrote that "ethical conduct is what sets our military apart. I have believed that every day since joining the Marine Corps in 1976."[10]

Retired Army Brigadier General Anthony J. Tata disagreed. He wrote that "the president was right to intervene to prevent a biased, small-minded person like Spencer from spitefully tilting the weight of the bureaucracy on top of a single sailor. Servicemen and women enjoy the same due process rights as the civilians of the country they serve." Tata predicted that Spencer and his hashtags would soon fade while "the president's support of warfighters over bureaucrats will increase the morale of those in the rank and file. The critics will angrily accuse the president of supporting a war criminal, but the real crimes in this case have been papered over by a secretary of the Navy eager to avoid embarrassment at the expense of a sailor who, on the whole, served honorably."[11]

Whether or not Gallagher might deserve some sympathy for his actions, what excuse could anyone make for Trump? He overruled the very military professionals pledged to serve the country and him. The rules of war they support aim to protect civilians and military of every country, whether foe or friend or neither. Ultimately, Trump's behavior contributed to heightened dangers for U.S. servicemen and women.

Besides granting clemency to Gallagher on November 15, 2019, Trump also pardoned two other former military officers the same day—one convicted of murder and another (pardoned before he went to trial) charged with two murders. Earlier, on May 6, Trump also pardoned another officer convicted of murder.

A senior Navy official said that Navy leaders believed Trump was making decisions based on bad information. "Trump doesn't make decisions based on military experts," said the official. "He does it off his gut and how it plays in the media. He watches Fox News and believes whatever they say." Beth Peyton-O'Brien, a retired Navy captain and former military judge, said Trump's intervention

---

10 *The Washington Post*, November 27, 2019.

11 *The Washington Post,* December 1, 2019. For the parallel views of Gallagher's attorney, see *Navy Times*, October 7, 2019.

sent the wrong message to service members. "The message seems to be there are no rules—do what you want," she said. "You can commit any crimes as long as you're in combat." Another official recalled that when Trump was campaigning, he said that torture works and that when he's president, it's going to be 'gloves off.'"[12]

The President's Clemency to a Host of Criminals

Dealing with violations of federal laws, as of July 2020, Trump pardoned 25 convicted criminals and commuted the sentences of 11 more. Almost all of the beneficiaries of Trump's clemency had a personal or political connection to the president. Most of his actions could advance his own political agenda (at least 21 of 36 pardons or commutations). Some (5 of 36) were championed by Trump's favorite source of information and wisdom, Fox News. Very few (5 of 36) had been recommended by the Department of Justice Pardon Attorney. No president in American history comes close to matching Trump's systematically self-serving use of the pardon power.[13] (Obama pardoned 212 criminals and commuted 1715 sentences—most convicted on drug charges for which some received lengthy mandatory sentences.)

Trump's first pardon went to the hard-on-immigrants Arizona sheriff Joe Arpaio (8/25/17), found guilty of criminal contempt of court. Next was Kristan Soucier (3/9/18), discharged dishonorably from the Navy and found guilty of retaining national defense information. Soon after came Lewis "Scooter" Libby (4/13/18), a key aide of VP Dick Cheney jailed for perjury and obstruction of justice. Libby's pardon was followed by that of conservative commentator Dinesh D'Souza (5/11/18), found guilty of illegal campaign donations to a Republican Senate candidate. The former media mogul and Trump biographer Conrad Black was pardoned (5/15/19) for his mail fraud and obstruction of justice.

On February 18, 2020, the president commuted the fourteen-

---

12 Andrew Dyer, "Did Trump disrupt military justice?" *The Los Angeles Times*, November 27, 2018.

13 Jack Goldsmith and Matt Gluck, "Trump's Aberrant Pardons and Commutations," *Lawfare*, July 11, 2020 at https://www.lawfareblog.com/trumps-aberrant-pardons-and-commutations (accessed 7/15/20).

year sentence of Rod Blagojevich, a former contestant on Trump's reality TV show and governor of Illinois, jailed for extortion (four counts); corrupt solicitation of funds; conspiracy to corruptly solicit funds (two counts); and making false statements.

In November 2019, a jury found Roger Stone guilty of making false statements to Congress (five counts), witness tampering, and obstructing an official proceeding. The sentencing judge stated that Stone had been "prosecuted for covering up for the president" in the investigations into Russian interference in the 2016 elections. On July 10, 2020, Trump saved Stone from 40 months imprisonment and eliminated any restrictions on his home confinement and erased a penalty Stone was to pay.

Republican Senator Mitt Romney called Stone's commutation "unprecedented, historic corruption." Stone said he would write a book to help his friend Donald Trump win the next election. California Democrat Adam Schiff introduced legislation that would make it a crime for pardons to be issued in return for something of value as a violation of bribery statutes. Schiff's bill would also require evidence be turned over to Congress if a president uses pardon powers in cases involving the president or a president's family, or in cases of obstruction of Congress. During a contentious interview after his release, Stone called black radio host Morris O'Kelly a "Negro."

Murders by Friends of the President

Trump's indifference to human rights, law, and basic morality was on display on many occasions. He seemed also to be Ok with murders by Saudi, Russian, Philippine, and other foreign strongmen. The dissident Saudi journalist Jamal Khashoggi walked into the Saudi Arabia consulate in Istanbul on October 2, 2018, and did not leave except as his body parts were carried out by Saudi agents. In November 2018, the CIA concluded that Crown Prince Mohammed bin Salman had ordered Khashoggi's assassination. The U.S. government sanctioned seventeen Saudis for the murder but not bin Salman himself. President Trump disputed the CIA assessment. In the weeks following Khashoggi's death, Trump spent more time praising Saudi Arabia as a very important ally and purchaser of U.S. weapons and goods (the value of which Trump wildly overstated) than he did reacting to the killing. Defending the crown prince, Trump complained that some were calling him "guilty before being proven innocent." A UN investigation in 2019 concluded that Khashoggi's murder was "a brutal and premeditated killing, planned and perpetrated." No matter. As if nothing terrible had happened, Trump son-in-law Jared Kushner, Treasury Secretary Steven Mnuchin, along with top executives of BlackRock and Goldman Sachs attended the 2019 Investment Initiative, the Saudi regime's annual money fest ("Davos in the Desert") to promote doing business with the kingdom.[14]

Trump chose to defend Saudi Arabia again in December 2018, when a 21-year-old Saudi officer and trainee at the Pensacola Air Base shot and killed three Americans and wounded eight others before he was put down. Speaking at the White House the day after the shooting, Trump said Saudi Arabia's King Salman bin Abdulaziz Al-Saud told him they "are devastated," and that the King would be involved "in taking care of the families." The President promised that "we will get to the bottom" of what happened. The shooter and many other Saudi trainees at Pensacola were found to be reading jihadist tirades. Some of the more than 800 Saudi trainees were sent home, but most continued their training in Florida.

Hoping to get Saudi Arabia to pump more oil, long-time Saudi critic President Biden pumped fists with Crown Prince "MBS" in July 2022.

Trump's "ignore human rights" syndrome also extended to North Korea, where the U.S. delegation to the United Nations for a second year refused to put North Korea's human rights on the Security Council agenda for Human Rights Day, December 10, 2019. Eight of the Council's 15 members signed a letter to schedule the meeting but needed a ninth signature, which the United States again refused to provide. Louis Charbonneau, the UN director for Human

---

14 In June 2022, a House committee said it was investigating whether Kushner traded on his former government position to land a $2 billion investment in his new private equity firm from a prominent Saudi Arabian wealth fund. During his time in government, Mr. Kushner developed a close rapport with Prince Mohammed, even as the prince faced criticism over his human rights record and Saudi Arabia's war in Yemen.

Rights Watch, complained: "Once again, the U.S. has prevented the UN Security Council from scrutinizing North Korea's abysmal human rights record, apparently because of President Trump's special relationship with Kim Jong Un." Charbonneau said that "by blocking this meeting ... the Trump administration is sending a message to Kim Jong Un that the U.S. no long considers arbitrary detention, starvation, torture, summary executions, sexual violence and other crimes against the North Korean people a priority." The upshot: "North Korea and many other abusive governments can now rest assured that they have little to fear from the Trump administration when it comes to human rights."[15]

The president seemed indifferent even when he learned that employees of his comrade and likely creditor Vladimir Putin killed American soldiers. In 2020, he downplayed or ignored evidence that Russian military intelligence was paying a bounty to Taliban militants for every U.S. soldier killed. Why not punish or at least complain to the Kremlin? His silence corroborated John Bolton's claim that Putin played the U.S. president "like a fiddle."

How any Republican patriot could support such a hypocrite is nearly unfathomable. The president did not distinguish between love of country and love of himself. On July 18, 2015, the notorious draft dodger said of Navy veteran John McCain: "He's not a war hero. He was a war hero because he was captured. I like people who weren't captured." In July 2016, Trump belittled the Muslim parents of Capt. Humayun Khan, killed in Iraq. Ohio's governor John Kasich castigated Trump, saying "There's only one way to talk about Gold Star parents: with honor and respect."

More hypocrisy: After Lt. Col. Alexander Vindman, a Purple Heart recipient, testified in the impeachment proceedings, Trump questioned his loyalty to the country. Trump often spurned veterans'

---

15 The South Korean government also joined the effort to buy the North's good will by appeasement. In mid-November 2019, Seoul withdrew from a list of more than forty co-sponsors of a General Assembly resolution condemning "the grave human rights situation" in North Korea. This was the first time since 2008, the era of South Korea's Sunshine Policy toward North Korea, that Seoul declined to co-sponsor the resolution. Still striving for some kind of deal with Pyongyang, South Korean and U.S. leaders tried to humor Kim Jong Un by keeping silent about human rights.

events and memorials; used tombstones of the fallen as a political backdrop; and suggested that those who did not applaud his State of the Union speech may have committed treason.

American Oblivion

Nearly two hundred years ago the Russian diplomat and poet Fyodor Tyuchev wrote a poem that helps describe how Trump's penumbra impacts all of life. Tyuchev's poem "The Vision [*Videnie*]" (1828) begins with four lines about a starry night when "the living chariot of the universe rolls openly into the sanctuary of the heavens." But then the "night thickens, like chaos on the waters, and *oblivion [bespamiatstvo]*—like Atlas—crushes the earth.[16] President Trump and many of his associates display ingrained habits of deception as well as *bespamiatstvo*—literally "without memory" or the state of being forgotten.

Tyutchev offers an apt description of the effect upon Americans of the flagrant deceptions of Trump and his team. A blizzard of lies, falling incessantly upon the public discourse and infecting our imaginations, makes truth itself a suspect. *Bespamiatstvo* threatens to crush and obliterate all that is sharp and clear in our minds.

The poet Tyutchev anticipated what Nobel laureate in economics Robert J. Shiller has written about the climate of lies and distrust enveloping the United States (*The New York Times*, November 10, 2019). "An atmosphere generated by a steady flow and variety of lies is like a dark cloud over the facts." Surveys by the Pew Research Center find that Americans trust each other less than 40 years ago and that trust in the U.S. government is at historically low levels. Shiller complains that "businesses can't plan effectively when they don't know who or what can be trusted." Indeed, this is true of Americans in all walks of life, reducing their capacity for cooperative reciprocity.

John Dryden in 1700 described a similar situation.

> *Among our crimes oblivion may beset;*
> *But 'tis the King's perfection to forget.*

---

16 *Bespamiatstvo, kak Atlas, davit sushu.*

A century later, Thomas Carlyle in 1872 asserted: "The deeper oblivion of the Law of Right and Wrong ... is by no means beautiful." Another observer, T. Sinclair, added in 1878 that "the oblivionists do not clearly see the whole truth here."

Robert Shiller worries that lying erodes trust, and that this process can be accelerated when publicity is given to lies. Long-term differences in economic and social achievement reflect cultural values. Young people in the United States who are just becoming interested in politics have seen only this period of rampant lying. This impression may affect them for the rest of their lives. Attitudes toward trust can linger for generations.

Trump's display of blatant, persistent, and unapologetic lying could inspire young people, who, with no basis of comparison, adopt knee-jerk attitudes of cynical disdain, while persons who still attempt to engage in honest debate may lose credibility—as when bad money drives out good.

THE OPERATIONAL CODE OF AMORAL POLITICS

The Model President and Model Party

Our teenage daughter often asks, "Is this song *vulgar*? "Is this singer's low-cut dress *appropriate*?" Her parents' opinions count for something within our four walls, but what if she looks onto our surroundings? What could our daughter or any child learn from Trump's presidency and the party that follows him? The short answer: Most everything he does or says is vulgar, while almost nothing is appropriate. As for his party, it just plays along—*exactly what we tell our daughter not to do.* Our daughter (adopted from China), like most American children, goes to school with kids of many colors and cultures. If she follows Trump's example, she will shun and make fun of those who look different from her.

Here is what kids can learn from today's leader of the free world. First, lie or distort the facts whenever it suits your needs. *The Washington Post* found that President Trump lied a few times nearly every day. He pushed off informed criticism as fake news and sometimes referred to major newspapers as the "enemy of the people." With just a few exceptions, hardly any Republican leaders chastised the president for abusing the truth.

Second lesson: Do whatever it takes to please your backers—big tax breaks and de-regulations for the ultra-rich; small tax breaks and empty promises for the hoi polloi. Most Republicans know that the 2017 Tax Cuts and Jobs Act will add mountains to public debt while other legislation reduces health insurance for many Americans.

Third lesson: Have illicit fun so long as you don't get caught. Enjoy yourself but cover your tracks. Whenever possible, get your kicks on the public dime.

Fourth, use "strong" language (more vulgar than "vulgar") to make a point. It's OK to call your foes ugly names so long as most of your followers go along.

Fifth, don't worry about the three R's. TV is better than books. Tweets are more powerful than pen and pencil or keyboards. Bad grammar and self-centered language ("I'm the greatest," etc.) are OK if they appeal to your supporters. Don't bother with history. All the morals and contradictions don't add up.[17]

Sixth, eat whatever you want and avoid the gym. Whip down fast food and take extra scoops of ice cream. Avoid real exercise so your knees and hips won't need replacing. Don't bother to enjoy nature unless, like son Donald Jr., you like to shoot big game.[18] The president's body, his doctors said, is in good shape; about his soul, little news from official sources.

Seventh, claim that you are following God's will. It's good PR to attend church from time to time (like comrade Putin) don't worry

---

17 The misplaced apostrophe in the subtitle of the self-published book by Donald Jr. *Liberal Privilege: Joe Biden and the Democrat's Defense of the Indefensible* (2020) suggests that an indifference to grammar is shared by father and son.

18 Donald Trump Jr's rare sheep hunt in Mongolia in August 2019 cost U.S. taxpayers over $75,000 for his Secret Service detail. Researchers say the Trump family take 12 times as many trips as did the Obamas. Critics accuse the Trump family of draining the Secret Services' finances with their average of 1,000 more trips per year, many for leisure. Donald Jr. met with the president of Mongolia and did not get permission to kill a rare Argali sheep *after* he did so. BBC June 10, 2020, at https://www.bbc.com/news/world-us-canada-52999375 (accessed 7/10/20).

about the lame and the halt. The poor you will have always with you. Let them learn to take care of themselves. As for those who are not white-skinned or Christian, kick them out of the country and don't let more in.

Eighth, be tough with so-called friends and as well as foes. Speak brashly and carry a big stick. If somebody does something you don't like, call them out on it loud and clear. If they have a weak spot, dig in there and press till it hurts. But if somebody has embarrassing stuff on you, as probably happens in Moscow, take it easy on them. Give them treats as needed.

MASS MURDERERS IN HIGH PLACES

Like other authoritarians, President Trump has consistently tried to suppress accurate information about the lethal results of his policies. Hitler killed millions in gas chambers as well as on battlefields, but informed estimates of the toll did not appear until years after his suicide. Nearly one-hundred million Soviet citizens lost their lives prematurely thanks to Lenin and Stalin. The toll of purges, gulags, and collectivization in Ukraine and Kazakhstan went unreported for decades. Mao Zedong hid the starvation from his Great Leap Forward, 1958-1962, but the estimates came out after his demise—20 million to 40 million dead. The world still does not know how many North Koreans starved in the 1990s. Was it 10% or 20% of the population? The common thread? Each putative Great Leader ignored wise counsel and did what he believed useful for his personal power and regime.

Trump did not praise Hitler or Mao Zedong, but he exchanged "love" letters with Kim Jong Un; seemed to approve whatever Putin did; and endorsed Xi Jinping's crackdown on Hong Kong and concentration camps for Uyghurs.

Lives lost to today's dictatorships number in tens or even hundreds of thousands—not yet in millions. But the world's authoritarian regimes today suffer from the same malaise as those in the past. Their evil is on a smaller scale but still amount to *democide*—mass murder of their own subjects (China's Tibetans and Uyghurs) or genocide—as in Putin's effort to extinguish Ukraine.

Authoritarian regimes drive policies in the world's largest powers—China, India, and Russia. Dictators also rule Iran, Syria, and North Korea as well as sometime U.S. partners including Pakistan, Mexico, and many African countries. All have been slow to acknowledge the dangers of the novel coronavirus. In Belarus the president prescribed vodka, saunas, and soccer. Even after recognizing the threat, all the ostensibly strong men have been reluctant to mobilize the needed resources to fight Covid-19. All ignored the advice of medical professionals and complaints of local governments that they were poorly equipped. Eventually, however, Beijing resorted to lockdowns of entire communities. As in Beijing and Moscow, the Trump White House tried to make the media a cheerleader for bad policies. As in Brasilia, the Trump presidency scorned public health guidelines in his quest for GDP and stock market highs. He lied about the dangers and what he did to cope.

Devoted to free-market remedies, the Trump administration cut funds for science and withdrew from the World Health Organization. It discouraged research and dissemination of information that might protect the public. Alert to the president's priorities, the Department of Health and Human Services in January-February 2020 failed to make early use of commercial labs; it even enforced regulations that prevented them from assisting in testing. Embarrassed by reports on the rising toll of Covid-19 and frustrated by warnings of its dangers, the White House labored to silence Dr. Anthony Fauci—director since 1984 of the National Institute of Allergy and Infectious Diseases. In July 2020, the White House ordered hospitals to send data on the virus—not to the CDC, as in the past—but to the Department of Health and Human Services, where the data could be sugarcoated and spun for public consumption. He ordered Dr. Fauci and other experts not to testify to Congress. He presses the CDC to modify its school opening guidelines because they were too stringent and expensive. To show their devotion to the Trump party line, many Republicans made it a point not to wear protective face masks.

Trump may not have intended to promote mass murder, but his words and deeds produced that effect. He permitted and helped an epidemic to spread—one that killed more Americans than all the country's wars since 1945. Following his denial of the epidemic's warning signs, his bad example (face masks and social distancing optional) and irresponsible claims ("it will soon disappear; meanwhile, we have plenty of protective gear and lots of testing") led many Americans to dangerous behaviors.

The lassitude of the Trump White House encouraged the fifty states and Puerto Rico to compete for scarce resources. High level indifference encouraged big businesses, small businesses, and unemployed workers to feud for federal relief dollars.

Besides the direct medical impact of Covid-19, there are also two major side effects: the economy and education. Since much of the economy had to shut down, millions lost their jobs. Their wages and often their health insurance suspended, many Americans went hungry; and many suffered intense stress, which can and does kill. The federal government tried to compensate the unemployed and to subsidize small businesses—in the process adding trillions to the national debt while enriching many large firms that claimed to be small.

America's not too great school system also deteriorated. Distance learning, especially without the appropriate hardware, is usually inferior to classroom learning. If most kids lose months of schooling, everybody suffers. We should again blame much of those losses on Trump and his Education Secretary Betsy DeVos, who continued to focus on helping private and charter schools. When the president actually did act, he tried to keep away foreign students from universities. With one stroke, he could limit the spread of knowledge and foreigners. Having provoked more stress and chaos, Trump relented after facing lawsuits by Harvard and MIT. Here is another tale triggered "by an idiot, full of sound and fury, signifying nothing."

Had the United States taken a more proactive approach, its leadership might have also saved lives abroad. Since some foreign governments and publics also took away incorrect information from the U.S. president, Trump is also responsible for a large number of foreign deaths.

Authoritarian rule is bad for the United States as well as the rest of humanity. There are mass murderers in high places.[19] Many American presidents have actively harmed their own people and the world by their military campaigns, as in Indochina and the Middle East. But the Trump White House warred against its own body politic—not just by its Covid-19 policies, but also by cutting protections of clean air, fresh water, and health.

Hear No Evil, See No Evil, Just Do It!

Most Republicans appeared deaf, dumb, and blind to their president's predatory past, his use of office for his own profit-making, his peculiar links to Putin's Russia, his attacks on the FBI and the U.S. intelligence community, and his various trespasses against the Constitution. Long before Trump's presidency, crime by Republicans far exceeded that by Democrats. A survey of corruption from 1961 to 2016 (28 years of five presidents, five from each party), found that Republicans were indicted, convicted, and sent to prison far more often than Democrats--eighteen times more indictments, 38 times more convictions, and many times more individuals sent to prison.[20]

Table 4.1 Republican Leadership in Criminal Behavior, 1961-2016

	Democrats	Republicans
Indictments	7	126
Convictions	3	113
Prison Time	2	39

The Mueller investigation garnered 199 criminal charges, 37 indictments or guilty pleas, and 5 prison sentences—three of which Trump and his attorney general overturned. As of early 2023,

---

19 Nobel laureate Amartya Sen has pointed out that democratic systems do not permit their peoples to starve. Not only dark-skinned Indians but white Irish and other British subjects starved under the "famine queen" Victoria and her imperial successors. There has been no mass starvation in India under self-rule, though today's PM Narendra Modi persecutes Muslims.

20 Rand Engel, "GOP Admins Had 38 Times More Criminal Convictions Than Democrats, 1961-2016," at https://rantt.com/gop-admins-had-38-times-more-criminal-convictions-than-democrats-1961-2016 (Accessed 7/10/20).

the former president faced dozens of active investigations.[21] Given the president's ability to obstruct, to pardon, and to appoint judges, the outcomes of these investigations could not be predicted.

Republican attitudes toward gender abuse are part of a larger indifference to basic morality and patriotic love of country. What explains Republican apathy to amoral or, rather, immoral behavior in high places? *Too Much and Never Enough* by the president's niece Dr. Mary L. Trump helps explain how Trump got that way. But what of other Republicans? As with "The Donald," elemental avarice rationalized by a sense of privilege certainly plays a role. As Chaucer rightly noted in the 14th century: "Greed is the root of evil."[22]

Table 4.2   The Amoral Code of Republican Elites

- Jigger the tax system to reward donors to our party regardless of the impact on national debt and collateral damage to health, welfare, and education.

- Subvert comprehensive medicine by removing any obligation to acquire health insurance.

- Remove tax exemptions for graduate student tuition grants and university endowments.

- Gut restrictions on oil, coal, gas, and chemical industries. Tear down environmental protection rules that favor alternative energy or protect public lands and water.

- Ignore and throttle science that warns about global warming, pollution, or perils of nuclear war.

- Denounce mainstream media as "fake news." Tear down net neutrality and let the biggest companies rule the airwaves.

- Remove Obama-era efforts to protect learners from for-

---

21 *The New York Times* on September 25, 2019, reported that Trump faced 30 investigations into his businesses, his campaign, his inauguration, and his presidency—12 Congressional, 10 Federal criminal, and 8 state and local. See https://www.nytimes.com/interactive/2019/05/13/us/politics/trump-investig ations.html. These numbers sharply increased in 2022.

22 As the hypocritical "Pardoner" put it in the *Canterbury Tales*: "*radix malorum est cupiditas.*"

profit colleges like the erstwhile Trump University.

- Support charter schools including the many that teach creationism and say nothing about pollution and global warming.

- Raise walls against immigration—especially by Muslims, blacks, and Latinos. Get rid of "DACA" protections from deportation and authorization to work for undocumented immigrants brought to the U.S. as children.

- Back white supremacists and weaken "Black Lives Matter" and other forms of protest by non-whites. Do not punish racist police actions or alt-right demonstrators.

- Appoint judges who share our "values." Question the patriotism and honesty of any courts that rule against us, especially if the judges are Hispanic or black. Tear down consumer, investor, and work-place protections; let free enterprise and the market do their thing. Subsidize big farms but defund the Supplemental Nutrition Assistance Program (SNAP).[23]

- Put "America First!" material interests above "values." Downplay our alliances with democracies and work with strong, if authoritarian, partners such as Saudi Arabia and Russia. Downsize the State Department. Diplomats are superfluous since it is the president who makes policy.

- Degrade arms control restraints and transfer trillions of dollars to industry to modernize our strategic and other arms. Permit carrying loaded weapons in every state. Fight any restraint on gun sales.

- Get a blessing on our actions by offering evangelicals a bargain. We install judges, laws, and subsidies Evangelicals favor. They, in turn, should look the other way as Republicans self-aggrandize.

---

23 In 2020, Iowa-based seed companies owned or partially owned by billionaire Harry Stine won six loans for many millions in the first round of the federal government's pandemic aid program for "small" businesses.

- Our all-encompassing rule is this: Do whatever helps us retain and use power in Washington and across the country. Never mind what might be good for the country and most of its people. Foster indifference to facts, truth, and moral standards. Make it seem that all politics is what it is and nothing can be done about it.

This amoral code of behavior continued even after Trump left the White House. In 2021 and early 2022 Republican Senators allied with two Democrats, West Virginia's Senator Joe Manchin and Arizona's Kyrsten Sinema, blocked much of President Biden's legislative agenda. Campaigning for another six-year term, Arizona's other Senator, Democrat Mark Kelly. also joined the schism. He helped sink one of Joe Biden's labor nominees, pushed the president to open new drilling in the Gulf of Mexico, and hammered the administration over lifting pandemic-era restrictions on the southern border.

Fossil fuel interests and holding on to a cushy job outweighed any devotion to the common good.

4

Injustice in High Places

A Murder Gets the President to Church

Donald J. Trump is not known for being a regular churchgoer. Still, one hour before a curfew was set to take effect on June 1, 2020, throngs of police officers in riot gear spilled out from the northeastern corner of Lafayette Square to cut a path through crowds of protesters so the president could walk across the street from the White House to St. John's Episcopal Church. He then stood in front of the church and held up a Bible. Striking different poses, he held up the book for cameras, at times upside-down.[1]

To get the picture, Attorney General William Barr and the president called in 5,000 National Guard troops from many states, two helicopters, and federal officers from at least a dozen agencies— all this against peaceful demonstrators. In addition, Task Force 504, an infantry battalion from the 82nd Airborne, was flown into the area, in case its services were requested. For the photo op the president and Barr were accompanied by Secretary of Defense Mark T. Esper and Chairman of the Joint Chiefs of Staff General Mark A. Milley.[2]

What triggered these events? On May 25, 2020, four Minneapolis police officers arrested George Floyd, a 46-year-old black man, after a convenience store employee reported that Floyd had bought cigarettes with a counterfeit $20 bill.[3] Seventeen minutes after the

---

1 Asked in 2016 about his favorite lines from the Bible, he pointed to the Old Testament teaching of "an eye for an eye," which he said resonated with his view that the United States had been taken advantage of by rivals. The phrase originated in the Code of Hammurabi that aimed to promote order in his Babylonian empire, sited in today's Iraq.

2 Barr and Milley have master's degrees from Columbia University; Esper, an M.A. from Harvard and a Ph.D. from George Washington University. Milley has a second M.A. from the Naval War College and Barr has a law degree from George Washington.

3 Floyd's second-grade teacher in Houston retained an essay he wrote declaring his intention to become a judge on the Supreme Court, like Thurgood Marshall. David Remnick, "An American Uprising," *The New Yorker*, May 31, 2020.

first squad car arrived at the scene, Floyd was pinned beneath three officers and showed no signs of life. He had resisted arrest but was handcuffed and held down by one officer who knelt on Floyd's neck for nearly nine minutes. Floyd's last gasps, "I can't breathe!" resounded around the country and the world, sparking days and nights of multiracial demonstrations against police brutality.

The officer who killed Floyd was convicted of murder and got 21 years in prison; a second officer who took part got only 30 months.

The Episcopal bishop Mariann Edgar Budde immediately appeared on national television and said she was "outraged" that the president had used St. John's as a "prop," noting that Trump visited "without permission" or advance warning. The Roman Catholic Archbishop Wilton Gregory complained that the president was using holy sites as political props. The formerly conservative evangelist Rev. Rob Schenck also denounced the president's manipulation of religious symbols to win Christian support.[4] The American Civil Liberties Union announced it was suing Trump and Barr in connection with the federal response. The lawsuit was filed on behalf of Black Lives Matter D.C. and individual protesters.

Responding to criticism from many quarters, Barr said that federal intervention was necessary as televised images of rioting "conveyed the impression that the United States was on the brink of losing control of its capital city." For days the Attorney General took battlefield control over a hodgepodge of security forces from a command center he set up to facilitate the president's photo op.[5] Barr claimed on Fox News that the image of peaceful demonstrators was "miscreated" to ignore "all the violence that was happening preceding that." He alleged that there were two "bottles thrown at me" when he surveyed the scene, though footage showed him at a safe distance. He charged that previously "things were so bad that the Secret Service recommended that the president go down to the bunker." However, Trump later claimed it was merely a bunker "inspection."

---

4   https://www.pbssocal.org/programs/amanpour-co/rev-robert-schenck-evangelicals-listen-more-deeply-vtakbc/ (accessed 6/14/20).

5   Katie Benner and Sharon LaFraniere, "For Barr, Standoff with Prosecutor Adds to String of Miscues," *The New York Times*, June 22, 2020.

More than 1,200 former Justice Department staffers called for an internal review of the Attorney General's role in clearing a peaceful demonstration near the White House. Writing to Justice Inspector General Michael Horowitz, they said were "disturbed" by Barr's involvement in the action that opened a path for Trump to stage a photograph. "Based on what we now know, these actions violated both the First Amendment . . . which protects freedom of speech and the press, and the right to assemble; and the Fourth Amendment, which prohibits unreasonable seizures, to include objectively unreasonable uses of force by law enforcement officers," the group wrote. The former Justice staffers doubted "that the personnel deployed from these agencies are adequately trained in policing mass protests or protecting the constitutional rights of individuals who are not subject to arrest or have not been convicted of a crime." The former Justice Department staffers noted that "federal officers were blocking streets, guarding buildings, and interacting with civilians without displaying or otherwise providing identification, even when asked to do so by peaceful protesters."[6]

Former and still serving military officials joined in the protest. They recoiled at the sight of the Secretary of Defense and Chairman of the Joint Chief of Staff joining Barr and the president as armed forces pushed back peaceful demonstrators to facilitate a political gesture.

"If last night's blatant violations do not cross the line for you, what will?" This is the question that James N. Miller posed to Defense Secretary Esper on June 2, 2020. Miller, who served as Undersecretary of Defense from 2012 to 2014, went on: When you were sworn in on July 23, 2019, you pledged to "support and defend the Constitution of the United States." Yesterday, June 1, 2020, "you violated that oath. Law-abiding protesters just outside the White House were dispersed using tear gas and rubber bullets— not for the sake of safety, but to clear a path for a presidential photo op. You then accompanied President Trump in walking from the White House to St. John's Episcopal Church for that photo."

---

6 *USA Today*, June 10, 2020 at https://www.usatoday.com/story/news/politics/2020/06/10/bill-barr-ex-doj-staffers-want-review-ag-role-clearing-protesters/5334704002/ (accessed 6/11/20).

Trump's actions violated his oath to "'take care that the laws be faithfully executed,' as well as the First Amendment 'right of the people peaceably to assemble.' You may not have been able to stop President Trump from directing this appalling use of force, but you could have chosen to oppose it. Instead, you visibly supported it."

Miller then asked: How should people interpret your suggestion to the nation's governors yesterday that they need to "dominate the battlespace." "I cannot believe that you see the United States as a 'battlespace,' or that you believe our citizens must be 'dominated.' Such language sends an extremely dangerous signal. You have made life-and-death decisions in combat overseas; soon you may be asked to make life-and-death decisions about using the military on American streets and against Americans. Where will you draw the line, and when will you draw it?" For Miller, a line had been crossed. He resigned from the Defense Review Board.

Defense Secretary Esper soon tried to distance himself from that photo op. He publicly broke with the president and said he did not support Trump's calls to invoke the Insurrection Act (1897) and use active-duty troops to quell the protests that had broken out after Floyd's killing. CNN reported that Esper's statement went over "poorly at the White House, where his standing was already viewed to be tenuous."

Not a slave to consistency, the Defense Secretary on June 3 reversed a previous decision and opted to keep near Washington some of the 750 soldiers from the 82nd Airborne who were sent there—in case they were needed to cope with ongoing protests. Army Secretary Ryan McCarthy told The Associated Press that the reversal came after Esper attended a meeting at the White House.

The Chairman of the Joint Chiefs of Staff also issued an apology in a commencement address to the National Defense University. General Milley said, "I should not have been there. My presence in that moment and in that environment created a perception of the military involved in domestic politics."

Esper's predecessor as Secretary of Defense, retired General Jim Mattis, broke his long silence and attacked the President whom he served for two years. He stated, "Donald Trump is the first president in my lifetime who does not try to unite the American people—does not even pretend to try. Instead, he tries to divide us. We are witnessing the consequences of three years of this deliberate effort. We are witnessing the consequences of three years without mature leadership."

On June 3, retired Gen. John Allen, a former commander of NATO and U.S. troops in Afghanistan, wrote that Trump's use of military force to violently drive peaceful protesters from Lafayette Square might mark "the beginning of the end of the American experiment," and he called on U.S. voters to respond by driving change "from the bottom up."

Four former chairmen of the joint chiefs, going back to the administration of President George H. W. Bush, took the extraordinary step of publicly breaking with the president to condemn the use of violence against peaceful protestors. One of the former chairmen, retired General Colin Powell, told CNN's Jake Tapper that Trump lies "all the time."

Many strains of scandal intertwined here—the president's unflagging concern for his own image, racial discrimination, police brutality, the use of armed force against mostly peaceful civilians, and the politicization of Barr's so-called Department of Justice.

This complex of events was sufficient to justify impeachment. It was surely more serious than the events for which Bill Clinton was impeached. Instead, it served merely as one of many abuses of presidential power for which Trump escaped unscathed.

IMPOSING LAW AND ORDER WITH STORM TROOPERS

After the death of George Floyd, the president's re-election campaign returned to its earlier portrayal of Trump as defender of law and order. The Attorney General began to treat local issues, such as a demonstrator breaking a police cruiser window in Mobile, Alabama, as reason to send in federal armed forces. Barr's prosecutors stepped in and charged at least seventy people with crimes in connection with the Floyd protests. If a federal crime takes place, much longer sentences can be imposed—raising incentives for a guilty plea.[7]

---

7   Barr maintained that a new generation of reformist D.A.s soft on crime led to

The Trump-Barr intervention syndrome led to federal armed forces being deployed not only in Washington, D.C., but also in Seattle, San Diego, Buffalo, Las Vegas, and Portland. The Customs and Border Protection sent drones, helicopters, and planes to surveil protests in at least 15 cities.

Protests over police brutality continued in Portland nearly two months after Floyd's murder. In mid-July, the city saw federal agents dressed in camouflage and tactical gear unleash tear gas, bloody protesters, and pull some demonstrators into unmarked vans—what Oregon governor Kate Brown called a "blatant abuse of power." On July 17, the U.S. Attorney for the Oregon District, Billy J. Williams, requested an investigation into the masked, camouflaged federal authorities without identification badges arresting protesters. Oregon's governor and Portland's mayor demanded the troops be withdrawn. Their presence was not needed and only added to the tension, they said. "Authoritarian governments, not democratic republics, send unmarked authorities after protesters," tweeted Jeff Merkley, a Democrat representing Oregon in the U.S. Senate.[8] Oregon Attorney General Ellen Rosenblum complained that federal agents "have been using unmarked vehicles to drive around downtown Portland, detain protesters, and place them into the officers' unmarked vehicles." The protesters were neither arrested nor told why they were being held.

"Be wary of paramilitaries," warned Yale historian Timothy Snyder in his book *On Tyranny: Twenty Lessons from the Twentieth Century.* "When the pro-leader paramilitary and the official police and military intermingle, the end has come." When his book appeared in 2017, the idea of unidentified agents in camouflage snatching leftists off the streets without warrants might have seemed like a febrile resistance fantasy. In 2020 it was happening.[9]

---

more crime. But reformers have been winning elections around the country not because their constituents want "greater criminality," but because "they recognize that we have incarcerated too many people (and particularly too many people of color) for too long." Jeffrey Toobin, "The Halted Progress of Criminal-Justice Reform," *The New Yorker*, July 12, 2020.

8   Sergio Olmos et al., "To City's Alarm, Federal Officers Police Portland," *The New York Times*, July 18, 2020.

9   Michelle Goldberg, "Trump's Occupation of American Cities Has Begun," *The*

The Trump administration said it mobilized federal police in Portland to "protect Federal property" from "anarchists and agitators"—two years after Trump pardoned two men serving sentences for arson that burned 139 acres of federal property in Oregon in a case that inspired armed militias to seize federal land.[10]

The agents in Portland were part of "rapid deployment teams" put together by the Department of Homeland Security after the president ordered federal agencies to protect statues, monuments, and federal property during the continuing unrest. The teams include 2,000 officers from Customs and Border Protection, Immigration and Customs Enforcement, the Transportation Security Administration, and the Coast Guard—all in support of the Federal Protective Service, responsible for security at federal properties.

So much for state's rights and the division of power between central and local government! Trump encouraged armed protesters in Michigan who stormed the statehouse because the governor had the temerity to shut down non-essential businesses and require people to wear masks in public. Continuing the top-down orientation, Georgia's governor Brian Kemp sued the mayor of Atlanta, Keisha Lance Bottoms, to block the city's mask requirement. Like many Republican governors, Kemp saw a mask requirement as an infringement of individual liberty. He seemed indifferent to the death toll when no masks were worn.

A Teen-age Bully Becomes the Top Law Officer in the Land

The future attorney general followed his parents in reacting to a liberal consensus around them. Barr (born 1950) grew up on Riverside Drive, in Manhattan, among the bookish élite of the Upper West Side. But his was a very conservative upbringing. While his neighbors hoped Lyndon Johnson's Great Society would flourish, the Barr family supported Barry Goldwater for President. The young Bill Barr, a devout Catholic like his mother and father (a

---

New York Times, July 20, 2020.

10 Dana Milbank, "America is flunking its cognitive assessment," *The Washington Post*, July 20, 2020.

converted Jew), was strong on law and order—except that he seems to have bullied others with a different outlook.[11] A fellow student at the Horace Mann School and later at Columbia University, Jimmy Lohman (later a death row defense attorney and musician in Austin), recalled that Barr, a "sadistic kid" then 15 years old, "put the crunch" on the twelve-year-old Lohman every chance he got.

Barr "lived to make me miserable," Lohman wrote, with a "vicious fixation on my little Jewish 'commie' ass." Barr did so, Lohman thought, because, at age twelve, he wore peace and racial-equality pins. One was distributed by the Student Non-Violent Coordinating Committee—"a small black button with a white equal sign in the middle that I thought said it all." Bill and his three brothers had a thing about blacks as well as war protestors. They picketed the school's "Junior Carnival" because proceeds went to the NAACP. The four brothers "teamed with the New York City riot police to attack anti-war protesters and 'long hairs.'"

Lohman's account is consistent with Marie Brenner's reporting in *Vanity Fair:* She found that a few of Barr's Horace Man classmates recalled that they called Bill and his brothers "the bully Barrs" and said they could be "intimidating."[12] At Columbia College, the seventeen-year-old Bill Barr helped lead a self-styled "Majority Coalition" that fought antiwar demonstrators.[13] Barr told Marie Brenner that his experiences at Columbia proved crucial to focusing his priorities. If leaders at Columbia "had taken a stronger stance, up front," Barr told Brenner, "it would not have degenerated so much."

Barr went on to get a B.A. and then an M.A. from Columbia in international affairs and Chinese area studies. He served in the CIA from 1971 to 1977 while obtaining a law degree at George

---

11 In the early 1970s, William's father, Donald Barr, was forced to leave his job as headmaster at the prestigious Dalton School in New York's Upper East Side because parents there saw him as autocratic, insular, and obsessed with adherence to rules. Dana Milbank, "So this is why Bill Barr is such a bully," *The Washington Post*, June 9, 2020.

12 "The Education of Billy Barr," *Vanity Fair* (December 2019).

13 Paul Cronin, "The Time That Bill Barr Faced Down Protesters—Personally," *Politico*, June 7, 2020.

Washington University. Law degree obtained, he began in 1977 to work as an attorney and, intermittently, in the Justice Department.

When President George H.W. Bush nominated Barr to be Attorney General in 1991, Lohman wondered: "Could it be that the sociopath from my childhood is really about to become the highest legal official in the land?" After George Floyd's death in 2020, Lohman noted that Barr, the lifelong racist, declared that there is "no systemic racism in policing." As Americans cry out for racial justice, "the 15-year old who hated me for believing in equality is now in charge of enforcing racial justice."[14]

Lohman wrote that Barr has been and still was a bully. Witness his flouting congressional authority with brazen contempt and when ordering the forceful removal of peaceful protesters from a public space. The conservative Catholic is also a would-be theocrat. Speaking at the Notre Dame Law School on October 11, 2019, Barr made a case for ideological warfare. He claimed that secularists and other progressives sought the "organized destruction" of religion and its replacement by moral relativism.

Why did Barr act as an instrument of Trump's whims? By wheedling his way into the confidence of a "demented, suggestible, Nero-like emperor," Barr could become supremely powerful. A multimillionaire, he did not need money, but he may think he is doing good.

The president wanted a U.S. attorney general who would serve as his personal attorney. Barr made clear his willingness to serve in June 2018 when, as a private citizen with no formal ties to the U.S. government, he sent an unsolicited 19-page memo to Deputy Attorney General Rod Rosenstein. In it, Barr disparaged Robert Mueller's investigation into possible Russian interference in the 2016 U.S. presidential election. Barr also defended Trump's firing of James Comey as FBI Director in May 2017 as "facially-lawful" exercise of "Executive discretion."[15]

---

14 Jimmy Lohman, "Bill Barr Bullied Me Because I Backed Civil Rights," *Daily Beast,* June 15, 2020.

15 A life-long Republican, Comey was named FBI Director by President Obama in 2013.

This was the kind of unwavering support Trump craved. He was glad to get rid of his Acting Attorney General, Jeff Sessions, whom he forced to resign in November 2018. Trump often vented his anger at the failure of Sessions to "un-recuse" himself from Mueller's investigation. Barr's letter did not come to light until December 2018—after Trump nominated Barr to be his chief legal officer.

Like no attorney general since the Watergate era, Barr acted as the president's political sword and shield.[16] Barr seems to be the one senior Trump official over whom the president does not project a show of superiority. But there he was on the cover of the *New Yorker* on June 3, 2019, shining the president's shoes, squeezed between Senate Majority Leader Mitch McConnell and Senator Lindsey Graham—a recent recruit to Trump's team of Big Lie sycophants. Barr was confirmed by the Senate in a party-line vote on February 14, 2019. Less than a month later, Barr had to deal with the first of many challenges.

THE MUELLER REPORT ON RUSSIAN INTERFERENCE IN THE 2016 ELECTION

June 8, 2018: Private citizen Barr submits memo to Justice Department denouncing the Mueller inquiry.

December 7, 2018: President Trump nominates Barr as his second attorney general following the ouster of Jeff Sessions.

March 22, 2019: Robert S. Mueller, III concludes his nearly two-year-long investigation and submits his confidential report, more than 400 pages long, to AG Barr.

March 24, 2019: Two days later, Barr releases a four-page summary stating that the "investigation did not find that the Trump campaign or anyone associated with it conspired or coordinated with Russia" and stated that "the evidence developed during the Special Counsel's investigation is not sufficient to establish that the President committed an obstruction-of-justice offense."

---

16 David Rohde, "William Barr, Trump's Sword and Shield," *The New Yorker*, January 12, 2020.

March 27, 2019. Mueller counters that Barr's account "did not fully capture the context, nature, and substance" of the investigation and had created "public confusion about critical aspects" of its results. Nonetheless, Barr's words shape public interpretation of the report and Trump himself claims the report exonerates him.

April 18, 2019: A heavily redacted version of the Mueller report, now 448 pages long, is made public. Its findings do not match Barr's March 24 summary, particularly on the matter of obstruction of justice. Mueller's report made clear that "if we had confidence after a thorough investigation of the facts that the President clearly did not commit obstruction of justice, we would so state. Based on the facts and the applicable legal standards, we are unable to reach that judgment. Accordingly, while this report does not conclude that the President committed a crime, it also does not exonerate him."

March 6, 2020: Reggie B. Walton, a Republican appointed a federal district judge by George W. Bush, has been asked by a privacy and civil liberties group to review the Mueller Report. A week later and having read the redacted version of the report, he criticizes Barr's summary as "distorted" and "misleading."[17] The attorney general, Walton says, cannot be trusted. There are "inconsistencies" between Barr's summary and the report's actual contents. Walton orders the Justice Department to privately show him the portions of the report blacked out in the publicly released version.

May 1, 2019: Barr defends his handling of the Mueller Report, while some Democrats demand he resign.

May 2, 2019: Barr is a no-show for a hearing before the House Judiciary Committee.

June 8, 2020: Having read an unredacted (or less redacted) version of the report, Judge Walton wants to question Justice officials. He orders a hearing in July.

---

17 The plaintiffs were the Electronic Privacy Information Center (EPIC), BuzzFeed, and BuzzFeed News reporter Jason Leopold. See Matt Naham on April 24, 2019 at https://lawandcrime.com/high-profile/federal-judge-sets-target-deadline-for-review-of-the-unredacted-mueller-report/ (accessed 5/20/19).

June 19, 2020: A version of the Mueller report, redacted but with fewer redactions, is released to the public. It showed again Trump's drive to weaponize information stolen by Russian hackers and funneled to WikiLeaks to use against his 2016 opponent Hillary Clinton. The newly released passages show that investigators suspected that the president feared Roger Stone, his intermediary with WikiLeaks, might incriminate him by linking Trump to Stone's quest for dirt on Clinton. The disclosures reveal the prosecutors' doubts about whether Mr. Trump told them the truth when he was questioned during their two-year investigation.

Although the Mueller investigation led to many indictments, it did not change politics in Washington. Barr's dishonest summary of the report and its later redacted release permitted the president and Republican leaders to hide Trump's dependence on Russian help in 2016 and his many obstructions of justice. The partisan divide in Washington grew deeper.

Meanwhile, nearly concurrent with the Mueller report, the president and his AG had to cope with serious efforts to remove Trump from office.

IMPEACHMENT GOES NOWHERE

January 23, 2018: Two Democratic congressmen again file an article for Trump's impeachment that they first presented in July 2017. House Speaker Nancy Pelosi is reluctant to pursue impeachment while Republicans control the Senate, because they are sure to acquit their leader.

April 18, 2019: Barr releases Mueller's 448-page heavily redacted report. Its details give more ammunition to Democrats who called for Trump's impeachment.

April 19, 2019: House Judiciary Committee Chairman Jerrold Nadler issues a subpoena for Mueller's full, unredacted report and underlying evidence.

July 25, 2019: Trump phones newly elected Ukrainian President Volodymyr Zelensky and tells him, "I would like you to do us a favor though"—thereby making delivery of military aid and a White House meeting with Zelensky conditional on Ukrainian investigations of Trump rival Joe Biden and his son and whether Ukraine [not Russia] interfered in the 2016 election.

August 12, 2019: An anonymous whistleblower complains to the Senate and House intelligence committees accusing Trump of "using the power of his office to solicit interference from a foreign country in the 2020 election." But the complaint is withheld from Congress by the new acting director of national intelligence.

September 18, 2019: House Intelligence Committee Chairman. Adam Schiff learns of the complaint from Inspector General Michael Atkinson (fired in 2020, probably in revenge) and demands the administration turn over the complaint.

September 24, 2019: House Speaker Nancy Pelosi announces the start of a formal impeachment inquiry. She says Trump is "calling upon a foreign power to intervene in his election." The president must be held "accountable," she says. "No one is above the law."

November 13, 2019: Impeachment hearings begin in the Intelligence Committee. Witnesses include Lt. Col. Alexander Vindman, a National Security Council expert on Ukraine; the former ambassador to Ukraine Marie Yovanovitch; and the U.S. ambassador to the E.U., Gordon Sondland. All three were soon shifted to other jobs or fired. John Bolton, Trump's National Security Assistant from April 9, 2018, to September 10, 2019, declines an invitation to testify, saving his revelations until his memoir appears in June 2020.

December 13, 2019: The House Judiciary Committee approves two articles of impeachment: abuse of power and obstruction of justice.

January 16, 2020: The House submits the two articles to the Senate, initiating the trial. Republican senators refuse Democrat requests for additional witnesses and documents.

February 5, 2020: Trump is acquitted on both counts by a party-line vote. Republican Mitt Romney, the only senator to break party lines, becomes the first U.S. senator to vote to convict a president of his own party in an impeachment trial. He votes for the article on abuse of power.

Bottom line: Republicans managed again to protect a president who deserved to be thrown out of office and into a federal prison.

PRYING LOYALISTS OUT OF JAIL WHILE KEEPING A "RAT" IN

At the president's behest, Barr launched an investigation of the F.B.I.'s Trump-Russia probe and the intelligence community's assessment that Russia intervened on Trump's behalf in the election. When the Justice Department's inspector general found no evidence of political bias in the F.B.I. investigation, Barr misrepresented its findings and claimed that the Russia probe was "consistently exculpatory"—ignoring that five people connected to Trump's campaign were indicted for lying to investigators.[18] Trump and Barr did what they could to ease the sentences of three of them—Paul Manafort, Michael Flynn, and Roger Stone.

Paul Manafort. Trump's campaign manager for much of 2016, Paul Manafort, is a convicted felon. He was serving a seven-year sentence for tax fraud and conspiracy, witness tampering, and foreign-lobbying violations. But Trump expressed sympathy, because Manafort has had a "very, very tough time" since being wrapped up in Mueller's investigation. In May 2020, the Bureau of Prisons released Manafort from federal prison because of Covid-19 concerns. In August 2020 his image darkened further. The Senate Intelligence Committee report on Russian meddling in the 2016 election described him as a "grave counterintelligence threat." It said that Manafort collaborated with Russians, including oligarch Oleg Deripaska and "Russian intelligence officer" Konstantin Kilimnik, before, during, and after the election. The committee found that Manafort's role and proximity to Trump created opportunities for Russian intelligence. His "high-level access and willingness to

---

18 Robert Mueller's team indicted or got guilty pleas from six former Trump advisers, 26 Russian nationals, three Russian companies, one California man, and one London-based lawyer. Seven of these people (including five of the six former Trump advisers) pleaded guilty. See Andrew Prokop at *Vox*, https://www.vox.com/policy-and-politics/2018/2/20/17031772/mueller-indictments-grand-jury, updated 12/17/19 (accessed 2/2/20).

share information with individuals closely affiliated with the Russian intelligence services . . . represented a grave counterintelligence threat."

Roger Stone. Aged 67, Stone was convicted of seven felony counts including lying about his attempts to get details of Hillary Clinton's private emails from the anti-secrecy group WikiLeaks, then threatening a witness who could contradict his story. Federal prosecutors urged that Stone be sent to prison for seven to nine years for impeding congressional and FBI investigations into connections between the Russian government and Trump's 2016 campaign. But Trump blasted the prosecutors' sentencing recommendation as a "horrible and very unfair situation." Barr's Justice Department then submitted a revised filing that called the prosecutors' proposal "excessive and unwarranted." The four attorneys who shepherded Stone's prosecution proceeded either to resign or notify the court that they were stepping off the case. Trump tweeted that "Roger was a victim of a corrupt and illegal Witch Hunt, one which will go down as the greatest political crime in history. He can sleep well at night!" On July 10, 2020, President Trump commuted the sentence of his former aide and confidante. Stone's conviction, however, remained on the books.

Lt. Gen. Michael T. Flynn. The Justice Department announced in May 2020 that it was dropping the criminal case against the former national security adviser, who had twice admitted to lying to the F.B.I. about his phone conversations with the Russian ambassador. Barr was asked: "Was Flynn guilty of lying?" Barr replied: "Well, you know, people sometimes plead to things that turn out not to be crimes." He added that Flynn's infamous phone conversations during the Trump presidential transition could be seen as "laudable." Trump and his allies accused the F.B.I. of framing Flynn—part of the president's effort to tarnish the Russia investigation and settle scores against perceived enemies.

Former F.B.I. Deputy Director Andrew McCabe commented that "the Department's position that the FBI had no reason to interview Mr. Flynn pursuant to its counterintelligence investigation is patently false and ignores the considerable national security risk his contacts raised." McCabe said that the move by the Justice

Department had nothing to do with the facts or the law —"it is pure politics designed to please the president."

John Gleeson, a former federal judge and prosecutor, complained that the attorney general was giving special treatment to a presidential ally and undermining public confidence in the rule of law. Reviewing the Justice Department's effort to undo Flynn's conviction, Gleeson wrote: "The Government's ostensible grounds for seeking dismissal are conclusively disproven by its own briefs filed earlier in this very proceeding. They contradict and ignore this Court's prior orders, which constitute the law of the case. They are riddled with inexplicable and elementary errors of law and fact." Accordingly, "leave of court should not be granted when the explanations the Government puts forth are not credible as the real reasons for its dismissal of a criminal charge."

Gleeson implied that Barr himself broke the law. "The government may not enlist a court in dismissing a case solely because the defendant is a friend and political ally of the president— and where the ostensible reasons advanced for dismissal amount to a thin and unpersuasive disguise . . . . If the executive wishes for the judiciary to dismiss criminal charges—as opposed to issuing a pardon or taking other unilateral action—the reasons it offers must be real and credible."[19]

The Justice Department responded on June 17, 2020, that the judge overseeing the Flynn case had no authority to reject Barr's decision to drop the case. In a 41-page brief to Judge Emmet G. Sullivan, who had called in Gleeson to review the matter, the Justice Department argued that—even if the department refusal to prosecute rested on an improper motive, the court had no mechanism to force the executive to prosecute a case against its will. The brief also suggested reasons to suspect actions by the agents who investigated Flynn. What the department defended as its own "prosecutorial discretion" was just politically motivated subjectivism.

Since the Justice Department had no sound reasons for intervening, it claimed that it did not need to explain its reasoning.

---

19 Charlie Savage and Adam Goldman, "Outsider Tapped in Flynn Case Calls Justice Dept. Reversal a 'Gross Abuse' of Power," *The New York Times*, June 10, 2020.

On June 24 an appeals court ruled that Sullivan had intruded on the Justice Department's "charging authority" by seeking further investigation after the department moved to dismiss Flynn's case. It ordered Sullivan to throw out the Flynn case.[20]

In May 2020, some 2,000 former Justice Department officials signed a letter urging Barr to resign over his actions in the federal cases of Stone and Flynn. House Judiciary Committee Chairman Jerrold Nadler said that Barr "has abruptly reversed course on prosecutions against the President's allies and friends. He has pursued pretextual investigations against the President's perceived political enemies. He has failed to defend the Affordable Care Act, and he has helped to roll back important civil rights protections."

The evidence pointed to this evaluation: Under President Trump, the Justice Department has been deformed and corrupted, becoming the unbridled defender of Trump's personal interests. Barr says that he is upholding law and order, but he has undermined criminal investigations and even sought to undo convictions of Trump allies. Whether misleading the courts on the 2020 Census, giving Trump a free pass on his impeachable conduct regarding Ukraine, or mischaracterizing the Mueller report to conceal Trump's illegal conduct, Barr's Justice Department has shredded the principle that no one is above the law.[21]

Michael Cohen. Another of Trump's former associates indicted by Mueller and sent to prison was Michael Cohen. Trump's long-time personal attorney was jailed for lying to Congress about plans for a possible Trump Tower in Moscow and his hush-money payments on Trump's behalf to two women. Having completed one year of a three-year sentence, he returned to his New York home

---

20 Responding to this ruling, Jessica Roth, a professor at Cardozo School of Law and former federal prosecutor in the SDNY observed: "It is not typical for an appeals court to short-circuit a lower court's ongoing proceedings . . . . Judge Sullivan might well have decided to grant the motion to dismiss, but now the court of appeals has preemptively directed him to do that," Roth said. "To justify this extraordinary intervention, the court of appeals in effect said Judge Sullivan's plan to scrutinize the Department of Justice's reasoning and motives amounted to an irreparable harm such that appellate review could not wait."

21 Jennifer Rubin, "The rule of law makes a comeback" *The Washington Post*, June 11, 2020.

in May 2020 after being released early from federal prison due to concerns of possible coronavirus exposure. Cohen, who once said he would "take a bullet" for Trump, later turned on his former boss and cooperated with Democratic-led congressional inquiries. Trump called Cohen a "rat," while Cohen termed Trump a "racist," a "con man" and "a cheat."[22] After Cohen was seen dining at a French restaurant, federal officials remanded him to prison, charging that he had broken the terms of his medical furlough.

Soon after, however, in July 2020, a federal judge in the Southern District of New York had Cohen returned to home confinement. Judge Alvin Kenneth Hellerstein stated. "The purpose of transferring Mr. Cohen from furlough and home confinement to jail is retaliatory, and it's retaliatory because of his desire to exercise his First Amendment rights." Exercising these rights, Cohen wrote *Disloyal: A Memoir: The True Story of the Former Personal Attorney to President Donald J. Trump,* published by Skyhorse in September 2020.

In August 2020, the Senate Intelligence Committee issued a 966-page bipartisan report on its Russia investigation.[23] Much of each volume is blacked out, but what remains is more damningly explicit than anything in the Mueller Report. It charges that Russia used Republican political operative Paul Manafort and the WikiLeaks website to help Trump win the 2016 election. The report found that President Putin personally directed the Russian efforts to hack computer networks and accounts affiliated with the Democratic Party and leak information damaging to Clinton. Trump said the report was another "hoax."

PANDEMIC LIBERALISM

Attorney General Barr also intervened to shape policy toward Covid-19. As Trump accused Democratic governors of denying

---

22 https://www.npr.org/2020/06/24/882787253/appeals-court-orders-lower-judge-to-throw-out-michael-flynn-case (accessed 6/22/20).

23 https://www.intelligence.senate.gov/press/senate-intel-releases-volume-5-bipartisan-russia-report (accessed 8/20/20). The committee was chaired by Republican Senator Marco Rubio and vice-chair Democratic Senator Mark Warner.

citizens their "freedom" and encouraged residents to "liberate" Michigan, Minnesota, and Virginia, Barr zeroed in on the legal case for "liberation": When two small churches filed lawsuits, seeking to hold live services despite state or local regulations, the Justice Department supported their First Amendment rights. Barr suggested that the federal government's interest went beyond protecting live worship. It included "disfavored speech and undue interference with the national economy."

Trump bragged that he held "total" authority over the states. When reporter Mattathias Schwartz asked Barr what Trump meant, the AG responded: "I think the federal government *does* have the power to step in where a state is impairing interstate commerce," "where they're intruding on civil liberties, or where Congress under the commerce clause—or some other power Congress has—has given the president under emergency authorities that essentially pre-empt the states in a particular area, if he chooses to use them." In short, yes, Trump has a claim to "total" authority.[24]

Mail-in balloting is another domain where Trump intervened. His AG called the distribution of ballot applications in Michigan "illegal" and warned that voting by mail "doesn't work out well for Republicans." He told a reporter that his department's role would be limited, as the power belongs to the states and their electors. But Barr also warned that foreign governments might conspire to mail in fake ballots. "I haven't looked into that," he cautioned, offering no evidence to substantiate that this was a real possibility. But he called it "one of the issues that I'm real worried about." Barr added: "We've been talking about how, in terms of foreign influence, there are a number of foreign countries that could easily make counterfeit ballots, put names on them, send them in. And it'd be very hard to sort out what's happening."[25]

Trump and Barr vs. the IGs, the Courts, and the SDNY

In the first half of 2020, the president got away with firing or

---

24 Mattathias Schwartz, "William Barr's State of Emergency," *The New York Times Magazine*, June 1, 2020.

25 Ibid.

replacing five inspectors general whose investigations threatened him or his associates:[26]

- *Michael Atkinson, Intelligence Community*, who passed on the whistleblower complaint about Trump and Ukraine to the House of Representatives.

- *Mitch Behm, Transportation Department*, one of twenty inspectors charged with overseeing the $2.4 trillion coronavirus relief package.

- *Glenn Fine, Defense Department*, who had been selected to head the accountability panel for the pandemic relief fund.

- *Christi Grimm, Health and Human Services*, who found major shortfalls in preparation for the pandemic.

- *Steve Linick, State Department*, who was investigating Pompeo for abuses of his office.

In June 2020, Trump and Barr tumbled in a perfect storm as the November elections approached. The Supreme Court ruled against Trump's efforts to discriminate against LGBTQ people and his campaign to deport DACA recipients. Other courts said that Barr could not stop distribution of John Bolton's tell-nearly-all book or the family memoir of Nancy Trump. A top prosecutor whom Barr tried to replace refused to resign or be fired, exposing the administration's efforts to shut down embarrassing investigations.

LGBTQ. The American Medical Association in 2019 said that killings of transgender women of color in the United States amounted to an epidemic. In many states it was still legal to refuse service to someone who is gay, bisexual, or transgender; deny them a home to rent; or decline them health care. The Trump administration was deeply hostile to transgender rights. Starting in 2017, it worked to ban transgender people from serving in the military. In early June 2020, in the middle of the pandemic, the Trump administration

---

26 Established by the Inspector General Act of 1978, the offices of inspectors general are responsible for identifying, auditing, and investigating fraud, waste, abuse, embezzlement and mismanagement of any kind within executive departments and agencies. Ronald Reagan and George W. H. Bush tried to fire many inspectors general when they became president; Barack Obama fired one.

acted to enable insurers and doctors to refuse coverage and care to transgender patients by rolling back nondiscrimination protections in the Affordable Care Act. The administration lifted a ban on civil rights protections for transgender patients seeking health care. It revoked Education Department guidance that told schools to respect students' gender identity in the use of bathrooms. The administration also proposed a new rule forcing transgender homeless people into shelters according to their biology, not their identity.

The court did not rule on these issues and they were left hanging. But in *Bostock v. Clayton County* (Georgia), five of the nine judges on June 15, 2020, ruled that an employer may not fire an individual merely for being gay or transgender. It said that Title VII makes it unlawful for an employer to fail or refuse to hire or to discharge any individual, or otherwise to discriminate against any individual because of such individual's race, color, religion, sex, or national origin." The court noted precedents making it illegal to discriminate against women with young children. The ruling was expected to support other kinds of claims, for example, by a professor denied tenure due to her sex change.

DACA. The Supreme Court on June 18, 2020, dealt a major blow to the Trump administration's immigration agenda. It found that the government improperly terminated the Deferred Action for Childhood Arrivals Program (DACA). The decision meant that, for now, nearly 700,000 young immigrants can live and work in the U.S. without fear of deportation. While immigrant advocates celebrated the outcome of *DHS v. Regents of the University of California*, the ruling was still problematic. The opinion written by Chief Justice John Roberts brushed aside the possibility that the decision to end DACA was motivated by discriminatory intent. By dismissing an equal protection claim, Roberts made it harder for future plaintiffs to challenge racist policies before the high court. Fox News said some conservatives felt buyers' remorse—let down by their chosen judges. But Trump told a rally on June 20 in Tulsa that the stay on deportation was only temporary. "Some people would say that we lost. We didn't lose. We're gonna refile it."

Against Investigations of Trump and His Inner Circle. The

Trump administration fired two strong federal prosecutors in the Southern District of New York who threatened Trump allies and the president himself. The first, Preet Bharara, was appointed U.S. attorney for the SDNY by Barack Obama in 2009, but Trump asked him to stay on after winning the November 2016 election. However, Bharara was fired on March 11, 2017, after refusing to resign.[27] Forty-five other Obama-appointed U.S. attorneys were also asked for their resignations.

On June 19, 2020, late on a Friday evening, when news cycles are often slow, Attorney General Barr tried to oust Geoffrey Berman, Bharara's successor in the Southern District of New York. Berman's office had been at the forefront of corruption inquiries into Mr. Trump's inner circle. It sent Trump's personal lawyer Michael Cohen to prison; convicted two partners of Trump's attorney Rudy Giuliani, and was continuing to investigate Giuliani himself as well as a state-owned Turkish bank, an operation that Trump had promised to end.[28]

Berman refused to step down. He and Barr had met earlier on June 19, but Berman said he had learned of his purported exit that night from a press release. He shot back: "I have not resigned, and have no intention of resigning, my position, to which I was appointed by the Judges of the United States District Court for the Southern District of New York. I will step down when a presidentially appointed nominee is confirmed by the Senate." He added that "until then, our investigations will move forward without delay or interruption." Berman's comment came an hour after the Department of Justice announced that Trump intended to

---

27 Preet Bharara, *Doing Justice: A Prosecutor's Thoughts on Crime, Punishment, and the Rule of Law* (New York: Knopf, 2019; on why Michael Cohen betrayed his long-time patron, see p. 102.

28 By a coincidence, John Bolton's memoir appeared at the same time as the Barr-Berman exchange, in which Bolton quoted Trump as promising the Turkish president in December 2018 that he would "take care of" an investigation into a Turkish bank, which was being carried out by "Obama people, a problem that would be fixed when they were replaced by his people." Trump erred, because Berman was appointed on his watch. Bolton surmised that "Trump was trying to show he had as much arbitrary authority as Erdogan." *The Room Where It Happened: A White House Memoir* (New York: Simon & Schuster, 2020), p. 191.

nominate Jay Clayton, the chairman of the Securities and Exchange Commission. Clayton had been a Trump golf-partner but never a prosecutor. As an attorney, moreover, he defended Deutsche Bank, one of Trump's most significant creditors, from allegations it facilitated Russian money laundering. The SDNY in 2020 continued to investigate possible criminal activities by Deutsche Bank. Barr said that Trump fired Berman and so he was out, but hours later Trump said he was "not involved," leading some legal experts to conclude that Berman still had his job. After nearly 24 hours of chaos, however, Berman said he would step down. New York state's two senators said that Clayton was unqualified to take over. Late on Saturday, June 20, assured that his well-regarded and principled deputy, Audrey Strauss, would take over the reins, Berman agreed to leave the SDNY.

Should the Confederacy Live On? The killing of George Floyd sparked a national conversation about the flag, customs, and artworks associated with racism and the Confederacy. Many Republican lawmakers joined a bipartisan push in June 2020 to rename military bases named after Confederate generals. Protesters toppled statues they perceived to have a connection to slavery. But President Trump opposed removing symbols of the Confederacy. He said he "will not even consider" renaming military installations such as Fort Bragg and Fort Hood.

The Wall. Trump got mixed support from the courts in summer 2020. An appeals court ruled that the administration does not have the authority to use military funding to pay for construction of a border wall. On June 26 in a 2-1 ruling, a 9th U.S. Circuit Court of Appeals panel found that diverting $2.5 billion Congress had appropriated for the military violated the Constitution and was unlawful.

Three Modest Victories. In July 2020, however, the Supreme Court delivered three victories for the administration. On July 8, it delivered two rulings that favor conservative religion. Justices upheld a rule allowing employers and universities to opt out on religious grounds from the Obamacare requirement to cover contraception. They also shielded faith-based groups from discrimination lawsuits over hiring and firing employees. On July 16 the Court's majority issued an order likely to help Florida Republicans suppress certain citizens' ability to vote. According to the decision, Florida can block ex-felons from voting if they have outstanding court fines or cannot pay all the costs associated with their convictions.[29] Justice Sonia Sotomayor, joined by Justices Ruth Bader Ginsburg and Elena Kagan, stated the consequences in their dissent: "This Court's order prevents thousands of otherwise eligible voters from participating in Florida's primary election simply because they are poor."

DOWN WITH THE INTERNATIONAL CRIMINAL COURT!

Not content with challenging law and order at home, the Trump administration also sought to undermine international law. Shortly after the United States withdrew support for the World Health Organization, President Trump in June 2020 signed an executive order authorizing sanctions and travel restrictions on officials of the International Criminal Court (ICC) investigating potential war crimes in Afghanistan by U.S. as well as Taliban, Afghan government, and other forces.[30] The United States was imposing sanctions not on those who commit atrocities, but on those who investigate such crimes. Washington was probably trying to shield Israeli actions against Palestinians as well as the U.S. treatment of Afghans.[31]

Both the U.S. president and the attorney general purported to be committed to law and order, but they consistently subverted national as well as international law. Their actions weakened the political culture and sense of national unity on which democracy depends.

---

29 Jen Psaki, "The Roberts court is striking at the heart of democracy," *The Washington Post*, July 21, 2020.

30 The United States signed the Rome Statute establishing the ICC in 1998, but never ratified it. The court said it could try U.S. troops because U.S. courts had not done so and because Afghanistan had signed and ratified the Rome statute. The Afghan government, however, also opposed the ICC investigation.

31 The ICC decision to investigate potential crimes in Afghanistan "vindicates the rule of law and gives hope to the thousands of victims seeking accountability when domestic courts and authorities have failed them," said Jamil Dakwar, director of the American Civil Liberties Union's Human Rights Project. The ACLU represented three detainees who said they were tortured in Afghanistan between 2003 and 2008.

The Courts Under Trump and After

Helped by Republican Senate leader Mitch McConnell, President Trump was able in his single term to fill 28% of the 816 federal **judicial** seats, including 30% of the appellate judgeships. He also nominated three of the nine justices on the Supreme Court bench: Neil Gorsuch (appointed 2017); Brett Kavanaugh (2018); Amy Coney Barrett (2020). They joined Clarence Thomas (appointed by President George H.W. Bush in 1991), Chief Justice John Roberts (by President George W. Bush) in 2005), and Samuel Alito (by President George W. Bush (2006). creating a strong conservative bloc likely to endure for decades.

In 2022, however, President Biden appointed Ketanji Brown Jackson an Associate Justice. She joined two other liberals (all of them female): Sonia and Elena Kagan (appointed by President Obama in 2009 and 2010). Eight of the justices graduated either from the Harvard or the Yale law schools; Barrett from Notre Dame. Barrett joined Roberts, Thomas, Alito, and Sotomayor to give Catholics a strong presence; Gorsuch is Episcopalian but was raised Catholic. Besides Gorsuch, there is one other Protestant, Jackson, and one Jew, Kagan, among the nine justices.

The impact of the conservative bloc was apparent in major court decisions in 2022:

In *West Virginia v. Environmental Protection Agency,* the court's (6-3) ruling curtailed the EPA.'s ability to regulate the energy sector, limiting it to measures like emission controls at individual power plants.

In *Biden v. Texas,* the court (5-4) cleared the way for the Biden administration to end a Trump-era immigration program that forces asylum seekers arriving at the southwestern border to await approval in Mexico.

In *Kennedy v. Bremerton School District*, the court ruled (6-3) that a football coach at a public high school had a constitutional right to pray at the 50-yard line after his team's games.

In *Dobbs v. Jackson Women's Health Organization*, the court ruled (6-3) that a Mississippi law that bans most abortions after 15 weeks is constitutional and overturned the constitutional right to abortion established by Roe v. Wade in 1973.

In *New York State Rifle & Pistol Association v. Bruen*, the court ruled (6-3) that states with strict limits on carrying guns in public violate the Second Amendment.

In *Carson v. Makin*, the court ruled (6-3) that a Maine program that excludes religious schools from a state tuition program is a violation of the free exercise of religion.

In *Shurtleff v. Boston*, the court ruled (9-0) that the City of Boston had violated the First Amendment when it refused to let a private group raise a Christian flag in front of its City Hall, although it had allowed many other organizations to use the flagpole to celebrate various causes.

In *United States v. Zubaydah*, the court ruled (7-2) that the government was not required to disclose the location of a C.I.A. black site where a detainee at Guantánamo Bay, Cuba had been tortured.

In *National Federation of Independent Business v. Department of Labor*, the court found (6-3) that the Biden administration's vaccine-or-testing mandate for large employers was not lawful.

In *Trump v. Thompson*, the court ruled (8-1) (that former President Trump could not block the release of White House records to a House committee investigating the January 6 attack on the Capitol.

We shall see below in chapter 8 that the Justice Department in 2022 began to investigate whether Trump's handling of privileged documents violated the Espionage Act. Meanwhile, prosecutors and grand juries in New York weighed charges against the Trump Organization. It appeared that Trump was no longer beyond the law.

5

KAKISTOCRACY → FLAWED DEMOCRACY
→ AUTOCRACY → TYRANNY

Kratos was the Greek word for strength. We combine it with other Greek words to describe different forms of government. *Demos* (people) with *kratos* = democracy or rule of the people. Though Plato lived in the kind of democracy practiced in ancient Athens, he believed that a political system run by a "philosopher-king" would be superior to all others. Winston Churchill disagreed. He argued that democracy (people-rule) is the worst political system except for all the others. He could see what happened to Germany under the self-proclaimed genius of Adolf Hitler.

Donald Trump, like Hitler, sees himself as a kind of philosopher-king—"a very stable genius." In practice, however, he produced a *kakistocracy*—a government run by the worst, least qualified, and most unscrupulous individuals The term kakistocracy blends Greek *kratos*, "strength," with *kakistos* "worst," superlative of *kakos*, "bad." Many of Trump's appointees were ignorant, incompetent, and venal.[1] Trump's kakistocracy was both a cause and consequence of what the Economist Intelligence Unit called America's "flawed" democracy.

KLEPTOCRACY AND KAKISTOCRACY

Under Donald Trump, the United States became not just a kakistocracy but also a kleptocracy, a term that blends the Greek *klepto*—steal—with *kratos*. The major skill of these thieves was knowing how to exploit people, government funds, and natural resources to bolster their personal wealth and power. In the process, they made the United States a badly flawed democracy.

---

1   *Kakos* may be related to the Indo-European word *caco* "defecate." One cognate is "cacophony"—harsh or bad sound. Variants of "kakistocracy" have been used in Latin and Slavic languages. Lamenting the corruption of the pro-Russian Viktor Yanukovich regime in Kyiv, a writer in Ukraine addressed the *"kakistokratiya* of the transition period *(Politikantrop,* May 7, 2010)."

Here is the vicious cycle: Serving the wealthy few, Republicans supplant democracy with a klepto-kakistocracy. This operation weakens government by and for the many, pushing the country toward autocracy—the role of one person with absolute power or its most extreme form, tyranny.

History lives on. Puritan critics of the Church of England warned in 1641 that when "government of the church is in the hands of bad men, we have kakistocracy." In 1876 the poet and sometime diplomat James Russell Lowell worried that the United States was not a "government of the people, by the people, for the people" but a kakistocracy "for the benefit of knaves at the cost of fools." He added: "What fills me with doubt and dismay is the degradation of the moral tone. Is it or is it not a result of Democracy?"

How was the Trump administration a kakistocracy? Its operations combined many facets of "bad" (*kakos*)—willful ignorance, indifference to scientific and historical truth, erratic and thoughtless language, improvised decision-making with a drive to increase the power and wealth of Trump's family and Republican kleptocrats. The Trump regime bypassed institutional traditions— release of tax returns, disinvestment, avoidance of potential conflicts of interest, and press access to government deliberations. Narcissism overwhelmed prudence as the president used tax giveaways and Tweets to browbeat business entities from Carrier and Boeing to NBC.

Ignorance and Incompetence. Was the United States being run by a madman? "What can you say about a person who, before an adoring crowd, raises his eyes to heaven and calls himself the chosen one?" asked MIT linguistics professor Noam Chomsky, responding to President Trump's boast that he aced a mental acuity test.[2]

Donald J. Trump is an ignorant fool, according to the president's former National Security Assistant John Bolton, and so were many of the people around him. Some were know-nothings hired for their loyalty or their made-for-TV exteriors. Some were well-informed but sloppy thinkers such as former Defense Secretary Jim Mattis, who displayed his erudition by carrying around the *Meditations* of

---

2   Interview with Amy Goodman, "Democracy Now," on *Raw Story*, July 24, 2020.

Marcus Aurelius. Some were opportunists such as Michael Pompeo who, venting his exasperation, sent Bolton a note as Trump talked about Korea: He is "so full of shit."[3]

Bolton certainly makes the case that Trump was unfit to be president. Not only does the former president use social media to broadcast his latest whims but his instincts are often grounded in harmful ignorance. For example, Trump expressed surprise that the United Kingdom possesses nuclear weapons. Approaching a meeting with Putin in Helsinki, Trump asked if Finland is not "a kind of satellite" of Russia. His off-the-cuff comments on Taiwan, Jerusalem, North Korea, and other global issues rocked world politics.

Trump counts on his instincts as he defies or ignores science. What one thinks "self-evident" is seldom adequate for dealing with a complex world and its large-scale social and economic problems. Like other megalomaniacs such as Napoleon III, emperor of France, 1852-1870, Trump is reluctant to listen to experts lest they get credit for any achievement. But success in any field usually requires input from competent advisers. Decisions based on gut instincts are unlikely to anticipate the second- and higher-order effects of policy actions such as withdrawing from the Paris climate accord. Common sense often fails to understand reality because it neglects unconscious biases, background circumstances, and network dynamics. Yes, scientists often err, but decisions on serious matters should take account of the best science.

Kleptocracy with Kakistocracy. Trump and his entourage combined their kakistocracy with kleptocracy—the rule of thieves. The Donald gatecrashed Washington on a promise to "drain the swamp," but his regime riddled with conflicts-of-interest served as a front for grifters of all stripes. Not far from the White House, the Trump International Hotel sparked charges that the president was violating the emoluments clause of the Constitution, because he profited from the many foreign delegations that stayed there.[4] After

---

3   See my review of John Bolton, *The Room Where It Happened: A White House Memoir* (New York: Simon & Schuster, 2020) in *New York Journal of Books*, at https://www.nyjournalofbooks.com/book-review/room-where-it-happened

4   Documents show that six foreign government (including Malaysia, Saudi

the Trump presidency ended, the hotel joined a number of failed Trump ventures such as Trump Airlines, Trump casinos, Trump magazine, Trump steaks, Trump vodka, snd Trump University. Aged six years, the hotel changed owners on May 11, 2022, via a $375 million sale to a Miami investor group that planned to reincarnate the hotel as a Waldorf-Astoria.[5]

In 2018 Trump asked the U. S. ambassador in London (and N.F.L. owner), Woody Johnson, to see if the UK government could help Trump's Scottish resort to host the world's oldest golf tournament, the British Open. In 2019 he proposed that his Trump National Doral resort host a G-7 meeting. In 2019 Trump urged Vice President Mike Pence to stay at his resort in Doonbeg, Ireland, even though Pence's official business was far away. Whenever the president or some other official visits one of his resorts, he enriches himself as the Secret Services rents rooms (at more than $1,000 per night) and dines there. Trump visited his family-owned golf courses more than 275 times after he took office, bringing reporters with him, ensuring that the resorts got publicity.[6]

Trump used his dealings with Xi Jinping, Vladimir Putin, and Recep Tayyip Erdogan to advance his personal interests. Trump pleaded with Xi for help in winning reelection by buying up U.S. agricultural products. In early 2020 Trump endorsed China's assurances that it had the coronavirus under control, implying that America was safe. But when COVID-19 spread in the United States, Trump called it the "Chinese flu" or even "Kung flu."

Nepotism also took place. Cardiopathy, a Reston, Virginia-based company in which the president's brother Robert S. Trump (deceased in 2020) had a financial stake, received a $33 million contract from the U.S. Marshals Service in 2019. This led two competing firms to complain of favoritism. One told the Justice

---

Arabia, Qatar and the United Arab Emirates) spent more than $700,000 at the Trump International in 2017-2018. See https://www.cnn.com/2022/11/14/politics/trump-hotel-spending-foreign-governments/index.html.

5　Anna　Spiegel　at　https://www.washingtonian.com/2022/05/12/rip-trump-international-dcs-wildest-hotel/ (accessed 7/28/22).

6　Mark Landler et al., "Trump's Request of an Ambassador: Get the British Open for Me," *The New York Times*, July 21, 2020.

Department on July 22, 2019, that Cardiopathy had failed to disclose that "one of the President's closest living relatives stood to benefit financially from the transaction."

Was it an accident that the Pentagon in October 2019 awarded a $10 billion cloud computing contract to Microsoft over Amazon? The contest was closely watched after President Trump ramped up his criticism of Amazon's founder, Jeff Bezos (owner of *The Washington Post*), and said he might intervene in the deliberations. An assistant to former Defense Secretary James Mattis reported that Trump personally got involved in who would win the contract. Trump called the Defense Department boss in summer 2018 and directed him to "screw Amazon" out of the opportunity to bid on the contract.[7]

Several cabinet members saw no problem with taking their wives on taxpayer-funded European vacations, using a government plane to get a better shot of the solar eclipse, plunking down $31,000 on a dining room set, and planning work travel based on a "desire to visit particular cities or countries." Scott Pruitt, the former Environmental Protection Agency head, used his post to travel widely on taxpayers' dimes and find a job for his wife. Health and Human Services Secretary Tom Price resigned under pressure in September 2017 after racking up at least $400,000 in travel bills for chartered flights. Ryan Zinke, the former Interior Secretary, awarded a contract to restore Puerto Rico's electrical grid to an ill-equipped two-person company run by his neighbor. Wilbur Ross, Trump's Commerce Secretary, promised to divest from his stocks but did not, and saw those shares increase in value. Treasury Secretary Steve Mnuchin similarly vowed to divest from his film company, Storm Chaser Partners, but merely sold his ownership interest to his wife.

Even as the Donald prepared to announce his candidacy for the 2024 elections, his family struck a deal with a Saudi-based real estate company to license its name to a housing and golf complex to be built in Oman, renewing a swirl of questions about former President Donald J. Trump's mixing of politics and business.

---

7   Guy Snodgrass, *Holding the Line: Inside Trump's Pentagon with Secretary Mattis* (New York: Sentinel, 2019)..

Misfit Kleptocracy

Like the president, most of his selections for cabinet posts had no experience in the jobs they were to perform. For his first Secretary of State, the president chose Rex Tillerson, a successful oil company CEO but with no experience in government foreign policy. For Secretary of Education, Trump chose Betsy DeVos, a plutocrat who had seldom visited a public school but espoused school vouchers, a policy shown not to work. Treasury Secretary Steven Mnuchin championed tax cuts for billionaires on the long-debunked hope that such largesse would trickle down. Secretary of Housing Ben Carson (seen by many as the token black in Trump's cabinet) was an accomplished surgeon but had no relevant experience except to occupy a house. Scott Pruitt, Trump's first choice to head the Environmental Protection Agency, was a notorious climate-change denier. One of Trump's picks to head the Department of Defense, James Mattis, was nicknamed "Mad Dog," and famous for his determination to avenge Iran's support of the Hezbollah truck bombing that killed 220 Marines and twenty-one other soldiers in Lebanon in 1983. The president's first choice as National Security Assistant, Michael T. Flynn, was compelled to step down after twenty-four days on the job—jailed for lying about his lobbying for Turkey and his Russian connections.[8]

Trump's Secretary of Transportation Elaine Chao scored a trifecta for herself, for her husband Senator Mitch McConnell, and her extended family. She did all this at taxpayers' expense and to the detriment of U.S. national security. For herself, she did not divest but held onto stock in Vulcan Materials Company where she had been a director before becoming a Trump cabinet officer. Vulcan is the leading U.S. maker of crushed building materials. The more asphalt it sells, the more it profits. When Chao talked infrastructure with President Trump, Vulcan's stock jumped. Pressured by a revelation in *The Wall Street Journal*, Chao finally sold her shares in June 2019

---

8 In the weeks after the November 2020 presidential election, Flynn picked up a presidential pardon to forgive his guilty plea to lying to the FBI. He immediately became a chief promoter of the "Stop the Steal" effort and championed bogus claims about foreign interference and ballot tampering. His status as a retired general and top intelligence officer gave weight to the empty theories and his campaign for a kind of Christian nationalism.

for a gain of at least $40,000 since her April 2018 promise to divest.

Transportation Secretary Chao told her aide Todd Inman to advise Kentucky officials and husband Mitch of any grants with special significance to McConnell's backers, including a highway-improvement project. Though twice rejected in the past, these supporters of Senator McConnell received grants totaling at least $78 million. No other state got such help from the Transportation Department.

According to *Politico* (10/07/2019), in her first 14 months as transportation secretary, one in four of the scheduled meetings with local officials on Ms. Chao's calendar were with Kentuckians. Some of the meetings were set up at the request of McConnell staff members, who let his wife's office know which officials were "friends" or "loyal supporters." A spokesman for the department allowed that it could appear as though Ms. Chao meets with Kentucky folks a lot, but disputed that there was anything odd about this—or that the state received more than its share of federal dollars.

Chao's father and sisters own a shipping company called Foremost Group, which has a fleet of foreign-flagged ships that transport materials to and from China. In the Trump era, Chao had no formal affiliation or stake in the Foremost Group, but she had worked for the firm while getting her MBA at Harvard. The firm is based in New York but was founded by her father, James Chao, an immigrant from Shanghai and Taiwan. Both Chao and her senator husband received millions of dollars in gifts from her father, James, and her sister Angela, who became Foremast's chief executive. [9]

The House Oversight and Reform Committee investigated reports that Chao used her role in the U.S. government to boost the company's status, which federal regulations prohibit. It cited 2018 and 2019 budget requests in which her department wanted to cut millions of dollars from programs supporting U.S. ships and shipbuilders—actions that could benefit Foremost Group, which

---

9   The transportation secretary is part of a long line of individuals who've bridged China and the United States—and done well for themselves in the process. Jonathan Hunt, "Elaine Chao Learned From the Best," *Foreign Policy* (June 26, 2019) at https://foreignpolicy.com/2019/06/26/971797-elaine-chao-anna-chennault-china-united-states-mitch-mcconnell/ (accessed 4/6/20).

received hundreds of millions of dollars in low-interest loans from the Chinese government to purchase ships made in China. "Given the decline in the number of U.S. flagged vessels in foreign trade," the committee stated, the Transportation Department's "approach to these programs may threaten national security by increasing the likelihood that our military will be dependent on foreign-flagged vessels during times of war or emergency." The committee noted that Chao had appeared in media interviews with her father, founder of Foremost Group, with the Transportation Department's official seal behind them where her father "touted [her] influence within the U.S. government and boasted about his access to President Trump."

The committee also investigated Chao's travel for possible ethics violations. In October 2017, the State Department raised ethics concerns over Chao's upcoming trip to China because she was going to include some family members in official meetings with the Chinese government. The Transportation Department canceled that trip, but Chao did make the trip in April 2018. The committee requested documents related to both trips as well as other potential travel by family members in government vehicles or aircraft. A Transportation spokesperson said that media reports targeting the Secretary's family were stale, xenophobic, and sought only "to undermine her long career of public service." Husband Mitch McConnell also came under ethics scrutiny for lifting sanctions on a Kremlin-linked oil company in exchange for building a large aluminum plant in an area in Kentucky hit hard by job loss and the opioid crisis.[10]

Professor Laurence Tribe at Harvard Law School called Chao's potential conflicts of interest "extremely serious" given her proximity to the center of Republican legislative power and Senate confirmation power in her husband. But he did not expect prompt action to correct the situation. "The swamp that defines this entire administration will not be drained while the president himself is the

10 Courtney Bublé on September 16, 2019 in https://www.govexec.com/oversight/2019/09/house-investigating-transportation-secretary-elaine-chaos-possible-conflicts-interest/159914/; also https://www.nationalmemo.com/oversight-committee-demands-documents-on-chao-family-shipping-firm/

corrupter-in-chief and is essentially on the take from foreign powers in violation of the Foreign Emoluments Clause of Article I and continues to rob America's taxpayers in violation of the Domestic Emoluments Clause of Article II."[11]

Despite Chao's profits working in Trump's cabinet, she resigned immediately after the January 6 insurrection and later spoke with the January 6 committee, provoking Trump to denounce both her and husband McConnell as tools of left-wing Democrats.

The former hedge fund manager Treasury Secretary Stevin Mnuchin (estimated assets $400 million) helped rationalize the 2017 tax law that reduced taxes for the super-rich but saved only pennies for middle-class and poorer Americans. By 2019 it became clear that the tax breaks for the rich added greatly to the federal budget deficit—nearly one trillion dollars a year.

Tucked into the 2017 tax relief bill was an "opportunity zone" initiative that allowed investors to delay or avoid taxes on capital gains by putting money in projects or companies in more than 8,700 federally designated opportunity zones. Mr. Trump boasted the initiative would revitalize downtrodden neighborhoods. But the incentive was criticized as a gift to wealthy investors such as Mnuchin and real estate developers (such as the Trump Organization). The tax break targeted people with capital gains, owned mainly by rich investors. The Treasury permitted opportunity zones to encompass not only poor communities but some adjacent affluent neighborhoods. As of 2020, much of the money flowed to those wealthier areas, including many projects that were planned long *before* the new law was enacted. After Trump lost the 2020 election, Mnuchin established an investment fund, Liberty Strategic Capital. The fund obtained contributions from the Saudi, Emirati and Qatari sovereign wealth funds. The scale of Mnuchin's fund and its investments from countries where he traveled as Treasury secretary suggested that he exploited his government role to enrich himself.

Trump exceled at installing foxes to guard the chicken coop. He

---

11 Matthew Rozsa at https://www.salon.com/2019/09/17/congress-investigates-secretary-of-transportation-elaine-chao-over-possible-conflicts-of-interest/

appointed a former coal lobbyist to administer the Environmental Protection Agency; a former lobbyist for Raytheon Technologies as defense secretary; a lobbyist for the auto industry to lead the Energy Department; and a former oil and gas lobbyist to head the Department of the Interior.

Do these ex-lobbyists shape policy? In July 2020, the Trump administration lifted a ban on sales of silencers to private overseas buyers that was intended to protect U.S. troops from ambushes in Afghanistan and elsewhere. The change was championed by a White House lawyer Michael B. Williams who for two years had worked for a firearms trade group, the American Suppressor Association, founded and directed by his brother. Operating in the private sector, however, Williams failed to overturn the ban. Then, in 2017, attorney Williams joined the Trump administration. Operating from the West Wing, Williams pushed to overturn the prohibition by raising the issue with administration officials and creating pressure within the State Department. On July 10 the State Department lifted the ban. The change paved the way for as much as $250 million a year in possible new overseas sales for companies that Williams had championed as general counsel of the American Suppressor Association. When the former Eagle Scout from Georgia returned to the ASA as its General Counsel, in March 2021, he got a warm welcome from the gun industry.[12] "We are absolutely thrilled to have Michael back on the team at ASA," said Knox Williams, President and Executive Director of ASA. "Over the years, he has proven himself as one of the great minds in Second Amendment advocacy, effectively championing firearm and suppressor rights at the State and Federal levels." Several years in D.C. had helped his brother Michael learn how to get around pesky laws.

Trump's campaign manager in 2016 and chief strategist in 2017, Steve Bannon, was arrested in August 2020 and charged with fraud over a fundraising campaign to build a wall on the U.S-Mexican border. The U.S. Department of Justice charged that Bannon and three associates defrauded hundreds of thousands of donors in connection with the "We Build the Wall" campaign, which raised

---

12 Michael LaForgia and Kenneth P. Vogel, "White House Lawyer Delivers for Ex-Patrons in Gun Industry," *The New York Times*, July 14, 2020.

$25 million but built only 300 feet of wall--so flimsy it had to be replaced. Bannon siphoned off at least $1 million to cover personal expenses. Bannon's right-wing anti-immigration ideology fueled Trump's "America First" campaign. He was arrested on a 150-foot yacht owned by a business partner, Chinese billionaire Guo Wengui, also being investigated on criminal charges.[13]

Bannon was the sixth former aide to Donald Trump to face criminal charges, most of whom Trump pardoned in 2020 and had released from prison. On August 20 the president said he felt "very badly" about Bannon's arrest. Trump also said he had had no involvement with "We Build the Wall," despite having flown to El Paso in 2019 to speak before the privately funded section of the wall, describing it as "private enterprise at its finest." When the El Paso wall appeared unstable, the Trump administration hired the same firm that the nonprofit had employed to rebuild the wall.[14] Outsiders wondered whether Trump would pardon Bannon as he did other malefactors.

Bannon and one associate were jailed in October 2022 for defrauding donors to their online campaign to build a wall along the U.S.-Mexico border.

New York's attorney general sought to dissolve the National Rifle Association, a major contributor to Trump's campaigns, claiming that its leadership "looted" it.

On August 20, 2020, Politico reported that another Trump supporter, Jerry Falwell Jr., recently suspended as president of

---

13 The Senate intelligence report on Russian campaign interference quotes Bannon disparaging Trump's eldest son. Donald Jr. Bannon thought "very highly" of the son but also called him "a guy who believes everything on Breitbart is true." Bannon, of course, ran the right-wing media outlet Breitbart before joining the Trump campaign, and then for several months after leaving the White House. See Michelle Goldberg, "Trumpism Is a Racket, and Steve Bannon Knew It," *The New York Times*, August 21, 2020.

14 Many Trump associates were part of the "We Build the Wall" scheme. Kris Kobach, a hardline anti-immigrant Kansas politician, was listed as the group's general counsel. The group's advisory board included the Blackwater founder and Trump ally Erik Prince; Curt Schilling, the ex-Red Sox pitcher whom Trump encouraged to run for Congress; and Robert Spalding, former senior director for strategic planning on Trump's National Security Council. See Goldberg, "Trumpism."

Liberty University, repeatedly used a 164-foot yacht owned by NASCAR mogul Rick Hendrick for family vacations after the university committed to a lucrative sponsorship deal with Hendrick Motorsports.

Were there links between kleptocracy, inefficiency, and conservative ideology? Did have-gots *want* the government to be inefficient so people would lose confidence in it, and have to rely solely on private enterprise? Republican activist Grover Norquist campaigned for decades to reduce taxes and the size of government. He quipped, "I don't want to abolish the government. I simply want to reduce it to the size where I can drown it in the bathtub."[15] Before the 2012 election he secured a pledge from most Senate and House Republicans to "oppose any and all efforts to increase the marginal income tax rate for individuals and business; and to oppose any net reduction or elimination of deductions and credits, unless matched dollar for dollar by further reducing tax rates." Devoted to conservative Republican causes, he cooperated with Oliver North (indicted on 16 felony counts stemming from the Iran-Contra affair) and Jack Abramoff (jailed for defrauding Native Americans). But Norquist could not be accused of ignorance. He was an editor of the Harvard college newspaper and a graduate of the Harvard Business School.

MARX. LENIN, AND STALIN IN REPUBLICAN WASHINGTON

Karl Marx, Vladimir Lenin, and Joseph Stalin would be pleased if they could see how-- thanks mainly to Republicans—their doctrines have been realized in the United States. Of course, rich liberals such as George Soros and Michael Bloomberg also use their wealth to try and shape U.S. politics, but not to enrich themselves or friends.

Superstructure and Base in Marxism

Marx taught that the economic base—*who owns what*—determines the superstructure of politics and culture. The superstructure creates an educational system and mass media that foster a "false ideology." This is an illusion that the present arrangement between haves

---

15 Interview on NPR's *Morning Edition*, May 25, 2001.

and have-nots is inevitable and as good as it gets. Institutions of government may appear to serve the people, but they are tools of those who own the means of production and control workers and farmers.

This Marxist vision has been validated by many trends in the United States. Ronald Reagan's defense outlays pleased the military-industrial complex. His tax cuts, deregulation of industry, and anti-welfare policies benefited the upper classes while harming most Americans. Like Reagan, George W. Bush also spent wildly on defense, widened the gaps between rich and poor, and broadened the budget gap. Meanwhile, the Supreme Court increasingly acted as a servant for the ruling elites. It threw the 2000 election to George W. Bush. In 2010, the court ruled in *Citizens United* that the government may not limit what non-profit and for-profit corporations and unions spend on "electioneering communication."

In June 2018, the Supreme Court upheld President Trump's Executive Order 13769 imposing limits on travel from five predominantly Muslim nations plus Venezuela and North Korea. The court's liberals denounced the decision. In a searing dissent, Justice Sonia Sotomayor said the ruling was no better than *Korematsu v. United States*, the 1944 decision that endorsed the detention of Japanese-Americans during World War II. Riding high politically in January 2020, Trump added Africa's biggest country, Nigeria, as well as Myanmar, Eritrea, Kyrgyzstan, Sudan, and Tanzania, to his restricted travel list. This gave a "two-fur" to xenophobes, because most residents of these countries were black or Muslim or both. The exception was Myanmar, which was not black and most of its Muslims had fled.

Given the results of the 2010 census, Republicans used their control of many state governments to redraw the lines of electoral districts ("gerrymander") to weaken the impact of minority votes and give the GOP a structural advantage in elections. The Supreme Court had ruled in 1995 (*Miller v. Johnson*) that racial gerrymandering violates the constitution and upheld lower court bans on redistricting based on race. But on June 27, 2019, the Court ruled 5-4 *(Rucho v. Common Cause)* that "partisan gerrymandering claims present political questions beyond the reach of the federal courts."[16] Justice Elena Kagan dissented with a warning: "The practices challenged in these cases imperil our system of government. Part of the Court's role in that system is to defend its foundations. None is more important than free and fair elections."

That same day in June 2019, the court issued another ruling that favored the Republican cause. By another 5-4 vote, it opted to gut public sector unions *(Janus v. AFSCME Council 31)*.

The court headed by Chief Justice John Roberts issued some judgments that kept alive Democratic initiatives such as the Affordable Care Act. On July 9, 2020, the court issued two rulings that appeared to help Democrats but did not. The Supreme Court on July 9, 2020, ruled that no one—not even the president—is above the law and that lawful subpoenas must be answered. By remanding these cases back to the lower courts, these rulings permitted the president's lawyers to keep stalling so that his tax returns could remain hidden until after the November elections.

Zero-sum Leninism

What does Leninism add to Marxism? While Marx expected the dynamics of materialism to destroy capitalism, Lenin shunned determinism. Politics, he argued, is an active, no-holds-barred fight to the death. The idea in Russian is brief and to the point: *kto kovo,* which means 'Who, whom--? Who will destroy whom?" For Lenin, politics is zero-sum combat.

What is ethics in politics, according to Lenin? Not some commandment that flashes down from heaven, but anything that promotes the class struggle—Communist objectives.[17]

---

16 Two judges appointed by President Trump, Neil Gorsuch and Brett Kavanagh, joined Chief Justice John Roberts and Associate Justices Clarence Thomas and Samuel Alito. Roberts wrote that partisan gerrymandering can be distasteful and unjust, but that states and Congress have the ability to pass laws to curb excessive partisan gerrymandering.

17 So politically sensitive was Lenin's view of morality that my academic adviser in Moscow, a retired diplomat, tried to keep the relevant document from me—a speech by Lenin in 1920 to the League of Young Communists, which I remembered reading in a Columbia University library.

Who whom? Lenin would not have been surprised by the amoral, zero-sum campaign waged by Republican leaders against Democrats since the Richard Nixon years. In 1968, for example, candidate Nixon and Henry Kissinger scuttled talks to end the Vietnam War, an outcome that could have helped Democrat Hubert H. Humphrey to win the presidency that November.[18] Nixon also opened a "Southern strategy" to convince southern whites that Republicans would do better than Democrats at keeping down blacks—an approach later adopted and embellished by presidential candidates Ronald Reagan and George H. W. Bush. In 1994 Republican Congressman Newt Gingrich (Tulane Ph.D., 1971) proclaimed a "Contract with America" calling for lower taxes. The contract's demagogic slogans, fine-tuned by the Heritage Foundation, helped Republicans regain control of the House of Representatives for the first time since 1952. Like Donald Trump in later years, Gingrich strongly influenced Republicans despite a troubled personal story involving debt, philandering, and double-dealing.[19]

Senator Mitch McConnell deepened the struggle in 2008 by committing Republicans to making the incoming Obama administration fail at whatever it assayed. Republicans proceeded to throttle many Obama initiatives. Members of what used to be the Grand Old Party continue striving to weaken if not kill the Affordable Care Act. But McConnell's supreme victory was preventing Senate hearings in 2016 on Obama's recommendation to make Merrick Garland, a political moderate, the ninth judge on the Supreme Court after the death of conservative Justice Antonin Scalia.

Trump's first appointment to the court was Neil Gorsuch, seated in April 2017.[20] In October 2018, while Republicans still controlled

---

18 John A. Farrell, "Anna Chennault: The Secret Go-Between Who Helped Tip the 1968 Election," *Politico* (December 30, 2018) at https://www.politico.com/magazine/story/2018/12/30/anna-chennault-obituary-vietnam-back-channel-nixon-1968-223299 (accessed 4/6/20).

19 Julian E. Zelizer, *Burning Down the House: Newt Gingrich, the Fall of a Speaker, and the Rise of the New Republican Party* (New York: Penguin, 2020).

20 Usually siding with conservative judges, Gorsuch aligned with liberals in *McGirt v. Oklahoma.* in July 2020. He wrote that the federal Major Crimes Act of 1885 could not be applied to a possible crime committed by a Native American on a

all branches of government, the Senate approved a second Trump nominee, Brett Kavanaugh. McConnell managed to cut short investigations into Kavanaugh's behavior toward women.

These dirty tricks broke with democratic principles supposed to guide American politics. They were aided and abetted by a leading follower of Lenin, former KGB agent Vladimir Putin. True to Lenin's operational code, Putin used every tool and trick to advance his objectives—from Kremlin politics and Crimea to the White House. Reversing Karl Marx's expectations, however, Putin—somewhat like Trump–also used politics to influence and profit from his country's economy. Blending political and economic power, both Putin and Trump worked to create a false ideology for their subjects.

In the Trump era, Lenin's operational code has been implemented not just by the White House but by most Republicans in Congress. In 2020, many Republicans probably accepted that the president had committed high crimes and misdemeanors, but they still voted to exonerate him. They put their own jobs and the Republican Party above truth and principle. With the single exception of Mitt Romney, all Republican Senators voted to squash the House impeachment charges.

Stalinism Lite

Trump validated Marxist economics and Leninist politics plus a mild version of Stalinism. Like Stalin, Trump held that the Party's leader knows everything. All Party members hsd to follow his lead or be purged. Any opponent was an "enemy of the people." Stalin's propaganda machine, like Fox News today, preached that the great leader could do no wrong. Millions starved in Ukraine and Kazakhstan, but *Pravda* (*"Truth"*) declared that everyone was happy. Trump too proclaimed that things in America had never been better, even as the country's COVID-19 deaths topped the global tolls.

As Stalin collaborated for a time with Adolf Hitler, Trump gets

---

former Native American reservation unless Congress specifically dis-established the reservation when passing the act. Therefore, the State of Oklahoma had no right to prosecute McGirt on what had been an Indian reservation.

along well with other "strongmen"--beginning with Vladimir Putin. Stalin's secret accords with Hitler in 1939 were not published in Russia for half a century. Any records of Trump's talks with Putin have been deep-sixed. Researchers from the National Archives were evicted from the Trump White House. After losing the White House in 2021, Trump took many boxes of official documents with him to Mar-a-Lago and fought every effort to get them to the National Archives.

In good Stalinist fashion, Trump purged any government officials who testified on impeachment, as detailed in the chapter "Injustice in High Places."

Rules—who needs them? If Congress votes to aid Ukraine, as it did in 2018, the president can make a "perfect" phone call to leverage the aid for his own needs. If Congress authorizes money for "Defense," Trump can divert it to a border wall that appeals to his base. Is the president limited to two terms by the Constitution? The president joked—or hinted—that he might stay indefinitely. After all, his comrade Vladimir had already run Russia for more than twenty years and manipulated the constitution so he could stay longer.

Out of office in 2022, Trump continued to stand by his comrade Vladimir—even in his blood-thirsty war to destroy Ukraine and its fledgling democracy.

With the highest court and the Justice Department in the pocket of the Trumpists, where could critics turn to challenge policies they saw as illegal or downright crazy? Leninists don't care how bad things get. For them, "the worse, the better." A Marxist would predict that decisions of a reactionary Supreme Court will intensify the contradictions within capitalist society and lead it to explode into socialism.

Can voters be brain-washed? Fox News functioned as an arm of the Trump administration, but America's major newspapers and some TV channels still strove to report accurate and complete— not false—news. In May 2020, even Twitter began to fact-check and sometimes block presidential statements. Nonetheless, the fact that many American voters still support President Trump no matter what he says or does—even if it hurts their interests—shows that the basics of Marxism, aided by some Leninist tactics, have permeated American life and may be hard to erase.

Two days after the events of January 6, 2021, Twitter announced: "After close review of recent Tweets from the @ realDonaldTrump account...and how they are being received and interpreted...we have permanently suspended the account due to the risk of further incitement of violence." Banned by Twitter, Trump created his own social media platform, "Truth Social." By September 2022, however, it had flopped as a money raiser—having brought in only $4 million. Still, it kept the Q'Anon mythology alive, now embraced by the ex-pres himself. In October 2022, Trump used his account to blast Senator McConnell for approving some Democrat-sponsored legislation; Trump denounced the wife of Mitch, Elaine, as "China-loving Coco Chow." He also ranted at reporter Maggie Haberman for her inside stories in *The Confidence Man: The Making of Donald Trump and the Breaking of America* (New York: Penguin, 2022).

Good-bye Plato, so-long, Jefferson; welcome Marx, Lenin, Stalin!

The actions of the Trump administration validated many of the forecasts of Karl Marx and shown the effectiveness, at least in the near term, of Leninist and Stalinist politics. Commenting on these thoughts, Boston University historian Igor Lukes noted that Plato argued that only the most exquisitely educated among us should govern. Lenin, in sharp contrast, said that "revolutionary sailors" can master the art of government in twenty-four hours. Trump acted like one of Lenin's revolutionary sailors, confident that being president is not much different from buying and bankrupting a casino. The president and his backers may not grasp that they are the revolutionaries who have come up from the street and lack the know-how to run a huge and multifaceted government. Alternatively, they may choose to act incompetently to show that government is incompetent. Like Stalin, however, Trump believes himself omniscient.

Ignorance. Impetuosity. Avarice. Thin skin. No ideas, fixed ideas, and false ideas. What a combination in and around a White House where the president can fire nuclear weapons in less than fifteen minutes and destroy much of civilization in an hour!

Flawed Democracy—How and Why?

Democracy in the United States withered under President Trump. Since 2016, when Trump was elected, the Democracy Index of the Economist Intelligence Unit has downgraded the United States from a full democracy to a flawed democracy. In 2019 The EIU rated the United States the 25th most democratic country in the world, just below Japan and South Korea and just above Malta, Estonia, and Israel; in 2022, the 26th most democratic—well below the "full" democracies in Norway, New Zealand, Finland, Sweden, Denmark, Australia, Denmark, Australia, Canada, Germany, Japan, South Korea, and the United Kingdom. The decline stemmed from many factors, some dating back to the late 1960s, each of them eroding Americans' trust in their governmental institutions.

The Democracy Index gave the United States relatively high grades for electoral process and pluralism. Its grade for "civil liberties," however, was only medium-high and just medium for government functioning, political culture, and political participation (voting turnout). Its score for political participation was boosted by the greater representation of women in the 116th Congress.[21] The global march of democracy stalled in the 2000s and retreated in the second decade of the 21st century. The score for democracy across the globe declined from 2010 through 2020. The Economist Intelligence Unit found that only 4.5% of the world's political systems were full democracies; nine (43,2%) were flawed democracies (including the USA); 36.6% were authoritarian; and 16.7% were hybrid. The authoritarian regimes include Russia which, under Trump's friend Vladimir, ranked 134th in 2019; China, under Trump's sometime friend Xi Jinping, placed 153rd. Trump's frequent partner Saudi Arabia ranked 159th, while North Korea,

---

21 "Democracy Index 2019" at https://www.eiu.com/topic/democracy-index (accessed 6/7/20).

whose leader Trump "loved," placed 167th—the least democratic country in the world.[22]

To call the governments headed by Xi Jinping, Vladimir Putin, and Kim Jong Un "authoritarian," is misleading. They are *tyrannies* led by one-man and a single party subservient to him, one individual and his closest associates who have usurped power for their own benefit.[23] Authoritarianism could be beneficent in some ways. as in Singapore, but it can lead to autocracy which can escalate to brutal tyranny.

America's status as a democracy is flawed for many reasons, most of which endured even after Biden succeeded the Trump presidency. A major problem is that government in the United States no longer functions very well. Public frustration with institutions has been building for years. Gallup polls show that the number of Americans who approve of how Congress is handling its job fell to 21% in 2019—down from 40% in 2000. The highly partisan nature of Washington politics contributed to this trend. Republicans and Democrats are increasingly seen as focused on blocking each other's agenda to the detriment of constructive policymaking. Partisan tensions have left Congress in a stalemate. The slightly revised U.S.-Mexico-Canada Agreement on trade was the only piece of major legislation to get through the divided Congress in 2019.

President Trump turned out not to be the dealmaker he promised to be. His response to the hostility of opposition to his presidency was to go on the offensive and up the ante. The president dismissed as a "hoax" and a "fraud" the impeachment case against him launched by Democrats over his dealings with Ukraine. Most Republican politicians closed ranks to shield him. Trump's freewheeling approach also strained relations between the executive and legislative branches. Major foreign policy moves—the trade war

---

22 On a scale 0-10, the average global score fell from 5.48 in 2018 to 5.44 in 2019—the sharpest decline since the Democracy Index began in 2006. Four out of five categories of the Democracy Index, electoral process and pluralism, the functioning of government, political culture, and civil liberties, also deteriorated in 2019. The exception was political participation, for which the average global score went up.

23 Timothy Snyder, *On Tyranny: Twenty Lessons from the Twentieth Century* (New York: Tim Duggan Books, 2017), p.10.

with China, the abrupt redeployment of U.S. troops from northern Syria, the assassination of a senior Iranian general—were executed without consulting Congress. Whenever courts challenged Trump's policy directives on immigration and other issues, the president repeatedly called into question the independence and competence of the U.S. judicial system

A slightly more positive picture of U.S. democracy appeared in the 2020 and 2021 reports on *Freedom in the World* by Freedom House, a nonprofit think tank founded in New York in 1941 to promote democracy. It ranks political systems as "free," "partially free," or "not free" based on their performance on political rights and civil liberties.[24] The 2021 report ranked the United States "free," with a score similar to that of South Korea and Trinidad, but observed that U.S. democratic institutions eroded in recent years. The reasons included partisan manipulation of the electoral process, bias and dysfunction in the criminal justice system, flawed new policies on immigration and asylum, and growing disparities in wealth, economic opportunity, and political influence.

The U.S. electoral process suffers from the power of the Electoral College to give the presidency to a candidate who loses the national popular vote, as happened in 2000 and 2016. The whole system is vulnerable to foreign meddling. Congress tried to reduce this vulnerability but has little to show for it.

The quality of the voting and counting processes varied as elections are administered by a patchwork of state and local authorities, though evidence of deliberate fraud is rare. Additional federal funding for voting-system upgrades was allocated in 2019, and some social media firms announced new limits on political advertising, but many analysts argued that election security provisions were still inadequate ahead of the 2020 and 2022 elections.

Partisan gerrymandering remains a problem. The Voting Rights Act of 1965 prohibits racially discriminatory voting rules, but partisan maneuvers continue to limit the electoral impact of black

---

24 Wendell Willkie, the Republican presidential nominee who ran against Democrat Franklin Roosevelt in 1940, served as an honorary co-chair along with the president's wife, Eleanor Roosevelt.

and other minority voters likely to support the Democratic Party. Radical partisanship, mostly by local GOP officials, may be more harmful than foreign meddling.

Freedom House noted that the Trump administration sought to ramp up arrests and deportations of undocumented immigrants, regardless of whether they had committed crimes, and legal immigrants or refugees who committed crimes in the United States, even if they had long since completed their sentences.[25]

The Trump administration's enforcement drive added to a backlog of cases in immigration courts—more than a million were pending in December 2019—double the number when Trump took office. The number of people in immigration detention was at record levels in 2019—more than 52,000 people in custody. Overcrowding brought multiple reports of inadequate living conditions.

Freedom House noted that trust in the "American dream" was fading—in part due to worsening inequality and declining upward mobility.

The high living standards of the United States and Europe evolved as an interplay of interests--labor, capital, learning, entrepreneurs, government. Wealth creation included empowering the middle class and providing a route out of poverty for those on the bottom, systematizing and applying the rule of law, and creating the conditions for discovery and innovation. But democratic capitalism in the last fifty years has failed a broad part of the population. If it is supplanted by tribal populism, the political economy will fail more broadly. Americans need a better social safety net, unemployment insurance, job retraining, good education, and health care. The shrinking of these resources dooms the system for many Americans.

Freedom House in 2022 included the United States with other full democracies, but its combined score for political rights and civil liberties was only 83—far below the United Kingdom 93, Taiwan

---

25 The previous practice was to deport the most dangerous criminal aliens with the weakest ties to American communities. In September 2019, a judge suspended a policy unveiled in July that allowed expedited deportation—without a court hearing—of undocumented immigrants detained anywhere in the country if they could not show more than two years of residence in the United States.

94, Canada 98, Ireland 97, and Norway 100. Most Republican voters and most Republicans in Congress continued in 2022 to deny the legitimacy of Biden's election in 2020.

Could democracy give way to absolutism? The ingredients were there—vulture capitalism, perpetual war, corruption, economic fissures, know nothing-ism, the top-down suffocating of political opposition. All this is conducive to strong man rule. If Americans are ruled by klepto-kakistocrats, however, everybody will eventually lose.[26] The trend in U.S. politics toward flawed democracy followed by autocracy is supported by the V-Dem (Varieties of Democracy) Project based in Sweden and by the Bright Line Watch at Dartmouth College. The V-Dem Project finds that the United States experienced "substantial autocratization" --the loss of democratic traits —under President Trump. The traits at issue are clean elections, freedom of association, universal suffrage, an elected executive, freedom of expression, and alternative sources of information. Setbacks for democracy used to occur suddenly, as in a military coup, but now they take place gradually under a legal façade. Since about 1993, such changes have taken place in countries so diverse as Brazil, Burundi, Hungary, Russia, Serbia, and Turkey. The global trend is ominous. Only 1 in 5 democracies that started down this path have reversed the damage before becoming a full-blown autocracy. The V-Dem *Democracy Report 2022* found that negative trends continued in 2021-2022. The Director of the V-Dem Institute, Staffan Lindberg, warned, "It's really time to wake up before it's too late."[27]

Bright Line Watch routinely surveys hundreds of political scientists to issue periodic assessments of the health of democracy in the United States. Those assessments show a post-2016 decline

---

26 Rand Engel, "28 Reasons Why The Rich And Super-Rich Should Vote For Democrats," *RanttMedia*, May 5, 2018 at https://rantt.com/28-reasons-why-the-rich-and-super-rich-should-vote-for-democrats (accessed 7/12/20.

27 Anna Lührmann and Staffan I. Lindberg, "A third wave of autocratization is here: what is new about it?" *Democratization* 26, 7 (2019). The East European specialist Igor Lukes at Boston University told me by e-mail in September 2020 that he is profoundly depressed by developments in the Czech Republic, Slovakia, Hungary, and Poland. As noted above, German authorities are deeply concerned about alt-right movements—particularly in the former East Germany.

in democratic performance similar to V-Dem's data.[28] "Democracy depends on both sides accepting the results of free and fair elections and willingly turning over power to the other side if they lose," But Trump warned he might not accept defeat at the polls and—after the 2021 election—did not. Dartmouth professor Brendan Nyhan said, "We've never had a president attack our electoral system in this way."[29]

CAN IT HAPPEN HERE?

Did Trump want to replace democracy with an authoritarian dictatorship? Based on Trump's words and deeds, there are many signs that he did.[30]

- With Fox News promoting Trump's lies as truth, the president enjoyed one of the most powerful propaganda machines ever created.

- President Trump talked and acted as though he had the power to do what he wants, regardless of Congress or the courts.

- Trump acted as if he owned the U.S. government and could fire any official who defends the law and pardon anyone who breaks the law.

- Trump used federal prosecutorial powers to investigate his opponents and anyone who dared to scrutinize him or his allies for the many crimes he and they may have committed.

- Trump viciously attacked his critics and implied the Ukraine whistleblower should be hanged for treason.

- Trump's messianic pretensions are supported with religious fervor by millions of his supporters.

28 http://brightlinewatch.org/bright-line-watch-august-2020-expert-survey/ (accessed 9/15/20).

29 Quoted in Christopher Ingraham, "The United States is backsliding into autocracy under Trump, scholars warn," *The Washington Post*, September 18, 2020.

30 Jonathan Greenberg, "Twelve signs Trump would try to run a fascist dictatorship in a second term," *The Washington Post*, July 10. 2020.

- Trump subscribes to a doctrine of genetic superiority and incites racial hatred to scapegoat immigrants and maximize his own power.

- Trump finds common ground with the world's most ruthless dictators while denigrating America's most steadfast allies.

Can authoritarian politics come to America? Absolutely. It has happened before. To many Americans, something like it is happening now. This is the verdict of Harvard law professor Cass R. Sunstein and most of the contributors to his book *Can It Happen Here? Authoritarianism in America.*[31]

For starters, the U.S. Constitution allowed slavery. Then, in 1798, the Federalists enacted the Alien and Sedition Acts. In the 1860s President Lincoln suspended the writ of habeas corpus and imposed martial law. Lynchings went unpunished for decades into the 20th century. The 1917 Espionage Act made it a crime to refuse military duty or obstruct recruitment. The Sedition Act of 1918 prohibited abusive language about the U.S. government or its military forces. In 1942, more than 110,000 individuals of Japanese descent were sent to internment camps. Courts upheld the 1954 Subversive Activities Control Act. During the Vietnam War, the FBI infiltrated and tried to neutralize civil rights and antiwar movements.

If President Trump wanted to be a dictator, he would have to sweep away powerful institutions. Here is a *Dictator's Handbook*, U.S. Edition. To get started, attack the press. Get courts and congress to undermine First Amendment protections. Curtail use of the Freedom of Information Act. Attack the bureaucracy. Make certain appointments and fail to make others. Attack the courts. Adapt and adopt many techniques earlier employed by Mussolini and Hitler. Attack state and local governments. Stir up the mob, as modeled by Sinclair Lewis in the novel *It Can't Happen Here* (1935). "When fascism comes to America," Lewis warned, "it will be wrapped in the flag and be carrying a cross."

---

31 Cass R. Sunstein, ed., *Can It Happen Here? Authoritarianism in America* (New York: Dey Street, William Morrow, 2018). The sixteen contributors are distinguished professors of law, social science, and psychology.

But if it happens here, it won't happen all at once. A large, diverse society with democratic traditions and a strong civil society is unlikely to become an autocracy overnight. Authoritarian rule may be checked by courts, elections, and wide (though not universal) support for democracy. Just the sheer size and complexity of the U.S. government make it difficult for any radical group to capture. So, the more feasible scenario is a gradual erosion of liberal democratic norms. The institutions will have been hollowed out; much of what we value in a liberal democracy will have been lost. Courts can push the limits of existing principles in response to extraordinary circumstances.

Trump has nourished a cascading intolerance. He panders to intolerant constituents and stokes fear and anger against other groups. He emulates not just Hitler but also Vladimir Putin and Recep Tayyip Erdoğan. Each has used state resources to reinforce and deepen popular prejudices instrumental in their own ascent. It can be difficult for those in the "mushy middle" to check the identitarian and native intolerances that have grown in recent decades and may get stronger as automation and globalization worsen job insecurity. The pollster Nate Silver pointed out that "Education, Not Income, Predicted Who Would Vote for Trump."

How do democracies perish? Democratically elected governments can use their constitutional authority to bulldoze democratic institutions and tarnish the idea of accountability to voters. This process took place as Hitler transformed Germany's Weimar Republic into his Third Reich. It happens now in Hungary and other parts of Eastern Europe. Once elected, even by a slim margin, a government can exploit simmering discontent to slander and harass independent media, turn TV channels into propaganda machines, deploy government agencies against internal enemies, and use the law selectively to attack opposition politicians and decrease funds for opposition parties, populate the judiciary with ideological extremists, enrich loyalists by the procurement process, and pass voter suppression laws. Elections then become not choices about policy but a way to highlight the differences between "them" and "us." Populist voters vote to avenge themselves against out-of-touch elites and under-the-radar immigrants. The indifference of many Americans to real news and their dependence on social media create vast opportunities for foreign bots and trolls to shape public opinion. Collective solutions to shared problems are not on the GOP agenda.

Conspiracy theories, long a staple of the Trump repertoire, spread as rapidly as COVID-19 among Trump supporters, inducing mass delusion. Trump called fears of the virus a Democratic "hoax." He treated mask-wearing as effete political correctness and said that the pandemic's spread merely proves that "our TESTING is much bigger and better" (which it was not).[32]

His tone became more somber in July 2020. The pandemic was growing unchecked where people followed Trump's example and shunned masks and social distancing. Tulsa, where Trump insisted on having an indoor rally, suffered a surge in new cases— "more than likely" spurred by the rally and protests according to the local medical authorities.

Reality collided with Trump's fantasies. As he became more desperate, his inclination to manipulate the levers of power increased. When the 2020 election went against him, Trump demanded that officials in Georgia and other states "find" more votes for him, which they refused to do.[33]

LESSONS FROM THE TWENTIETH CENTURY

Based on his study of Nazi and Communist takeovers, Europe, Yale historian Timothy Snyder recommended that citizens in democracies practice these safeguards:[34]

Refuse to obey in advance, aware that kow-tows to would-be

---

32 Dana Milbank in *The Washington Post*, July 10, 2020 at   https://www.washingtonpost.com/opinions/2020/07/10/trumps-gop-is-becoming-garish-opera-paranoia/

33 In September 2022, however, a federal judge (appointed by Obama) ruled against a voting rights group founded by Georgia Democratic gubernatorial nominee Stacey Abrams. This group, known as Fair Fight Action, challenged state laws regarding "exact match" voter registration policy, absentee ballot cancellation practices, and registration inaccuracies, all of which impeded voting by many blacks.

34 Snyder, *On Tyranny: Twenty Lessons from the Twentieth Century.*

dictators cannot be easily reversed.

Defend democratic institutions, as many Jews failed to do in 1933, hoping that Hitler would appreciate their loyalty.

Beware the one-party state, as in Communist systems and facilitated in the USA by courts that allow unlimited spending by the wealthy to influence elections.

Beware of symbols such as swastika pins or MAGA hats.

Uphold professional ethics, unlike the lawyers, physicians, industrialists who executed the Holocaust or the Federalist Society perverting the U.S. court system.

Beware of paramilitaries--not just Nazi storm troopers and Putin's mercenaries but Trump's use of private security forces and armed Oathtakers to fight dissenters and peaceful protestors.

Be reflective if you carry a weapon in public service--avoid evils of the past such as abetting Stalin's purges and Hitler's Holocaust and unwarranted violence against minorities in the USA.

Stand out, like Rosa Parks. If you set a positive example and break a spell, others may follow.

Look out for dangerous words such as "temporary emergency measures" and "terrorism."

Do not fall for tricks to expand emergency power such suppression of opposition parties and free press.

Contribute to good causes. Pick up one or two charities and support them by autopay. Your free choice will support civil society and help others to do good.

Do not abuse language and believe in truth, Cultivate clear and honest thinking and expression. If the main pillar of a tyranny is living a lie, Vaclav Havel wrote, "the fundamental threat to it is living in truth."

Establish a private life. Totalitarians try to eliminate the barriers between public and private life. Do not allow the world to know and manipulate your every thought and deed.

Investigate complexity and learn from peers in other countries,

Be a patriot (not a blind nationalist) *and courageous.*

6

THROWING AWAY LIVES, FRIENDS, TREASURE, AND HONOR IN WORLD AFFAIRS

The "best countries" ranking by *U.S. News and World Report* placed the United States 7th in the world in 2020—still 1st in power but only 15th in quality of life. In 2016, the last year under President Obama, the United States ranked 4th.[1] The decline in U.S. standing derived from many factors—among them, Trump's words and deeds on the global stage.

GOALS AND TOOLS OF FOREIGN POLICY

Foreign policy should strengthen a country's overall fitness—its ability to cope with complex challenges and opportunities at home and worldwide.[2] The Trump administration lowered U.S. fitness in the world as well as at home. Since its founding, the United States has experienced many successes and many failures in world affairs. Most presidents leave a legacy of achievements that his/her successor can build on as well as problems to ameliorate. President George H. W. Bush left a positive legacy of international cooperation that Bill Clinton enhanced but that George W. Bush later demolished. "W" then bequeathed Obama a huge mess to clean up. Obama did not end the Middle East catastrophes launched by George W., but Obama fostered the Paris climate accords and the Iran nuclear deal—both of which Donald Trump soon neutered. Obama improved alliances in Europe and Asia, which Trump derided and nearly destroyed.

Success in foreign affairs requires the skillful and consistent application of smart power, using soft power assets to persuade and

---

1   https://www.usnews.com/news/bestcountries/overall-rankings (accessed 8/6/ 20). The top countries in 2020 were Switzerland, Canada, and Japan. China placed 15th in 2020—up from 17th in 2016. Russia ranked 23rd in 2020, up from 24th in 2016.

2   On fitness, see Walter C. Clemens, Jr., *Complexity Science and World Affairs* (Albany: State University Press of New York, 2013).

coopt and hard power tools to coerce and compel. A smart foreign policy blends ideals such as human rights with political and economic realism. It works for what is both desirable and do-able. Trump did none of these things. He flattered a Russian dictator whose evil ways were manifest already in the early 2000s. He also appeased and flattered China's president even as he claimed for China the South China Sea, locked Uyghurs in concentration camps, and turned Hong Kong into a police state. Trump was rightly concerned with China's theft of intellectual property. To cope with this problem, however, he made things worse by launching a tariff war. Diverting attention from his own neglect of Covid, he called it the Chinese flu. Trump increased U.S. defense spending but did nothing to reduce the threats posed by China, Russia, Iran, and North Korea—nothing to control their arms buildups or aggressive foreign policies.[3]

The Trump administration frittered away some of the strongest assets of any country:

- an educated population enriched by continuous flows of intelligent and enterprising immigrants;

- geographic isolation from hostile adversaries;

- near self-sufficiency in natural resources;

- the world's largest and most innovative economy;

- a dynamic framework and culture for science and technology;

- unprecedented soft power—the ability to persuade and coopt others to adopt policies you favor;

- and a military establishment second to none.

Most failures on the world stage, as within the United States, stemmed from Trump's myopic cult of self-seeking. Like Hitler and other dictators, Trump views all of life as a zero-sum struggle. In his view, any gain for other parties means a loss for the United States, for his administration, and for him personally. His outlook

---

3   He staged showy meetings with Kim Jong Un but offered him nothing to curb his arms buildup.

would have *precluded* two of the greatest achievements of U.S. foreign policy: The Marshall Plan for the reconstruction of Europe, 1948-1952, and the Fulbright exchanges (1946-- and 1961--) of international students and faculty.[4] These and other successes aimed at *mutual* gain—not unilateral advantage. The Marshall Plan for European recovery created the foundation for strength and solidarity across the Atlantic to counter the threat of Soviet aggression.[5] The cultural exchanges fostered friendship and respect as well as mutual understanding between Americans and people on every continent. Many future leaders of other countries took part in those exchanges.[6]

The United States has gained from its contributions to a liberal world order' It managed to contain the USSR without a nuclear cataclysm, but it has also squandered its assets in wars and other interventions not needed for national security. Since 1945 no other country has been engaged in so many wars—Korea, Vietnam, Cambodia, Afghanistan, Iraq, Syria, along with lesser interventions in Iran, Guatemala, Cuba, Dominican Republic, Lebanon, Chile, Grenada, and Panama. Each operation had its justification, but most were optional. Most cost the United States dearly and netted little for America's security and well-being.

Republicans and Force, 1898-2020

President Trump's actions around the globe built on an "America-first" mentality among Republicans that, for more than a century, has harmed U.S. interests and undermined world peace. Of course, the picture is not black and white. Democratic administrations also made major blunders such as the Bay of Pigs and entering and

---

4　On the patient and persistent efforts of State Department officials, Congressional Democrats and Republicans, along with business leaders to win public and official support for the Marshall Plan, see Robert B. Zoellick, *America and the World: A History of U.S. Diplomacy and Foreign Policy* (New York: Twelve, 2020), pp. 272-276. The Louisiana Purchase was another major achievement.

5　Under the European Recovery Program, the United States extended to Europe $14.2 billion in loans and credits (nearly $140 billion in today's terms)—nearly 3% of U.S. GDP in peak years but only 1.1% from 1948 to 1952.

6　Walter C. Clemens, Jr., *America and the World, 1898-2025: Achievements, Failures, Alternative Futures* (New York: St. Martin's, 2000), pp. 54, 110, 144, 224.

escalating the Vietnam War.[7]

Ignoring the positive actions of previous Republican presidents,[8] Trump's "us-first" policies followed a long chain of myopic policies under Republican administrations that harmed U.S. interests as well as world peace, and contributed to the Republican virus sickening America's body politic.

1898: President William McKinley launched America's overseas empire in 1898 by taking Hawaii from the Hawaiians and the Philippines and Puerto Rico from Spain and their native peoples and soon turning Cuba into a U.S. protectorate.

1903: President Theodore Roosevelt helped Panama split from Columbia and let the United States build and control the Panama Canal.

1905: Under TR the Taft-Katsura Memorandum traded Japanese rule in Korea for U.S. in the Philippines.

1906-1909: TR occupied Cuba for a second time.

1908: TR started U.S. occupations of Nicaragua that continued until 1933.

1920: Senate Republicans kept the United States from joining the League of Nations—crippling at birth the one institution that could

---

7　A Democrat was president when the United States joined the Korean War and, a few years later, the Vietnam War—each seen in Washington as a spearhead for global Communist expansion. North Korea's aggression, we now know, was reluctantly backed by Stalin and Mao Zedong. North Vietnam's war on the South was driven more by nationalism than by ideology. That engagement was America's greatest blunder until the George W. Bush invasion of Iraq.

8　Teddy Roosevelt won the Nobel Peace award for mediating the Russo-Japanese War. Even before Woodrow Wilson proposed a League of Nations, William Howard Taft called for a League to Enforce the Peace. William Harding in 1921-1922 sought to prevent a naval arms race by limiting the battleship tonnage of the five major naval powers. When Japan invaded Manchuria in 1931, Herbert Hoover's Secretary of State Henry Stimson declared that the United States would never recognize political or territorial changes made by force—a stance followed by the League of Nations. President Eisenhower worked to relax Cold War tensions. Nixon began a dialog with China and signed the first strategic weapons arms control treaty with Moscow. Reagan and George H. W. Bush helped end the Cold War.

have prevented a second world war.

1930s: Congressional Republicans were reluctant to prepare for coping with aggression.

Post-1945: Top Republicans went along with most foreign policy initiatives of Democratic president Harry Truman, but Republican Senator Joe McCarthy spawned great chaos in the 1950s by false claims that the U.S. State Department was infested by Communists.

1953-1960: President Eisenhower's CIA helped overthrow nationalist leftist regimes in Iran and Guatemala. Ike's Radio Free Europe encouraged Hungarians to count on U.S. help if they rebelled against the USSR, a hope proved illusory in 1956. In 1960 Ike lied about a U.S. spy plane over the USSR. His CIA prepared the Bay of Pigs invasion that led to a disaster under JFK in 1961.

1968: Presidential candidate Nixon helped sabotage Vietnam peace talks that, if they succeeded, could have boosted election prospects of Democrat Hubert Humphrey.

1970s: Nixon and Kissinger expanded the Vietnam War into Cambodia, setting the stage for Khmer Rouge rule there and democide. To get a deal on strategic weapons in election year 1972, Nixon and Kissinger authorized the USSR to keep building nuclear submarines able to launch multiple warheads. In 1973 the United States helped overthrow President Salvador Allende in Chile.

1980s: President Reagan launched the Strategic Defense Initiative ("Star Wars") boondoggle. His Iran-Contra affair violated U.S. and international law. In 1986 Reagan withdrew U.S. acceptance of International Court of Justice compulsory jurisdiction after Nicaragua complained about U.S. mining of its harbors.

1990s: George W. Bush ignored warnings of the terrorist strike that happened on 9/11/91. He then launched the Iraq war on false pretenses in 2003. His "shock and awe" invasion of Iraq generated America's greatest blunder abroad--one that has spread its ramifications across the Middle East for nearly two decades. The ensuing wars have killed and maimed thousands of Americans and millions of other human beings; cost the United States trillions of dollars; debased the U.S. image abroad; and alienated America's friends and allies. These wars ruined the economies of the Middle East and drove millions of its people to despair. If any parties have gained, it has been the vultures picking at the debris—the Taliban and the dictatorships in Russia, Iran, Syria, and Turkey.

Another major blunder: In 1992 Bush unilaterally abrogated the 1972 ABM treaty that made it possible to limit U.S. and Soviet strategic weapons. He then revved up spending for antimissile defenses—a project that could never outpace improvements in enemy attack forces.

THE UNDERLYING PROBLEM OF MILITARIZATION

The Global Peace Index (GPI) ranked the United States in 2020 the world's third most militarized society.[9] Israel topped the list, followed by Russia, the USA, North Korea, and then France. To evaluate "militarization," the index asks what is the share of defense spending in a country's GDP. This percentage is important— particularly when compared with outlays for health and education. Israel says it must spend heavily on defense to protect against hostile neighbors. Circumstances also help justify America's large defense budget. Since U.S. allies count on "extended deterrence," America's outlays will be higher than those in Costa Rica. For their parts, Russian and North Korean leaders say their countries are encircled by hostile powers. France can say that its *mission civilisatrice* often requires it to help its former colonies. An historic quest for *grandeur* is also a driver.

The GPI reported that peacefulness in the United States declined under President Trump. The peacefulness rank is set by a country's level of conflict at home and abroad. Of 163 countries studied, the United States ranked 128th in 2019—down from 88th in 2012 and

---

9   *Global Peace Index 2019* at https://reliefweb.int/report/world/global-peace-index-2019 (accessed 6/4/20). The GPI is produced yearly by the non-profit Institute for Economics and Peace based in Sydney, Australia. The index employs three filters: domestic safety and security; domestic and international conflict; and militarization.

103rd in 2016. In 2019 the United States placed just below South Africa, 127th, and above Saudi Arabia, 129th. China ranked 110th; Mexico, 140th; and Russia, 154th.[10] The least peaceful countries included several where the United States was active--Afghanistan, Syria, Iraq, Yemen, and Somalia.[11]

The U.S. defense budget under President Trump increased to some $732 billion in 2020. Critics complained that the budget was bloated to please the defense industry and politicians in states with bases and military employment. Critics worried that the very existence of such large forces increased the proclivity to use them, even when national security was not at stake.

The White House has long claimed that U.S. defense spending consumes just over 3 percent of GDP, but this calculation omits government outlays for nuclear weapons research, weapons in space, satellite and other intelligence gathering and analysis, current and future veterans' benefits, and interest due on debts incurred by previous military activities. When these are included, the burden of defense swells to between 6 and 7 percent of GDP. Similar omissions deflate the official defense outlays of China and Russia. Their numbers are deflated also by the minuscule wages paid to their military personnel, the abbreviated training and low levels of creature comforts provided, and the state-controlled profits of defense industries. Neither China nor Russia spent much for veterans' benefits or interest charges on past debts.

At 38 percent of the world total, the USA spends as much on the

---

10 Iceland remained the most peaceful country in 2022, a position it held since 2008. It was joined at the top of the Index by New Zealand, Ireland, Denmark, and Austria. For the fifth consecutive year, Afghanistan was the least peaceful country, followed by Yemen, Syria, Russia and South Sudan. Seven of the ten countries at the top of the GPI were in Europe, and Turkey was the only NATO member placed in the bottom half of the Index. Two of the five countries with the largest deteriorations in peacefulness were Russia and the Ukraine.

11 Peacefulness deteriorated in all the Americas in 2019, with Central America and the Caribbean showing the largest deteriorations, due to crime and political instability; followed by South America, and then North America. Increasing political instability has been an issue across all three regions, exemplified by violent unrest in Nicaragua and Venezuela, and growing political polarization in Brazil and the United States.

military as the next nine or ten countries combined.[12] The leading military spenders in 2021 were the USA, China, India, the United Kingdom, and Russia.[13] These five accounted for 62 percent of global military spending of about $2.1 trillion—the first time such spending exceeded $2 trillion, even as the major economies took a hit because of COVID. Taking account of the many uncertainties, total U.S. spending on defense in 2022 was probably three to four times greater than China's and ten times more than Russia's.[14] U.S. funding for military research and development (R&D) rose by 24 per cent between 2012 and 2021, reflecting a major focus since Obama's time on new weapons, such as next-generation nuclear weapons, deemed too destructive to use by many analysts.

Defense spending is one element among many that help to shape national security and well-being. Military outlays compete with the human development priorities in health, education, and income, as well as research and development and eldercare. In 2020, defense spending amounted to *half* of all U.S, discretionary spending—all federal outlays for transportation, veterans, education, health, justice, international affairs, housing, environmental protection, science, space, technology, and social services! The very modest defense budgets of most NATO members in Europe—about 2 percent of GDP—permitted them to spend a much greater share of their wealth on social benefits than in the United States. Many Republicans did not care, because they loathed social welfare and did not care much for education. The GOP's biggest backers traveled in their own limos and private planes. They expected payback in tax relief, juicy contracts, subsidies, and lowered environmental standards.

---

12 Peter G. Peterson Foundation, "U.S. Defense Spending Compared to Other Countries," May 13, 2020 at https://www.pgpf.org/chart-archive/0053_defense-comparison.

13 https://sipri.org/media/press-release/2022/world-military-expenditure-passes-2-trillion-first-time

14 China, the world's second-largest spender, allocated an estimated $293 billion to its military in 2021, an increase of 4.7 per cent compared with 2020. The official number of $293 billion hides considerable unofficial spending on weapons R&D and the paramilitary People's Armed Police. China's more assertive foreign policy in 2021 drove up military spending increases all around Asia, starting with Japan (7% increase), Australia (4% increase), and India (0.9%).

The world is awash with weapons. The Stockholm Peace Research Institute reports that the USA remains the world's leading arms exporter at 39 percent of the world total, followed by Russia and France. China and Germany are a distant fourth and fifth. Europe accounts for 13 percent of global arms transfers and is the major growth region in arms imports.[15]

Thanks to U.S. aid to war-ravaged Ukraine, the U.S. share of weapons exports keeps increasing. Speaking in 2022 at a Lockheed plant in Alabama where the *Javelin* antitank missile is made, President Biden boasted that such weapons make the USA "the arsenal of democracy." Kyiv has become the largest yearly recipient of U.S. military aid in recent decades—more than twice the largest yearly total ever provided to Afghanistan and seven times Israel's annual military assistance package.[16] Just one arms package of about $47 billion for Ukraine in mid-2022 dwarfed the U.S. budget for combating climate change.

Under Trump and then Biden, the USA remained the principal military power in world affairs. The intersecting interests of the Pentagon, national security think tanks, relevant congressional committees, and arms makers ensure that debates over weapons will always result in higher military budgets and arms sales.

The USA is a weapons foundry and arsenal for weapons at home as well as abroad. With more guns in Americans' hands than there are people (roughly 400 million privately owned, with 11 million manufactured in 2020 alone), with mass shootings each year, with murderous attacks on schools that politicians cannot or will not stop, the American body politic teeters on chaos.. Demand for guns keeps increasing while gun manufacturer profits reach all-time highs. The driving forces build on each other--right-wing paranoia, Congressional support for an unregulated gun market, the obeisance of right-wing politicians to the National Rifle Association, pro-

15 https://sipri.org/media/press-release/2022/global-arms-trade-falls-slightly-imports-europe-east-asia-and-oceania-rise (accessed 7/31/22). For further analysis, see Mel Gurtov, *In the Human Interest* at https://melgurtov.com/2022/06/04/post-340-the-arsenal-but-not-of-democracy/

16 https://responsiblestatecraft.org/2022/04/28/putting-bidens-new-whopping-33b-ukraine-package-into-context/ (accessed 7/31/22).

gun lobbyists, and the impunity of gun manufacturers when mass shootings occur.

Weapons vs Real Security

The U.S. weapons may help protect Ukrainians but have also bolstered dictators. At home America's uncontrolled weapons arsenal is a menace to national security, democracy, and public health.

The Trump administration cut the State Department/USAID budget from $53 billion in FY2018 to $40 billion in 2020, of which only $15 billion was for development aid. The comparison is mind-boggling—$732 billion for war and $40 billion for peace and development, a ratio of 18 to 1.[17] Meanwhile, Trump reduced U.S. contributions for UN peacekeeping by one-third and, as the Covid-19 pandemic gathered steam, stopped contributions to the World Health Organization in April 2020.[18]

The Trump administration increased defense spending while lowering taxes paid by large corporations and the richest Americans. More spending on defense combined with lower taxes widened the gap between spending and revenue. This expanding gap meant less money for health, elder care, and education.

The national debt poses a security threat as well as a growing financial problem. Current deficit spending adds to inflation and to the national debt passed on to future generations. Debt held by the public amounted to 70% of GDP in 2020 and, if present trends continue, will rise to 180% by 2050. In 2020 the government was paying nearly $400 billion a year in interest—a sum projected to

---

17 "Congressional Budget Justification, State Department, Foreign Operations, and Related Programs, Fiscal Year 2020" at https://www.state.gov/wp-content/uploads/2019/05/FY-2020-CBJ-FINAL.pdf (accessed June 4, 2020). The largest U.S. contributions to a UN agency went to the World Food Program, $2.5 billion; next, UN peacekeeping, $2.1 billion; refugee assistance, $1.6 billion; the World Health Organization, $0.7 billion. The administration of the Security Council and General Assembly got $0.6 billion.

18 President Biden's Fiscal Year (FY) 2023 Budget Request for the State Department and the United States Agency for International Development (USAID) was $60.4 billion. It included $29.4 billion for USAID—a trivial 6 percent above the FY 2022 Request.

reach $800 billion by 2030. From 2010 to 2019 the government paid $2.5 trillion for interest on its debt while investing only $1.1 trillion on education, $0.4 trillion for resources and environmental protection, and $1.5 trillion on veterans. Meanwhile, outlays for Medicare, Medicaid, Children's Health Insurance, and ACA subsidies rose to 5% of GDP in 2020 and were expected to steadily climb. In 2022 the national debt rose to $31 trillion—more than the year's GDP. Having doubled in the past decade, the debt burden approached its highest levels since World War II.

Civilians Killing Civilians, Officials Killing Civilians

A high rate of domestic violence is another reason why the Peace Index rates the United States as not very peaceful. The United States leads industrial democracies in homicides—with 19,000 deaths in 2019, a ratio of 5.6 per 100,000 people, slightly down from 6 per 100,000 in 2017. It ranks 104th worst out of 163 countries, but El Salvador topped the world in homicides with 62 deaths per 100,000 people. Japan and Hong Kong had the lowest rates—0.2 and 0.3. China also reported a low rate—0.6. On the other hand, the U.S. suicide rate is low compared to many European and Asian countries. Total U.S. suicides of 47,173 in 2017 (nearly half by firearms) produced a rate of 14.5 per 100,000.[19] Guyana led the world in 2016 with 30 per 100,000. Russia was also high, with 26.5. Barbados had the lowest rate—0.4.

The Trumpist Supreme Court made it more difficult to control guns. Despite its ostensible devotion to "originalism,' it ignored the condition explicitly stipulated in the first words of the Second Amendment: "*A well regulated Militia,* being necessary to the security of a free State, the right of the people to keep and bear Arms, shall not be infringed." The Court's conservative supermajority in June 2022 declared for the first time that there is a constitutional right to carry a handgun in public for self-defense, even without a well-regulated militia. By a vote of 6-to-3, the court struck down a century-old gun law in New York that limited licenses to carry a gun outside the home to people carrying them for sports like hunting or shooting, and those with a special need, like messengers carrying

---

19 https://www.cdc.gov/nchs/fastats/suicide.htm (accessed 6/5/20).

cash. Writing for the court majority, Justice Clarence Thomas said that "the constitutional right to bear arms in public for self-defense is not a second class right subject to an entirely different body of rules," and just as the First Amendment doesn't allow the banning of unpopular speech, the Second Amendment is not limited to people who can demonstrate a special need to carry a gun in public.

The Supreme Court then sent several challenges to state gun laws back to lower courts. These cases included challenges to bans in New Jersey and California on high-capacity magazines that hold ten rounds or more, Maryland's assault weapons ban, and Hawaii's restrictions on open-carry. In each instance, the lower courts had upheld the restrictions.

The United States also leads developed countries in police killings. "U.S. police kill more in days than other countries do in years."[20] The number of police killings increased from 981 in 2017 to 1020 in 2020 to 1055 in 2021. Police killed blacks at the highest rate—from 30 to 40 per million; then Hispanics, 23 per million, and then whites, 12 per million.[21] Years after George Floyd's murder, the United States made little progress in preventing deaths at the hands of law enforcement. But police officers also get shot—48 out of 147 deaths while on duty in 2019; 22 of 96 deaths on duty in the first half of 2020.[22]

Trump and other GOP leaders encouraged political violence such as the January 6, 2021 attack on the Capitol and intimidation of Democrats that led to the break-in of Nancy Pelosi's San Francisco residence in October 2022.

HOW TO SUBVERT A SUPERPOWER: TRUMP-BORN CHAOS

Long before Trump, the United States erred in three major ways. *First*, the U.S. strategy of liberal hegemony sought to spread democracy, markets, and other liberal values to bring the whole world into a

---

20 *The Guardian,* June 9, 2015.

21 https://www.statista.com/statistics/585152/people-shot-to-death-by-us-police-by-race/(accessed 8/4/22); also https://www.washingtonpost.com/graphics/investigations/police-shootings-database/ (accessed 8/5/20).

22 https://www.odmp.org/search/year?year=2019 (accessed 6/5/20).

liberal order designed and led by the United States. This orientation provoked a wide backlash and led to the unnecessary and costly wars that squandered trillions of dollars and wasted key sectors of the U.S. economy. *Second,* Republican leaders pushed tax cuts and facilitated tax evasion with scant regard for the fiscal consequences. Wealthy Americans including Trump found countless ways to avoid contributing to public coffers. Instead of creating and funding robust, competent, and respected public institutions, Americans acted as though they did not need them. *Third,* starting with Newt Gingrich, Republicans weaponized partisan politics turning politics into a blood sport indifferent to the public interest.[23]

World leadership entails substantial sacrifices and requires a powerful bipartisan consensus and robust public support. Endless gridlock also made American democracy a less appealing model for other societies. These problems grew more acute under Trump. Then came his mishandling of the pandemic, which undermined America's smart, soft, and hard power. Aided by talk radio hate-mongers like Rush Limbaugh and fake news at the *Weekly Standard* and Fox News, conspiracy theories and slander replaced respectful debate and compromise.

On the world stage, as at home, Trump provoked more chaos.

Chaos in the Middle East. President Trump did nothing to cut U.S. losses in the ongoing conflicts. He redeployed U.S. troops from Syria, exposing America's long-time Kurdish partners to a Turkish onslaught. Trump threatened to destroy Turkey's economy if Turkish troops advanced too far, but he soon rewarded President Recep Tayyip Erdoğan with a White House visit. Now the armies of Bashar al-Assad and Vladimir Putin occupy more of the region, but two Trump Towers still stand in Istanbul—one for residences and the other for offices.[24]

A major contribution to chaos was Trump's withdrawal from the Iran nuclear deal—the Joint Comprehensive Plan of Action signed

---

23 Stephen M. Walt, "How to Ruin a Superpower," *Foreign Policy*, July 23, 2020, at https://foreignpolicy.com/2020/07/23/how-to-ruin-a-superpower/ (accessed 8/1/20).

24 The complex also holds a shopping mall with some 80 shops and a multiplex cinema. They are the first Trump Towers built in Europe.

in 2015 by Iran, the United States, Russia, the United Kingdom, France, China, and Germany. He proceeded to increase pressures on Iran—even assassinating an Iranian general. This approach neutered moderates in Tehran and pushed Iran to intensify nuclear weapon preparations, while doing nothing to restrain Iranian missile tests or meddling. Trump left Biden with hard-liners controlling Iran and enriching sufficient uranium for a nuclear bomb, their capacity to meddle in the region unfettered.

Trump supported Saudi Arabia in attacking Yemen to destroy forces there backed by Iran. Claiming that Saudi Arabia meant to buy U.S. arms worth billions, Trump said nothing about the mutilation murder of *The Washington Post* journalist Jamal Khashoggi by agents of Crown Prince Mohammed bin Salman in Turkey.

Trump's diplomats arranged an Afghanistan peace deal with the Taliban without engaging the Afghan government. Trump's legacy to Biden was a complete Taliban takeover of Afghanistan ending any hope for democracy and gender equality in Afghanistan. The abrupt departure of U.S. forces in 2021 left thousands of Afghans who had worked for Americans or as teachers at the mercy of medieval terrorists.

The president and his son-in-law Jared Kushner produced a peace plan that would permit Israel to expand while shrinking Palestinian land and rights. Most Palestinians saw no future for themselves under a Trump administration. Indeed, Trump's moves neutered any prospect of better relations between Israel and Palestinians.

In September 2020, the United States brokered a deal in which the United Arab Emirates and Bahrain established diplomatic relations with Israel but left the future of Palestinians unresolved.

Meanwhile, *The New York Times* (September 17, 2020) reported that many officials at the State Department and Pentagon were seeking legal help in case they are charged with war crimes for assisting the Trump-Pompeo sales of weapons to Saudi Arabia that killed more than 13,000 civilians in Yemen. "It's a moral issue and a criminality issue," said Representative Ted Lieu, a California Democrat and a former military lawyer, adding that it was clear that

State and Defense Department officials had "potential legal liability for aiding and abetting war crimes."

Chaos in Asia. The president opened wide the door to Chinese expansion by pulling the United States out of the Trans-Pacific Partnership negotiated by Obama's team. Meanwhile, the Trump administration did almost nothing either to contain China or to address Beijing's goals diplomatically. It presented a contradictory and confusing picture of U.S. policy. Trump combined assertions of his good personal relations with President Xi Jinping with tariffs that hurt all parties. Trump groveled asking Xi to buy U.S. soybeans so farmers would back him in the next election. Trump told Xi he was right to incarcerate Uyghurs and repress Hong Kong. At the same time, U.S. warships risked escalation by sailing close to Chinese-claimed islands in the South China Sea. Washington uttered not a constructive word about a possible division of the sea's resources among China and the other littoral states or an end to U.S. reconnaissance from the South China Sea—moves that could reward a Beijing pull-back. The Trump administration did little to forge a collective front against Chinese claims and actions in the South China Sea or elsewhere. Washington pressed its allies not to use China's 5G technology but failed to work with them to develop an alternative. Instead of coopting the European Union in a joint strategy, Trump treated the EU as an economic foe.

As in Europe, Trump demanded that Japan and South Korea pay a lot more (as much as 400% more) toward the costs of stationing U.S. forces on their soil. Stoking doubts about U.S. reliability as an ally, Trump in 2018 unilaterally canceled joint military exercises on the Korean Peninsula as a positive gesture to Kim Jong Un.[25] Anxious to carry on his "love" affair with Kim Jong Un, Trump downplayed North Korea's tests of short- and medium-range missiles. He blithely asserted the tests did not violate Kim's commitments made in Singapore, even though they certainly violated United Nations resolutions. The North's weapons may not yet reach the U.S. mainland, but they certainly menace South Korea and Japan and perhaps Guam. Meanwhile, Trump did not offer

---

25 In 2022 the exercises were conducted by way of computerized simulations.

North Korea any substantive incentive to begin limiting its nuclear-missile arsenal.

An administration that embraces "America First" should be doing a lot to make the country more competitive vis-a-vis China. Not until July 2022 did Republican Senators join Democrats in passing an expansive industrial policy bill to counter China's technological and manufacturing dominance, voting to advance legislation that included some $52 billion in subsidies for companies that build semiconductors in the United States. To the same end, the Biden administration encouraged some of the most talented and hard-working people in the world to come and stay, rather than pushing them away.

Reluctant to antagonize South Asia's two nuclear-armed powers, Trump stood aside as Pakistan seethed over Prime Minister Modi's clampdown in Kashmir and his anti-Muslim policies.

Russia and Eurasia. Despite the Soviet collapse, the Kremlin again threatens Europe as well as Russia's immediate neighbors. Trump said nothing about Russian troops still in Moldova or in Georgian territories that Putin seized in 2008. Trump ignored Russia's annexation of Crimea and occupation of eastern Ukraine. Desperate for U.S. support, Ukrainian President Volodymyr Zelensky sought an oval office meeting and delivery of military aid already appropriated by Congress. But Trump conditioned the White House meeting and delivery of the promised aid on Zelensky's public commitment to investigate Ukraine's role in America's 2016 election and possible corruption by political rival Joseph Biden and his son. As big-time donor to Trump and the erstwhile U.S. ambassador to the EU Gordon Sondland explained to Congressional investigators, Trump was more interested in Biden than in Ukraine.[26]

United States interests in Atlantic solidarity suffer from Trump's denunciation of the Paris climate accords and his backing for British exit from the European Union. On Brexit, as in other

---

26 Sondland was Trump's "point man" on Ukraine. The lead Russia expert on the National Security Council, Fiona Hill, told House investigators that Sondland did not intend to harm the country, but that the Trump-donor turned ambassador posed a national security risk because he was so unprepared for the job.

cases, Trump's actions advanced Putin's goals. Trump's brazen demand that Denmark sell Greenland and his occasional digs at President Emmanuel Macron and Chancellor Angela Merkel added to European doubts about the Atlantic alliance.

While Trump's relations with key EU leaders were frosty, he offered fulsome praise for human rights abusers Vladimir Putin, Kim Jong Un, Xi Jinping, Recep Tayyip Erdoğan, Benjamin Netanyahu, Narendra Modi, Brazil's Jair Bolsonaro, and Philippines President Rodrigo Duterte. Indeed, Trump openly coveted the autocratic powers they enjoyed. He also relished a mutual admiration relationship with authoritarians in Hungary, Poland, and the Czech Republic.

The depth of Trump's knowledge of European affairs is suggested by John Bolton's revelation that the U.S. president did not know the United Kingdom has nuclear weapons and his question whether Finland is a satellite of the Russian Federation. As for Russia, Bolton wrote that Putin played Trump like a fiddle.

Trump's main way of showing a tough stand toward Russia was to back out of major arms controls—the 1987 Intermediate-range Nuclear Forces Treaty and the 2002 Open Skies arms inspection treaty. He seemed unconcerned that the New START treaty was scheduled to expire in 2021. He did nothing to allay Russian and Chinese anxieties about possible improvements in U.S. antimissile defenses that push them to bolster their own strategic forces. All these moves and non-moves serve to enrich arms makers everywhere.

Latin America. More insults about Mexicans but a slightly modified trade deal with Mexico and Canada—ostensible proof that Trump had mastered the art of the deal. Cruel treatment of would-be immigrants continued. Also, much huffing and puffing about Venezuela's dictatorship. Breaking off most links to Cuba. Praise for Brazil as it decimates the Amazon and the indigenous people there.

Africa. More or less benign neglect toward what Trump called "shit-hole countries." There was no progress in U.S. efforts to mediate differences among Egypt, Ethiopia, and Sudan over what could be Africa's largest hydropower dam. On July 19, 2019, Trump condemned four minority congresswomen for being "racist" and "not very smart." Earlier he said the four, known as the "squad," should "go back" to the "totally broken and crime-infested places from which they came." His comments were publicly rebuked by Prime Minister Justin Trudeau, European Council President Donald Tusk, German Chancellor Angela Merkel, and by some UK politicians.[27] Only one of the "squad," Ilhan Omar, was born abroad—in Somalia. She came to the United States at age 12. Another, Alexandria Ocasio-Cortez was born in the Bronx—12 miles away from the Queens hospital where Donald Trump was born![28]

Soft Power Disappears. Who would wish to emulate or follow a country led by Trump Republicans? Many foreigners feared U.S. power, but the respect and affection many felt for the United States and its values nearly disappeared. As a citizen and then as a candidate, Trump often claimed, "The world is laughing at us." In his presidency, the claim came to fruition.

The Pew Research Center in January 2020 reported that views in other countries of the United States and its presidents had changed dramatically in the past two decades. At the end of Obama's presidency, 64% of adults abroad had a favorable view of the United States. From 2016 to 2020, that percentage dropped to 53%. In Germany, the UK, France, and Spain, attitudes toward the U.S. president moved downward during the George W. Bush era, surged in the Obama era, and fell again under Trump.[29] Pew reported in September that views of the United States and Trump in thirteen countries became more negative in 2020. Negative views of the United States among major allies such as Germany reached lows not seen in the last two decades.

Many people everywhere were critical of Trump's withdrawal from the Paris climate accord and his tariff policies. In 2019 positive

---

27 Peter Wade in *Rolling Stone*, July 20, 2019 at https://www.rollingstone.com/politics/politics-news/trump-worldwide-respect-for-america-861637/

28 Although we never met, I am proud that she graduated from Boston University where I taught for four decades.

29 https://www.pewresearch.org/fact-tank/2020/01/08/how-people-around-the-world-see-the-u-s-and-donald-trump-in-10-charts/ (accessed 8/8/20).

views of the United States were found in Israel, the Philippines, South Korea, and Ukraine (before news of Trump's "perfect phone call"). In Hungary, Poland, and Lithuania support for Trump came from the ideological right and members of right-wing parties. However, only 39% of Germans and 20% of people in Turkey had a positive opinion of the United States.

Pew surveys showed the share of people who see U.S. power and influence as a major *threat* increased between 2013 and 2018. That included increases of 30 percentage points in Germany, 29 points in France, and 26 points in Brazil and Mexico. In Germany and France, for instance, the share of people who saw U.S. power and influence as a major threat went up by 14 and 13 percentage points, respectively, between 2017 and 2018. Other notable year-over-year increases occurred in Tunisia (11 points), Canada and Argentina (8 points each), South Africa (7 points) and Brazil and Russia (6 points each).[30]

"The world is realizing the U.S. is no longer committed to basic standards of decency," declared a *Washington Post* editorial on July 27, 2020. Not so long ago, asylum seekers turned to the United States, seeking refuge from repressive states. Now the United States has become one of those repressive states. That was the gist of a Canadian federal court ruling, which would scrap a 16-year-old bilateral treaty called the Safe Third Country Agreement, under which Canada and the United States recognize each other as a safe place to seek refuge. The court ruled that Canada could no longer turn back third-party refugees at the border, because the United States is no longer a safe harbor. Instead, it denies decent and dignified treatment to asylum seekers. As the *Post* editorial lamented:"That a Canadian judge would give a failing grade to this country's commitment to human rights where they concern refugees is a damning rebuke."

Europe's confidence in U.S. policies increased after Biden succeeded Trump in the White House, but much damage done in the Trump years ran deep and could not quickly be undone.

---

30 Ibid. Also https://www.pewresearch.org/global/2019/02/10/climate-change-still-seen-as-the-top-global-threat-but-cyberattacks-a-rising-concern/#changing-threats-in-a-changing-world (accessed 8/8/20).

A DAMOCLES SWORD STILL HANGS BY A THREAD

Trump's failure to join international efforts to regulate climate change added to the threats facing the United States and the world.[31] But there remains another threat that could destroy humanity in hours or less. Despite fervent promises by U.S. and other leaders, nuclear weapons capabilities in many countries continue to grow, nearly unchecked. In August 2022, the UN Secretary-General warned the UN Conference on the Nuclear Nonproliferation Treaty of 1970 that the risks of more nuclear weapons are growing as guardrails to prevent escalation are weakening. "Today, humanity is just one misunderstanding, one miscalculation away from nuclear annihilation," Antonio Guterres told the opening of the Nuclear Non-proliferation Treaty (NPT) review conference. "States are seeking false security in stockpiling and spending hundreds of billions of dollars on doomsday weapons that have no place on our planet," he said. He warned that there are crises with nuclear undertones from the Middle East to the Korean Peninsula, as well as Russia's invasion of Ukraine. There are nearly 13,000 nuclear weapons stockpiled around the world. But the conference changed nothing.

The Damocles Sword that has hung over humanity for nearly 80 years shows no signs of being sheathed or turned into plowshares. In 1948, President Harry Truman summed up the problem: "You have to understand that this isn't a military weapon. It is used to wipe out women and children and unarmed people, and not for military uses. So we have got to treat this thing differently from rifles and cannons and ordinary things like that."[32] The nuclear war plans concocted in Washington and Moscow have verged on madness—complete neglect of morality as well as practicality. The story ranges from the beginnings of the nuclear age in the 1940s to the latest upgrades

---

31 Today Americans are more likely to identify climate change as the greatest man-made threat to the planet. In 2019 in the list of what Americans fear compiled annually by Chapman University, "North Korea using nuclear weapons" and "Nuclear weapons attack" ranked 27 and 29--far below "Corrupt government officials" (No. 1) or "Pollution of oceans, rivers and lakes" (No. 2). https://www.chapman.edu/wilkinson/research-centers/babbie-center/survey-american-fears.aspx (accessed 8/8/20).

32 Fred Kaplan, *The Bomb: Presidents, Generals, and the Secret History of Nuclear War* (New York: Simon & Schuster, 2020), p. 6.

of U.S., Russian, Chinese, and North Korean weapons and Putin's threats to use all his available weapons in the Ukraine conflict.

Briefed by the military in 2017 on the levels to which U.S. and Russian nuclear arsenals had been reduced through arms treaties, President Trump demanded that the United States increase its nuclear stockpile ten-fold. Some reports say that this prompted the then Secretary of State, Rex Tillerson, to call the president a "moron." The so-called "axis of adults"—many of them well-read, thoughtful, and battle-tested generals, could not correct Trump's ignorance of global realities or override his gut impulses. None of them accomplished nearly as much to restrain Trump as the President's critics thought they should have. But all of them—John Kelly, James Mattis, Joseph Dunford, plus H. R. McMaster, the national-security adviser, and Rex Tillerson, Trump's first Secretary of State—had served as guardrails in one way or another. Frustrated by them, Trump tried to replace them with more malleable figures. As Mattis observed, Trump was so out of his depth that he decided to replace most expert advisers with fawning yes-men.[33]

Why do the United States and Russia want thousands of nukes? Each is determined to keep an assured deterrent. If Side A shoots first and destroys much of Side B's forces, Side B wants sufficient redundancy to fire back causing unacceptable damage. [34]

Strategic planners still wrestle with the question of whether nuclear war can be "limited," for example, by striking the enemy's forces but not his cities, and whether the other side would *understand* that it need not reply with an all-out response. John F. Kennedy's

---

33 Susan B. Glasser and Peter Baker, 'Inside the War between Trump and his Generals, "*New Yorker*, August 15, 2022. For more, see their *The Divider: Trump in the White House, 2017-2021* (New York: Doubleday, 2022).

34 In 1960, the U.S. National Strategic Target List included 4,000 points as "targets" in the USSR, Eastern Europe, and China. At least one bomb was needed for each target. To destroy the two hundred most important targets with 90 percent certainty, several nukes would be needed. If the president ordered U.S. forces to strike first, the Pentagon would launch 3,423 nuclear weapons against 1,043 targets. The plan called for hitting a particular Soviet city the size of Hiroshima with more than six times the blast power of the Hiroshima bomb. The Defense Secretary and Joint Chiefs approved the plan just as the Eisenhower administration gave way to that of John F. Kennedy. Some officials protested "overkill," but the arms buildup proceeded.

Secretary of Defense, Robert McNamara, told his assistant Daniel Ellsberg in 1961 that he believed a "limited nuclear war" in Europe impossible, because it would quickly escalate to a general war. Having argued for a counterforce strategy, however, he did not advertise this deep concern.

Strategic planners argue about the right balance between nuclear and conventional arms. President. Eisenhower authorized a doctrine of massive nuclear retaliation as a cost-effective way to cope with Soviet advantages in conventional forces. Now the tables are turned, and Vladimir Putin seeks to compensate for Russia's weaknesses in conventional forces with advanced missiles and nukes.

There is no real barrier to stop any U.S. president from ordering U.S. forces from firing weapons of mass destruction on his/her own--without consulting Congress or even his/her own cabinet. Strategic bombers can be recalled if they are flying toward enemy targets, but not missiles. It would take roughly 12 minutes between an attack order and the irreversible missile launch. If radars say that enemy missiles have been launched, the president would have less than half an hour to decide whether to fire a retaliatory blow.[35] Leaders with their finger on the "button" (or computer codes kept in a "football") face a dilemma: If radars warn of an incoming missile attack, decision-makers must act quickly to retaliate. But what if the radars have sent a false signal? If leaders launch a counterstrike, they may needlessly start a nuclear war.[36]

All governments with nuclear weapons face a similar dilemma.

---

35 Former U, S, Defense Secretary William J. Perry and Tom Z. Collins, *The Button; The New Nuclear Arms Race from Truman to Trump* (Dallas: BenBella, 2020).

36 How a hair-trigger alert can lead to unwanted results is seen in Iran's shooting down a Ukraine International Airline Boeing 737-800 on January 8, 2020. Iranian defense crews feared an American attack but wound up killing the crew and 176 passengers, most of them Iranians. On July 17, 2014, Russian-armed troops in Ukraine shot down Malaysia Flight 17 with its crew and 283 passengers—probably due to some kind of misperception. On July 3, 1988, a U.S. cruiser shot down Iran Air Flight 655 killing all 280 people on board. The *USS Vincennes* crew said it had incorrectly identified the Airbus A300 as an attacking F-14 Tomcat, a U.S.-made jet fighter sold to Iran in the 1970s. Under pressure, the temptation is to shoot first and save questions for later—a formula for catastrophe when each side fears a nuclear attack.

In 1993 a U.S. expert warned of a Soviet doomsday system that could automatically launch a nuclear counterattack even if Moscow's military command posts were wiped out. The danger of a misinformed decision in Moscow has grown as Russia's early warning systems deteriorate. The late Bruce G. Blair warned that the greatest challenge today is not deterrence but a failure of control-- particularly in Russia.[37]

The reformulation of Russian strategic doctrine signed by President Putin on July 2, 2020, stressed that Russia's policy is strictly defensive but that it will crush any aggressor.[38] Clarifying the doctrine on the front page of the military newspaper *Krasnaia Zvezda (Red Star)* on July 8, two senior General Staff officers, A. E. Steplin and A. L. Khriapin, wrote that Russia's early warning system cannot distinguish incoming ballistic missiles armed with conventional warheads from ballistic missiles armed with nuclear warheads. Therefore, any attacking ballistic missile will be treated as a nuclear weapon. This information will be "automatically" relayed to the "military-political leadership" for the appropriate action.

Those who decide on war and peace in other nuclear-weapon states such as North Korea probably have early warning systems no better than Russia's. To guard against a too hasty response to a threat, some nuclear weapons states store their own warheads apart from their missiles, but this practice can change quickly.

As Russia's conventional forces performed poorly in Ukraine, Putin warned that Russia might use nuclear weapons to counter non-nuclear as well as nuclear threats to its sovereignty.

The only reliable answer to these problems is the complete or nearly complete elimination of nuclear weapons and stockpiles of highly enriched uranium and weapons-grade plutonium. Besides greater mutual security, economic gains could be another incentive.

If the international mood favored détente and arms control, the danger of a nuclear war, deliberate or not, could diminish. But this

---

37 Sam Roberts on Bruce G. Blair in *The New York Times*, July 31, 2020.

38 For the text of the nuclear strategy plan signed by Putin on June 2, 2020 see http://static.kremlin.ru/media/events/files/ru/IluTKhAiabLzOBjIfBSvu4q3bcl7AXd7.pdf (accessed 8/8/20).

is not the case in the 2020s. Instead, tensions are increasing between the United States and China, Russia, North Korea, and Iran. The same is true of relations between India and Pakistan; India and China; Israel with its neighbors.

With the end of the Cold War, the numbers of Russian and U.S. nuclear weapons were reduced, thanks to several treaties. Russia and the United States cut their nuclear arsenals to fewer than 6,000 warheads each, but they can still destroy the world in less than one hour. A harrowing and expensive new arms race is now accelerating. Moscow and Washington abrogated all but one of their previous arms agreements. Fortunately, the Biden and Putin governments in 2021 extended New START for five years, keeping in place the treaty's verifiable limits on the deployed strategic nuclear arsenals of the world's two largest nuclear powers. In September 2022, as fears rose that Putin might commit some desperate act, the Russian submarine Belgorod ("Beautiful City") left its base and was spotted in the Arctic near the Kola Peninsula. Some observers feared it might test one of its 80-foot long Poseidon missiles with a 100-megaton warhead.

Nine states have nuclear weapons—the United States, Russia, Britain, France, China, Israel, India, Pakistan, and North Korea. Iran and Saudi Arabia may be trying to join the club. Putin and Trump are committed to modernizing their arsenals. Trump's envoy for arms control Marshall Billingslea boasted in May 2020: "We know how to win these races, and we know how to spend the adversary into oblivion." This boast arises from the erroneous Republican claim that President Reagan's arms buildup destroyed a Soviet Union unable to compete. The reality was that the Soviet system had been deteriorating long before Reagan due to its inherent inefficiency. Reagan's hard line before Gorbachev's presidency probably helped keep the system alive.

On July 3, 2020, the Government Accountability Office estimated that the nuclear weapons modernization called for by the President Trump and being planned by the Pentagon would cost a minimum of $1.2 trillion over the next thirty years. This was surely an underestimate, because it did not take account of the usual cost overruns in weapons procurement. Apart from the harmful consequences for the federal budget, this emphasis on nuclear weapons would lead to painful tradeoffs in other areas of defense.[39]

A rational response to these dangers is the nuclear freeze sponsored by Senators Edward J. Markey and other Democrats in June 2020.[40] Their proposed *Hastening Arms Limitation Talks (HALT)* legislation created a blueprint for nuclear-weapons powers to reduce the risk posed by weapons of mass destruction. It called for negotiating a comprehensive and verifiable freeze on the testing, deployment, and production of nuclear weapons and delivery vehicles.[41]

On October 7, 2022, Senator Markey revived his HALT agenda by filing eight amendments to the National Defense Authorization Act. They addressed a world far more dangerous than just two years earlier—a world in which Russia's losses in Ukraine led Putin to threaten to use of nuclear weapons; a world in which Iran moved closer to a capacity to make nuclear weapons; a world in which North Korea fired missiles over Japan that could hit Guam and beyond; a world in which a U.S-China war over Taiwan became more likely. Having watched the spectacle of President Trump's whimsical approach to policy-making, Markey proposed to bar any U.S. president from launching a nuclear first-strike absent a declaration of war by Congress. A related amendment would require presidents to turn over all emergency action documents (PEADS) that may give the President extraordinary powers.

---

39 "The GAO's sober analysis makes clear what we already knew: we cannot afford well over a trillion dollars in gold-plated nuclear modernization programs," said Senator Edward J. Markey who, with Senator Dianne Feinstein, requested the analysis.

40 H.R. 7260 introduced by Representative James McGovern on June 18, 2020 and S.4045 introduced by Senators Markey and Feinstein on June 23, 2020 at https://www.govinfo.gov/content/pkg/BILLS-116s4045is/pdf/BILLS-116s4045is.pdf (accessed 6/25/20).

41 HALT also called on the U,S to ratify and bring into force the Comprehensive Nuclear Test Ban Treaty, being sure to include North Korea; negotiate a global ban on production of fissionable materials; negotiate a ceiling on all deployed shorter-range and intermediate range as well as strategic delivery systems and associated nuclear warheads at their August 2019 levels; ban configurations of nuclear forces to launch on warning; ban cyberattacks on nuclear command and control systems; and seek agreed limits on hypersonic cruise missiles and glide vehicles mounted on ballistic missiles.

Markey's proposals meant to uphold the principle affirmed by presidents Ronald Reagan and M. S. Gorbachev in 1987 that "a nuclear war cannot be won and must never be fought."

As Bob Dylan warned, *"The times they are a-changin."*

> *Come senators, congressmen*
> *Please heed the call*
> *Don't stand in the doorway*
> *Don't block up the hall*
> *For he that gets hurt*
> *Will be he who has stalled*
> *The battle outside ragin'*
> *Will soon shake your windows*
> *And rattle your walls*
> *For the times they are a-changin'*

7

WAS TRUMP'S AMERICA THE GREATEST?

HUMAN DEVELOPMENT IN TATTERS

President Trump's Republican backers have claimed to be making America great again. But the record shows that Republican politics are bad for most people. What the United Nations calls "human development" in the United States began to deteriorate under President George W. Bush and continued to go downhill under Trump, with negatives spilling over into the first years of the Biden administration. Every country's level of human development is ranked every year by the UN Human Development Index (HDI). The index measures each country's performance in health, education, and material well-being. For years Norway has been the highest ranked country on the HDI. In 2022, however, Switzerland was ranked tops and Norway 2nd. The United States ranking has steadily declined—from 3rd highest in the world in 2000 and 8th in 2015 to 15th in 2019 to 21st in 2022. Canada's placement has also declined--from 1st in 2000 to 9th in 2015 to 13th in 2019 to 15th in 2022 The Russian Federation ranked 49th in 2019 but fell to 52nd in 2022. China ranked 85th in 2019 but climbed to 79th in 2022. Ukraine ranked 77th in 2022—based on pre-war data.[1] The HDI says nothing about political freedoms or corruption—which are tracked on other indexes summarized here in other chapters.

IS AMERICA'S HEALTH SYSTEM THE BEST?

President Trump asserted that the United States has the world's best health system. Is this so? Health care systems worldwide face seven challenges:

1. Mounting costs as populations age and expensive new technologies emerge;

2. Rising drug prices;

---

1   https://hdr.undp.org/data-center/documentation-and-downloads

3. Inefficiency in delivery of health services and provision of unnecessary services;

4. Coordination between hospitals and outpatient health care providers;

5. Mismatch between health care delivery institutions and chronic care needs;

6. Provision of mental health care;

7. Long-term care--how to provide and pay for it?

The American system is an outlier in dealing with all seven challenges. U.S. health care costs consume nearly 18% of GDP— much greater any other country. With just 4.5% of the planet's people, Americans account for half the world's spending on prescription drugs!

America's health and its health system were substandard even before Covid-19. Some *40 other countries or territories had higher life expectancy than the United States in 2019*. Life expectancy at birth in the United States in 2019 was 78.9 (a few years more for women and less for men); by 2022 it fell to 77.2. U.S. life expectancy is more than eight years lower than in Hong Kong, 85.5 in 2022—despite Chinese repression there. In fact, average U.S. life expectancy is one year less than in China; it ranks just below the United Arab Emirates and Bahrain; it is barely above levels in Estonia, Czechia, Poland, and Algeria.[2]

Two other health markers are infant and maternal mortality. *Infant mortality in the United States in 2019 was 5.6 deaths per 1,000 live births*—a rate worse than in *forty-four* other countries. Finland had the lowest rate, 1.4. Even Bosnia had a lower rate than the United States--5. The U.S. rate was just slightly better than in Russia, 6.1, and in China, 7.4. But the U.S. rate was much worse than Cuba, 3.7. Republicans could boast only that the U.S. rate was much better than in the Central African Republic, 84.5; and lower than in two U.S. client states, Afghanistan, 47.9 and Iraq, 22.5, and

---

2   Life expectancy in China is 78.2; Ukraine, 71.6; Russia, 69.4; North Korea, 73.3, One of the lowest is South Sudan, 55. All these numbers differ slightly by source and date.

adversary North Korea, 13.7.[3]

Maternal mortality. It is becoming increasingly dangerous to give birth in the United States. From 2000 to 2017, the number of maternal deaths per 100,000 births *steadily increased—from 12 to 19.* In Norway, it decreased from 6 to 3.[4] In Canada, it hovered between 9 and 11.[5] Of course it is far more dangerous to give birth in many parts of the world. The maternal mortality ratio is more than 1,000 per 100,000 births in South Sudan and Chad. Thanks to a Supreme Court with several Trump-appointed justices, American women suffering miscarriages have been denied proper medical treatment because it resembles an abortion.[6]

America's social and public health malaise is also manifest in the high birth rate for females ages 15-19. The U.S. adolescent birth rate in 2018 was 19 in 100,000; in Canada, 8.4; in Norway, just 5.[7]

Lack of spending is not the reason for the poor U.S. track record in heath matters. For perspective, compare the United States with the 36 other industrialized countries members of the Organization for Economic Co-operation and Development.[8] The average per capita outlays for health in OECD countries was $4,000 in 2019—about 8.8% of their combined GDP. The United States spends far more—some $11,000 per capita, nearly 18% of GDP and projected to rise to 30% by 2030. The next highest spending country is Switzerland--at 12.2%. Canada spends about $5,000 per capita—just 10.7% of GDP; Norway, $6,18 7—10.2 % of GDP. A large group of OECD countries

---

3 https://www.macrotrends.net/countries/ranking/infant-mortality-rate (accessed 6/1/20).

4 World Health Organization statistics at   https://www.who.int/gho/maternal_ health/countries/en/ (accessed 6/1/20).

5 https://www.who.int/gho/maternal_health/countries/can.pdf (accessed 6/1/20).

6 The court reversed Roe vs Wade in 2022 but many states sought to interpret the ruling in their own way.

7 https://data.worldbank.org/indicator/SP.ADO.TFRT (accessed 7/25/20).

8 The OECD is an intergovernmental organization founded in 1961 to promote economic progress and trade. Its members in 2017 produced 62.2% of global GDP (US$49.6 trillion). China does not belong to the OECD. Russia was disinvited in 2014 because it took Crimea from Ukraine. Most former Soviet allies such as Poland belong but no former Soviet republics belong except Estonia, Latvia, and Lithuania.

spanning Europe, Australia, New Zealand, Chile, and South Korea, spend between 8 and 10% of GDP. A few OECD members spend less than 6% of their GDP on health care. They include Mexico, Latvia, Luxembourg, and Turkey, which spends only 4.2%.[9]

What do Americans get for these outlays? They have 2.6 physicians and 11.7 nurses for every 1,000 inhabitants--similar to Canada's 2.7 physicians and 10 nurses. But the OECD average for physicians is much higher—3.5. Norway has 4.7 physicians and 17.7 nurses per 1,000 residents. Here is a paradox: The U.S. system is highly complex but also "lean"—with ever fewer physicians and nurses, fewer hospital admissions, and fewer other services than any other developed country, despite U.S. bloated costs. Yet it is tremendously innovative—not just in new drugs and devices but also in efforts to improve how care is delivered and paid for. Government, private insurers, and venture capitalists are looking for ways to improve the system.[10]

The U.S. health care system underperforms in many ways and leaves millions uninsured or underinsured. In the 1940s and 1950s the U.S. government encouraged employer-based health insurance. This was better than nothing, but it left out retired, self-employed, and unemployed Americans. The government introduced Medicare for seniors in 1957; Medicaid for some of the poor in 1964; and the Affordable Care Act in 2010—the first structure for universal coverage. However, the Trump administration repealed the individual mandate for ACA, weakening its scope. The outcome of all this is a patchwork of complex insurance arrangements very difficult to navigate, with significant differences from one state to another.

Of 325 million Americans in 2020, most have private insurance—156 to 181 million employer-sponsored; 15 million individually purchased. Public insurance covers the next largest

---

9 See *Health at a Glance 2019 OECD Indicators* at https://www.oecd-ilibrary.org/ social-issues-migration-health/health-at-a-glance-2019_4dd50c09-en (accessed 6/1/20). For other comparisons of OECD countries, see https://en.wikipedia.org/ wiki/OECD#Former_members (accessed 6/2/20).

10 Ezekiel J. Emanuel, *Which County Has the Best Health Care System?* (New York: Public Affairs, 2020), pp. 50-54..

segment: Medicare, 55 million; Medicaid + CHIP (for children), 65 million; Veterans, 9 million; Indian Health Services, 2.2 million; Tricare, 9.4 million. This leaves 28 million Americans uninsured.[11]

If Americans spend more on health than any other country, why do they not live longer than countries that spend far less? The big picture is that medical care in the United States can be very high quality for those who can pay for it—by themselves or through their insurance. But millions of low- and medium-income Americans stay away from doctors because they are uninsured or reluctant to make high co-payments. As a result, many seek Emergency Room care (ultimately financed by taxpayers). Others simply avoid professional help until their ailments become severe. Some must choose between dialysis and food or rent.

The United States leads the world in deaths from Covid-19. Why? Chronic underfunding of public health has helped put the United States on track for the worst coronavirus response in the developed world—the most total cases, the highest death toll, and some of the darkest projections.[12] In summer 2020, the European Union banned Americans (along with Chinese, Russians, and others) from entering any EU member state. As Joe Biden observed on July 2, 2020, Trump transformed the United States "into a global health risk."

President Trump was slow to acknowledge and respond to the dangers posed by the virus. He muzzled government experts such as Dr. Anthony Fauci and set a dangerous example by scorning face masks and social distancing. He and many Republican governors pressed for opening public space before it was safe. Trump called on supporters to join him at rallies where they cheered cheek by jowl. With 4.5% of the world's population, by 2022 the United States suffered more than one million Covid deaths out of a global total of about six million.

To cope with a pandemic the world needs humane internationalism, but Trump abetted "medical nationalism."

---

11 Emanuel, *Which Country*, Fig. 3, p. 23.

12 Jeneen Interlandi, "Why We're Losing the Battle with Covid-19," *New York Times Magazine,* July 19, 2020.

The impulse of governments around the world has been to block exports of protective gear and stockpile supplies, leading to a mad scramble for life-saving equipment in a global black market overrun by fakes and fraudsters. Meanwhile, the Trump administration stopped funding the World Health Organization in the middle of this pandemic.

The Centers for Disease Control and Prevention and the National Institutes of Health struggled to contain the virus and get remedies to the public, but Trump sought to phase out funding for both, as well as for testing and contact tracing. State and local governments hemorrhaged cash fighting the virus. Instead of providing them relief, congressional Republicans focused on protecting private businesses from lawsuits if they made workers sick. None of this made sense.[13]

For the world's great cities, the incubators of the Covid-19 pandemic arise from inequality. Covid-19 infected many New Yorkers, but density was not the fundamental problem. Singapore is also densely populated but had relatively few infections. Covid-19 preys on the poor. Dilapidated housing and pollution breed asthma. Low incomes lead to poor diets, obesity, and pulmonary disease— all co-morbidities associated with Covid-19 fatalities.[14]

How can these disparities exist in one of the world's richest countries? President Trump and most Republicans opposed any form of government-backed medical care for all. Republicans have tried over and over to torpedo or weaken the Affordable Care Act since its enactment in 2010. Some Republicans have also talked of curbing the benefits provided by Social Security. They have cut back food stamp and school lunch programs. In short, they have opposed government interventions to bolster the health of the most-needy Americans. They resemble Marie Antoinette who, informed the masses lacked bread, is said to have replied, "Let them eat cake."

The numbers are shocking. Only 90.8% of Americans have access to core medical services compared to the OECD average of

---

13 Dana Milbank, "America is flunking its cognitive assessment," *The Washington Post*, July 20, 2020.

14 Bloomberg New Economy, "Turing Points," 6/13/20 at https://mail.google.com/mail/u/0/#inbox/FMfcgxwHNqFmLCZDjSqKhwZLMpFQgbbb

98.4%. In Canada, Norway, and many other OECD countries, the rate is 100%. The needs-adjusted probability of visiting a doctor for American adults is 65% compared to the OECD average of 78%. Where Americans do better than the OECD average is on one dimension of preventive care—cervical cancer screening. For Americans, the probability of cervical cancer screening is 80% against the OECD average of 73%. Norwegians fall below the average at 66%.

A large share of American outlays for medical care does not go to doctors and hospitals but to intermediaries—insurance agencies and the accountants who try to match medical services with those who may pay for them. Medical providers can demand high compensation because they have great leverage while government sets no ceiling on prices charged for new treatments or drugs and rarely investigates what providers charge Medicaid and Medicare. Republicans in Congress call it socialism to have Medicare negotiate prices for drugs with Big Pharma.

How to improve U.S. health care? One expert recommends: 1. Ensure universal coverage with auto-enrollment and larger subsidies. 2. Cover children at no additional cost to their families. 3. Simplify the system so patients and providers do not have to figure out what is covered and how. 4. Increase reimbursement for primary care doctors relative to specialists. 5. Adopt best-care practices for patients with chronic and mental health conditions. 6. Regulate drug prices. None of these reforms would be easy to implement. Most of them would require coordinated work by the federal government and private insurers.[15]

The *spirit* that underlies health care is also important, as Stephen Trzeciak and Anthony Mazzarelli argue in their book *Compassionomics: The Revolutionary Scientific Evidence That Caring Makes a Difference.*[16] How can a doctor develop or show

---

15 Emanuel, *Which Country*, pp. 387-404. Dr. Emanuel did not say which health system is best, but the American is surely one of the worst. He did say that Germany, the Netherlands, Norway, and Taiwan are in the top tier of health systems. China has one of the worst systems—overly focused on hospitals, with a poorly develop ambulatory care, very low patient trust, and very thin attention to rural areas. Taiwan has been particularly successful in containing Covid-19.

16 *Compassionomics: The Revolutionary Scientific Evidence That Caring Makes a*

much compassion when pressured to keep patient visits to 15 or 20 minutes?

What about prevention? Lifestyle does much to improve or shorten lives. *Americans lead the OECD in obesity*—43% of U.S. children and 71% of adults are overweight--much higher than the OECD adult average of 56%. Nearly 11% of Americans suffer from diabetes—the third highest rate in the OECD. Fast foods at McDonald's, Pizza Hut, and Kentucky Fried Chicken have widened waistlines around the world, but some societies have limited their impact. Japan and Korea are far below the OECD average in body mass scales—just 36% and 34% respectively.

Fatty calories, computer screens, and couch-potato habits combine with aversion to exercise to reduce life expectancy.[17] The example set by the White House also plays a role. First-lady Michelle Obama urged Americans to exercise and eat more fruit and vegetables, while enlisting children to help in the White House garden. Trump has avoided even walking and favors the burgers that sustain his girth.[18] A reflection of his reverence for life, the president in June 2020 lifted the ban on hunters luring bears to their death

---

Difference (Pensacola, FL: Studer Group, 2019).

17 The big picture is grim but there are three areas where Americans' lifestyles are better than the OECD average: First, some 10.5% of Americans continue to smoke daily, but this is far below the 18% OECD average. Second, Americans consume no more alcohol than the OECD average of 8.9 liters per year (equivalent to nearly 100 bottles of wine). Nearly 4% of adults in the OECD are alcohol dependent. Canadians, Latvians, and Lithuanians drink 11 or 12 liters, while Japanese and Koreans drink just 7.2 and 8.7 liters respectively. Third, despite President Trump's efforts to lower automobile emission standards, air pollution kills fewer Americans—24 per 100,000--than the OECD average of 40 deaths per 100,000 people. But Canada has an even lower death rate from air pollution—14.7. Two of the OECD countries with the greatest percentage of smokers, Latvia and Lithuania, suffer 98 and 82 deaths respectively from air pollution. Death rates from pollution are much higher in India and China—some 140 deaths per 100,000 people.

18 Dr. Harold Bornstein, Donald Trump's personal physician from 1980, wrote two letters vouching for Mr. Trump's health. In December 2015, he said that Mr. Trump would be "the healthiest individual ever elected to the presidency," and in September 2016, he reported that Mr. Trump was "in excellent physical health." In May 2018 he told CNN that Mr. Trump had dictated the contents of the first letter. See https://www.bbc.com/news/world-us-canada-43970908, May 2, 2018 (accessed 5/1/20).

with donuts soaked in fat.[19]

The United States has no national information campaign about diet and exercise as there has been about smoking; no large-scale education about Tai Chi and other gentle movement and mediation programs potentially beneficial for all ages; almost no serious research to distinguish useful forms of alternative medicine from crackpot schemes and snake oil.

America's health problems are aggravated by the failure of most doctors and the public to adopt a preventative approach to health and look for alternative approaches that could be more effective and cheaper than conventional practices. Low-income Americans often lack information about health matters and live in neighborhoods where KFC is close but fresh fruit and vegetables are distant. Vulnerability to all kinds of ailments grows where people cohabit a small space where clean water, heat, and air conditioning are scarce. All these issues help explain why black Americans die from Covid-19 and suffer from heart disease and diabetes at higher rates than whites. Sad to say, the same problems help explain high murder rates, single-parent families, and poor education in inner cities.

Are America's Schools the Best?

Education is another way to measure human development. Americans are exposed to more years of education than in most countries, but the results are poor and getting worse. As in health care, Americans spend more for education than most nations but do not get commensurate results. The top U.S. universities are widely seen as best in the world, especially their graduate programs. But U.S. schooling for persons aged three and up to college age is mediocre. Fewer Americans access pre-school education than in the most advanced OECD countries. Despite increasing awareness of the importance of high-quality early childhood education and care (ECEC), enrollment in ECEC at the age of 3 in the United States is 35 percentage points below the OECD average.

However, students in U.S. elementary and high schools do

---

19 The Obama-era restrictions were also loosened so hunters may invade a bear den with blinding lights to shoot a mother bear with her cubs.

poorly in math, science, and reading compared to those in other OECD countries as well as in Russia, and China. In 2016, the average reading score for fourth-grade students in the United States was lower than averages in twelve other countries including Singapore, Hong Kong, Finland, and Latvia. American students did better in comprehension of online information—inferior only to Singapore, Norway, and Ireland. Tests of U.S. students' knowledge of science and mathematics at different grade levels and on completion of high school produced lower scores than in five to ten other countries such as Hong Kong, Russia, Taiwan, Canada, and Norway. Students in Florida did much worse than the U.S. average and in Massachusetts much better. Even so, students in Massachusetts lagged those in Shanghai by two years. Students in Singapore, Japan, Korea, parts of China, and Liechtenstein have topped the rankings for math, reading, and science.[20]

Socio-economic class plays a larger role in the United States than in many other countries. Some 15% of the variation in U.S. academic achievement is explained by socio-economic differences between students. Less than 10% of score variations in Finland, Hong Kong, Japan, and Norway are due to socio-economic differences. The United States also has a lower-than-average number of "resilient" students. These are students among the 25% most socio-economically disadvantaged who nonetheless perform much better than predicted by their socio-economic class. On average, just 7% of American students are considered "resilient"—compared with 13% in Korea, Hong Kong, Macao-China, Shanghai-China, Singapore, and Vietnam.

Many U.S. teachers feel they are underpaid. Average salaries of teachers in primary and secondary education in the United States are higher than the OECD average, but much lower than the salaries of most U.S. college graduates. Some U.S. teachers feel compelled to buy classroom supplies with their own funds because school budgets are too low. Many teachers feel they are not appreciated. Relatively

---

20 Finland, known for its excellent school system, has continued to perform well, in recent years but has dropped several points in math, reading, and science. Prior to Covid-19, the biggest annualized score improvements came in Brazil, Tunisia, Mexico, Turkey, and Portugal.

few of the best students choose to enter the teacher profession. Low pay is one issue; lack of prestige and respect is another.

The United States ranks fifth in the OECD in spending per student. Only Austria, Luxembourg, Norway, and Switzerland spend more per student. But higher expenditures do not ensure good results. Students in the Slovak Republic achieve exam scores similar to U.S. students but at much lower cost. Education outlays there are less than half the American.

Rising tuition costs at public as well as private institutions keep many young people away from college or, while there, short of money for food and other basics. The United States spent over $30,000 per college student in 2018—more than any OECD country except Luxembourg. Many students and their families take on big debt to meet college costs. But Education Secretary Betsy DeVos pressured people struggling to repay student loans. Her Education Department worked to collect college loan payments from borrowers in default even though the Cares Act had suspended such collections and the department had promised to comply. She also fought efforts by colleges to include undocumented students among the recipients of money designated for helping students in need.

In July 2020 President Trump demanded that schools nationwide reopen that autumn regardless of their community's COVID-19 epidemic status. When reporters asked Secretary DeVos how this could safely be accomplished, she offered no guidelines and no financial support to strapped school districts. She said that school districts nationwide needed to create their own safety schemes and to realize that the federal government will cut off funds if schools fail to reopen. The Trump administration tried to bend schools bend to its will, without offering any expert guidance on how to reopen safely, much less the necessary financing.

Are Americans the Best Off in Material Wealth?

The third measure used by the UN Human Development Index is material well-being. Yes, the uman United States probably has the world's largest gross domestic product (GDP)—nearly $21 trillion in 2020, followed by China with $15 trillion) and then by Japan and Germany. But if you divide GDP by the number of a country's inhabitants, you get *per capita* income. By this ranking, the United States places 13th in the world, outpaced not only by oil-rich Qatar but by the more diversified economies of Singapore, Ireland, Switzerland, Norway, and Hong Kong. However, this calculation—GDP per capita—gives you only an *average*—a very misleading figure. It misleads because a tiny percent of the U.S. population takes in and possesses a huge share of intangible as well as material wealth. If the gap between the wealthiest Americans and the others were diminishing, the picture would be brighter. But the opposite trend emerged in the 1970s and is increasing.

Taking account of inflation, real incomes for most Americans have increased very little, if at all, in half a century. Intangible as well as material wealth is at stake. The more material wealth, the more education and culture can be accessed. The less that high quality education is accessible, the more the income gap spreads. This helps explain why social mobility in the United States has stagnated or decreased for decades.

The main sources for income equality and growth in productivity are education and investment in training and skills. The diffusion and sharing of knowledge are what the French economist Thomas Piketty calls the public good *par excellence*.[21] But the diffusion of knowledge is not automatic. It depends on educational policies and access to training. Market mechanisms and political decisions can help or hinder these processes,[22] China's excellent training programs have contributed to the country's rapid growth in recent decades, though millions in the countryside have lagged behind.

The gaps between the poor and the rich can narrow if the poor achieve higher levels of education and technological know-how. Knowledge diffusion depends on institutions that mobilize investment in education and training while guaranteeing a stable legal framework. All this requires a political system perceived as legitimate and efficient.

---

21 Thomas Piketty, *Capital in the Twenty-First Century* (Cambridge: Harvard University Press, 2014), p. 21.

22 But Piketty found that human labor plays no greater role in GDP today than in centuries past.

Why then has inequality in the United States continued or even increased? Some U.S. jobs have moved to Mexico and China, but the root problem is failure to invest broadly in education and skills training. This failure keeps large strata of the population from participating in economic growth. Even when minority skills have been honed, blacks and Hispanics have trouble getting access to financial services. When one black woman took her first paycheck to a bank, the teller phoned 911.

Have-gots tend to get more and to keep more than have-nots. In the United States and some other countries, top earners arrange things so that they get much heftier pay increases than those lesser down the ladder. They often set their own remuneration, independent of company earnings. The have-gots militate for tax laws that permit them to keep a greater share of what comes in. They can borrow more money and at lower costs than have-nots.

Here is what has happened in the last hundred or so years. The top 10% of U.S. earners received nearly half of national income in the 1910s-1920s before dropping to 30-35% by the end of the 1940s. Inequality stabilized at that level from 1950 to 1970. Starting in the 1980s under President Ronald Reagan, inequality rose again to its level in 1910-1920. The top 10% again possessed nearly half of national income.[23] This trend gained momentum under George W. Bush; slowed under Barack Obama; and accelerated under Donald J. Trump, when the wealth of the top 1% and especially the top 0.1% skyrocketed. In 2020 the OECD reported that America's richest 10% owned 80% of the country's wealth.[24] Just 400 families contributed half of the capital deployed in the last election.

The years 1950 to 1980 were the "glorious thirty" (*Trente Glorieuses*) for Thomas Piketty, because incomes rose for the lower and middle classes as well as the rich. Politicians voted to reduce the social influence of private property. Steeply progressive income

---

23 Piketty, p. 43.

24 Concentration of wealth at the top happens in many other countries. The wealth owned by the highest 10% in eleven other OECD countries exceeded 50% See https://www.oecd-ilibrary.org/docserver/077d9feb-en.pdf?expires= 1593305377&id=id&accname=guest&checksum=2B804BD1E979979CB4B 34B6A8D94BD27 (accessed 6/27/20).

taxes and estate taxes shaped income distributions. Tax rates on the rich have declined so much in the United States that the tax system are now flat—even regressive. France enjoyed strong economic growth, higher productivity and average wages, plus improved social benefits. According to Piketty, ten per cent of global financial sets are now stashed in tax havens such as Ireland.[25]

Here was the picture after eight years of George W. Bush:[26]

- Inequality in the United States increased substantially, as it had since the Reagan 1980s, with the overall level of inequality now approaching that of the Great Depression.

- CEOs in 1965 made 24 times more than the average production worker, whereas in 2009 they made 185 times more.

- In 2007 there were 750,000 Americans homeless on any given night with one in five chronically homeless.

- Only college graduates experienced growth in median weekly earnings since 1979. High school dropouts saw their earnings decline by 22%.

- The trend toward more equitable pay for women plateaued in 2005.

- High-school dropout rates were lowest among whites and highest among Hispanics; college enrollment rates are least among blacks and highest among whites.

- Over one-fifth of U.S. children lived in poverty, a rate higher than in all other rich nations.

- More than 8 million children had no health insurance.

Trump's policies aggravated income inequality and racial discrimination as well as income inequality, with each malaise

---

25 Thomas Piketty, *Capital and Ideology* (Cambridge: Harvard University Press, 2020).

26 "20 Facts About U.S. Inequality that Everyone Should Know," Stanford Center on Poverty and Inequality," 2011 at https://inequality.stanford.edu/publications/20-facts-about-us-inequality-everyone-should-know (accessed 6/25/20).

nourishing the other. According to the OECD, the United States in 2019 was one of the most unequal of industrialized countries with a Gini coefficient of 0.39 (where 0 meant complete equality and 1 complete inequality). Most of Europe placed much lower. The Slovak Republic ranked 0.24, Norway 0.26, Canada 0.31. Even Russia placed lower, 0.33. Despite dreams of equality, Costa Rica scored 0.48 and South Africa, 0.62.[27] Using other rankings, China placed about the same as the United States.

Data from the U.S. Census Bureau and other government agencies showed that, as of 2016, black wealth was less than one-tenth that of average white families ($13,024 vs. $148,703)—a ratio unchanged since 1968. The percentage of blacks living in poverty in 2018 was much lower—21%—than in 1970, but still more than twice the percentage of whites (8%). The employment rates for blacks (58.6%) nearly caught up with whites (61.0%), but average black wages were much lower.[28]

The white-black gaps in the United States in 2020 have been summarized by two Princeton University professors and a graphic artist:[29]

- Median household income for whites is $82,000; for blacks, $53,000. However, in in Minneapolis-St. Paul, whites' incomes are more than doubles blacks'; in San Francisco, whites triple blacks' incomes. In Boston, as noted below, the gap is even larger.

- Three-fourths of whites own their own homes; two-fifths of blacks are homeowners.

- Before the pandemic, 3.5% of whites and 6.5% of blacks were unemployed.

27 https://data.oecd.org/inequality/income-inequality.htm (accessed 6/27/20).

28 Tarni Luhby, "These charts show how economic progress has stalled for black Americans since the Civil Rights era," *CNN*, July 5, 2020 at https://www.cnn.com/2020/07/05/politics/inequality-black-americans-civil-rights-economic-progress/index.html (accessed 7/10/20).

29 Patrick Sharkey, Keeanga-Yamahtta Taylor, and Yaryna Serkez, "The Gaps Between White and Black America, in Charts," *The New York Times*, June 19, 2020.

- Some 35% of whites and 26% of blacks had completed four-years of college.

- Imprisonment ratios diverged sharply. Of 100,000 black males, 2,272 were incarcerated; of 100,000 whites, just 392.

- Partly as a result of these divergencies, average life expectancy for whites was 78.8; for blacks, 75.2. In Omaha, home to one of the world's richest individuals, Warren Buffet, the gap was *ten* years! (He rightly complained that federal tax breaks permitted him to pay taxes at a much lower rate than his secretary.)

The Princeton professors explained: "The costs of segregation are amplified by how we invest and disinvest in cities and neighborhoods. If black and white neighborhoods received the same resources and had the same political influence, segregation would not lead to so much inequality. These inequities have been not only an urban phenomenon but also a suburban phenomenon, following black families as they have moved into suburban communities."

Zip codes foretold the style of policing. "From the 1970s to the 1990s, segregated, low-income neighborhoods became the focal point for a new style of aggressive policing and prosecution. Although violence has fallen sharply since the mid-1990s, that style of policing has remained intact."[30]

Some cities and regions were more unequal than others. As noted above, whites in San Francisco were much more affluent than blacks. In Boston, another liberal bastion, wealth gaps are stark. The average black family in Boston had about $8 to its name in 2017; the average white household, $247,000. For every dollar the typical white household in Boston possessed in liquid assets (excluding cash), U.S.-born blacks had 2 cents, Caribbean blacks 14 cents, Puerto Ricans and Dominicans less than 1 cent.[31]

The future is unknown. But when population growth and economic productivity slow, as now expected in the United States,

---

30 Sharkey et al., "The Gaps Between White and Black America."

31 Federal Reserve Bank of Boston, "The Color of Wealth in Boston" at file:///C:/Users/walter/Downloads/color-of-wealth.pdf (accessed 6/25/20).

the have-gots tend to get wealthier while others run on a treadmill. The Congressional Budget Office estimates that post-tax inequality will continue to climb, with the country's top 1% earning 3.1% more each year while the bottom 20% earns just 1% per year. Established wealth grows because it takes only a small flow of new savings to steadily increase the stock of wealth. A mere 1% increase in $10 million brings in another $100,000—for another Mercedes. On $80,000 a 1% gain would net just $800—enough for a few weeks of groceries. As a result, inherited or recently acquired wealth among the rich can grow faster than overall economic output or income. Under such conditions, inherited wealth will far overshadow the earnings that others amass in a lifetime of labor. The concentration of capital with reach very high levels—levels that clash with meritocratic values and visions of social justice.[32]

Government hand-outs to big companies add to inequality. Corruption helps the have-gots. Corruption is not needed to keep the wheels turning in the United States, but business executives and other analysts believe the levels of corruption in the country are gradually increasing. In 2019, the United States was judged to be the 23rd most corrupt of 198 countries. From a possible 100 points, its score was 69—down from 73 in 2012. The least corrupt country in 2019 was Denmark, with a score of 87. Canada ranked 12th with a score of 77. China ranked 80th; Mexico, 130th; and Russia, 137th.[33] Honesty correlates strongly with high scores on the Human Development Index and other measures of societal fitness. The four Nordic countries score near the top on all measures.

Bloomberg opinion writer Matthew Winkler on July 8, 2020, blamed intensified economic woes on the president's poor handling of the pandemic. The April unemployment rate was the highest since 1948. The labor participation rate that month plummeted 2.5%—a downturn unprecedented since record keeping began. Other advanced economies had quicker rebounds after their shutdowns.

---

32 Piketty, *Capital and Ideology,* p. 26. Having inherited a fortune and multiple bailouts from his real estate tycoon father, Donald Trump could build on that foundation of money, buildings, and contacts to expand his own domain, even absorbing huge losses from failed investments in casinos and other projects. Corrupt practices, bullying, and sleazy lawyers also helped.

33 https://www.transparency.org/en/cpi/2019/results/dnk (accessed 7/3/20).

The Covid-19 pandemic exacerbated inequality. It hits poor people harder than the more affluent. Poor people are more desperate to work and earn again despite the threats to their health. Children in poor homes have fewer tools for distance-learning or quiet corners in which to study. The disease deepens stress for all Americans regardless of race. However, blacks and Hispanics suffer more than whites and all those who can work at home and still be paid. Workers in "essential" occupations--from meat packing to nursing and home care--are at greater risk, so their problems must be addressed as well as those of whites without a college degree.

VICIOUS CIRCLE: POOR HEALTH,
WEAK SCHOOLS, INEQUALITY

The interactions between health, education, and material well-being are underscored by the 2015 Nobel laureate in Economic Science Angus Deaton and his wife Anne Case. Well before the Covid-19 crisis, they found that death rates among middle-aged white Americans were increasing. Many suffered self-inflicted "deaths by despair"—by suicide (often with a gun), by drug addiction, or by alcohol. Most of those dying of despair had never finished college. They did not get the best jobs and did not benefit from the IT revolution. Indeed, many of their jobs can be swept away by robots and globalization. Few have the protections once afforded by labor unions; these individuals are less likely to marry or stay married than college grads—less likely even to *know* much less nurture their own offspring, and less likely to belong to a church.[34]

Life expectancy for most blacks is still lower than for whites, but black life expectancy is rising while that of middle-aged whites is decreasing. More blacks are acquiring higher education, but fewer whites. The socio-economic situation of many whites resembles that of blacks in the 1970s-1980s. Some Republicans tell whites: "You are not rich but at least you are white." Their minds and values distorted; many whites regard the rising equality of blacks as oppression of whites.

---

34 Anne Case and Angus Deaton, *Deaths of Despair and the Future of Capitalism* (Princeton NJ: Princeton University Press, 2020).

All these problems are sharpened by the rising power of capital and the for-profit nature of American medicine and drug-manufacture. Large companies such as Amazon are able to do their business relying heavily on IT. They make enormous profits while employing relatively few workers. Part-time employees at Amazon and many other businesses have no health insurance. Politicians—mainly Republicans—protect the interests of the rich and ignore the needs of others. They fail to use antitrust law to reduce exploitation by monopoly power. One variant of Covid-19 relief devised by Republican Senators in July 2020 cut weekly unemployment benefits from $600 to $200 while reinstating the 3-Martini lunch as a taxable business expense!

Health versus wealth? Many economists predicted that relaxing social distancing, as many GOP leaders urged, would lead to a brief period of job growth, but these gains would be short-lived. Premature reopening will be self-defeating even in economic terms, Paul Krugman warned.[35] In the summer of 2020 the predictable happened.

What had been a great country became less great as it sickened from the Republican virus. The Biden initiatives made law in 2002, described here in chapter 9, can change this orientation.

---

35 *The New York Times*, July 2, 2020.

Goethe's drama Faust has spirits of the earth chastise the dejected Dr. Faust for rejecting what is good. Their words could apply directly to Trump and Trumpists:

Woe! Woe!
You have shattered
The beautiful world
With your powerful fist.

The world is smashed, downward hurled!
A demigod has broken it to bits!
We carry

The ruins into the Void
And bemoan the beauty lost and gone!

—Choir of Spirits in *Faust* I, Lines 1607-1616

8

Before And After January 6

The GOP Campaign to Destroy Good Government

Leaders of today's Republican Party oppose Abraham Lincoln's proposition that "all men are created equal" and his hope that the United States shall have a "new birth of freedom" and "that government of the people, by the people, for the people, shall not perish from the earth."

Government of the People?

Starting with Richard Nixon's "Southern strategy" and continuing to current efforts to prevent blacks and other minorities frum voting, today's GOP does not accept that all people are created equal. Republicans do nothing to usher in "a new birth of freedom." Trump and his lieutenants repressed peaceful demonstrations for the support of causes such as "Black Lives Matter." They have sought a government *of* the upper classes, *for* the upper classes, and *by* the upper classes. To be sure, most of Trump's most avid followers—his base—are not from the upper classes. Most are from the lower and middle classes—individuals and groups who have been brainwashed into believing that Trumpism will benefit them and "make America great again"—MAGA.

Government by the People?

Gerrymandering keeps established elites—mostly middle-aged and older white men—in power. They can then set the rules for voting, making it difficult for minorities to vote; they can declare some ballots invalid; they even try to manipulate voting machines.[1]

The V-Dem *Democracy Report 2022* finds that the United States is only a fraction away from losing its status as a liberal democracy after substantial autocratization under Donald Trump.[2] The U.S. score as a "Liberal Democracy" dropped from a potential 1.00 to 0.85 in 2015 to 0.72 in 2020, driven by weakening constraints on the executive under the Trump administration. Simultaneously, polarization and government misinformation escalated and remained high in 2021.

Political use of social media exacerbated polarization. Fake news, hate speech, conspiracy theories, and distrust have intensified negative feelings, prejudice, and violence between Republicans and Democrats since the 2016 election. Polarization and misinformation culminated in a violent test for U.S. democracy: the storming of the Capitol on January 6th, 2021. Trump's false claim that he won the 2020 presidential election helped to instigate the riots. Though ultimately unsuccessful, the storming of the Capitol tested the foundations of U.S. democracy after an unprecedented post-election period of lawsuits and pressure from Trump to have the election outcome overturned. Liberal democracy in 2021-2022 was significantly weaker than before Trump came to power. Toxic levels

---

1 In states across the country, including Michigan, Colorado, Pennsylvania, and Georgia, attempts to inappropriately access voting machines sparked concern among election authorities that breaches by those looking for evidence of fraud could themselves compromise the integrity of the process and undermine confidence in the vote.

2 https://v-dem.net/media/publications/dr_2022.pdf (accessed 8/24/22).

of polarization continued to increase. Democracy survived in the United States, but under serious threat.

Of 179 countries surveyed, V-Dem found that the United States was one of 33 to have moved substantially toward "autocratization." From 2016, when Trump won the presidency, to 2021, when he involuntarily left office, the United States fell from 17th to 29th in the global V-Dem democracy rankings.

Government for the People?

The 2017 tax law ignored the decades-long stagnation of working-class wages and exacerbated inequality. By 2025 it will have raised the after-tax incomes of households in the top 1 percent by 2.9 percent—three times the 1.0 percent gain for most households in the bottom 60 percent. The tax cuts saved $61,100 for the top 1 percent and $252,300 for the top one-tenth of 1 percent. By contrast, average savings by 2025 for the lowest fifth would be just $70 and $910 for the second fifth.[3]

The tax law's tilt to the most well-off exacerbates racial inequities. While the highest-income (mostly white) households make up just 0.8 percent of all households, they receive 23.7 percent of the total tax cuts from the 2017 tax law—far more than the 13.8 percent that the bottom *60 percent* of households of all races receive. Unless modified, the 2017 law will cost $1.9 trillion over the next decade in lost revenues. The law created new opportunities for the well-advised to game the tax code to avoid taxes. The law moved U.S. international tax system towards a "territorial" system, where most profits that a U.S. parent company earns from its foreign subsidiaries are not subject to U.S. taxes.

Tax advisers and lobbyists referred to the law as a "bonanza" and a "giant present to the tax lobbying community." The creation and widespread abuse of tax shelters could cause the bill to lose even more revenue and to increase income inequality since tax avoidance is most valuable to the wealthiest individuals and corporations able

---

3   Testimony of Chye-Ching Huang, Director of Federal Fiscal Policy before the House Budget Committee, 2/27/2019 at https://www.cbpp.org/research/federal-tax/fundamentally-flawed-2017-tax-law-largely-leaves-low-and-moderate-income

to exploit those opportunities.

The 2017 law changed the Child Tax Credit in a way that largely left behind millions of working families, while doing much more for high-income families. It increased the maximum CTC from $1,000 to $2,000 per child but denied that full increase to millions of children in low-income working families. Eleven million children in low-income working families will receive just a token CTC increase of $1 to $75. However a married couple with two children making $400,000 is now newly eligible for a full $2,000-per-child CTC.

In 2021, the American Rescue Plan increased the Child Tax Credit from $2,000 to $3,600 for qualifying children under age 6, and $3,000 for other qualifying children under age 18. As of December 2021, the expanded child tax credit helped reduce child poverty by about 30%. In 2022, however, the child tax credit reverted to $2,000 per child under 17 with no advance monthly checks

The Impacts of Gerrymandering

Even in moderate states like Ohio (where this author grew up), redistricting by local authorities has let unchecked Republicans pass extremist laws that could never make it through Congress The laws being passed by Ohio's statehouse place it to the right of the deeply conservative legislature in South Carolina. How did this happen, given that most Ohio voters are not ultra-conservatives? The legislative-district maps in Ohio have been deliberately drawn so that many Republicans effectively cannot lose. As a result, the sole threat most Republican incumbents face is the possibility of being outflanked by a rival even farther to the right. David Pepper, former Chairman of the Democratic Party in Ohio explains in *Laboratories of Autocracy,* how, when a district is firmly controlled by one party, the primary process drives its representative   inexorably toward extremism until you have "a complete meltdown of democracy."[4]

The cry "Stop the Steal!" should be directed to Republicans

---

4   Because these statehouses no longer operate as functioning democracies, unknown politicians have all the incentive to keep doing greater damage and cannot be held accountable however extreme they get. This has harmed democracy in Ohio and other states across the country. David Pepper, *Laboratories of Autocracy: A Wake-Up Call from Behind the Lines* (Cincinnati: St. Helena Press, 2021).

who have used gerrymandering to win control of state governments and repress voting by persons likely to vote Democratic. Since January 2022 judges in Alabama, Georgia, Louisiana, and Ohio have found that Republican legislators illegally drew those states' congressional maps along racial or partisan lines, or that a trial very likely would conclude that they did so. In years past, judges who reached similar findings ordered new maps, or had an expert draw them, to ensure that coming elections were fair. But ideological shifts at the Supreme Court, combined with a new aggressiveness among Republicans who drew the maps, have upended that model. In November 2022 all four states used the rejected maps. Questions about their legality for future elections will be hashed out in court later.[5]

Nearly two dozen Republican state treasurers are working to thwart climate action on state and federal levels, fighting regulations that would make clear the economic risks posed by a warming world. They lobby against climate-minded nominees to key federal posts and use the tax dollars they control to punish companies that want to reduce greenhouse gas emissions.

Over the past year, treasurers in nearly half the "United" States have been coordinating tactics and talking points, meeting in private and cheering each other in public as part of a well-funded campaign to protect the fossil fuel companies that bolster their local economies.

The treasurer of West Virginia, Riley Moore, has barred several major banks—including Goldman Sachs, JPMorgan and Wells Fargo—from government contracts in his state because they are reducing their investments in coal. Moore along with the treasurers of Louisiana and Arkansas have pulled more than $700 million out of BlackRock, the world's largest investment manager, saying the firm is too focused on environmental issues. Treasurers in Utah and Idaho are pressuring the private sector to drop climate action and other causes they label as "woke."

Treasurers from Pennsylvania, Arizona, and Oklahoma have joined a campaign to thwart the nominations of federal regulators

---

5 Jane Mayer, "State Legislatures Are Torching Democracy," *The New Yorker*, August 15, 2022.

who wanted to require that banks, funds and companies disclose the financial risks posed by a warming planet. At the nexus of these efforts is the State Financial Officers Foundation, an ostensibly nonprofit organization in Shawnee, Kansas. The foundation pushes Republican state treasurers to stymie President Biden's climate agenda.[6]

At conferences, on weekly calls, and with a steady stream of emails, the foundation hosted representatives from the oil industry and funneled research and talking points from conservative groups to the state treasurers, who have channeled the private groups' goals into public policy. The Heritage Foundation, the Heartland Institute, and the American Petroleum Institute are among the conservative groups with ties to the fossil fuel industry that have been working with the State Financial Officers Foundation and the treasurers to shape their national strategy.

POLITICAL VIOLENCE: SUBVERTING TRUST IN U.S. ELECTIONS

A tectonic shift has emerged in American politics since about 2000. Differences between the two parties have become more distinct. Among voters, partisan identities have deepened. Polarization has led to calcification. Each party has become more rigid. These trends make it harder for Republicans and Democrats to compromise. For Republicans, it becomes harder to accept the result of an election if they lose.[7]

Trump and his followers approved and even encouraged violence to overthrow fully legal elections and to attack Justice Department and FBI officials for lawful exercises of government power such as the recovery of classified documents from Donald Trump's estate in Palm Beach.

---

6 David Gelles and Hiroko Tabuchi, "How an Organized Republican Effort Punishes Companies for Climate Action," *The New York Times,* May 27, 2022. The newspaper reviewed thousands of pages of internal emails and documents obtained through public records requests by Documented, a watchdog group (https://documented.net/), that shed light on the treasurers' efforts since January 2021.

7 John Sides, Chris Tausandovitch, Lynn Vavreck, *The Bitter End: The 2020 Presidential Campaign and the Challenge to American Democracy (Princeton NJ: Princeton University Press, 2022).*

The January 6 Attack: The GOP vs Liz Cheney

President Trump in 2021 and 2022 continued to assert that he won the 2020 presidential election and called on his supporters to "stop the steal." He urged them to invade the Capitol on January 6, 2021, and stop Vice President Pence from approving the Electoral College vote in favor of Joe Biden. The House Committee investigating the January 6, 2021, events found that Trump knowingly violated his constitutional obligations.

As Dana Milbank summarized the event: On January 6, 2021, an armed mob invited and incited by President Donald Trump smashed barriers, overpowered police, and stormed the Capitol. The insurrectionists scaled the scaffolding erected for President-elect Joe Biden's inauguration and proceeded to sack the seat of government for the first time since the War of 1812.

Summoned to Washington by Trump, who promised a "wild" time, and sent by him to the Capitol on January 6, 2021, to "fight like hell," the mob delayed Congress's certification of Biden's victory, sending lawmakers and staff fleeing for their lives. At least seven people died in the riot or its aftermath. And more than 140 police officers were hurt. Some 845 insurrectionists, several with ties to white-supremacist or violent extremist groups, faced charges including seditious conspiracy.[8]

Having dispatched armed attackers to Capitol Hill, Trump refused for 187 minutes to call off the assault. He agreed that Pence deserved to be executed for failing to shift the count to favor Trump. House Minority leader Kevin McCarthy and other elected Republicans initially condemned Trump's attack on democracy, but soon excused his actions and rationalized the violent insurrection itself as what the Republican National Committee called "legitimate political discourse."

Russian historian Nikolai Popov compares the invasion of the Capitol in 2021 with the storming of the Winter Palace in Petrograd by Bolshevik troops in November 1917.[9] The Bolsheviks overthrew

---

8 Dana Milbank, 'The GOP is sick. It didn't start with Trump—and won't end with him," *The Washington Post,* August 5, 2022.

9 Nikolai Popov, "Уроки трампизма [Lessons of Trumpism]," *Nezavisimaya*

the lightly protected Provisional Government that took power after Tsar Nikolas II abdicated in March. The Bolsheviks were not yet very numerous or well known in Russia. They won just 23.3 percent of the vote in nationwide elections for a Constituent Assembly held in November 1917, but they did seize power and a Communist regime held—and abused--it for the next 74 years.[10]

The January 6 chaos at the Capitol looked more like an 18th century Pugachev uprising than the relatively sedate revolution in November 1917. The January 6 events were far more violent and serious than anything done by Richard Nixon and his Watergate "plumbers." Indeed, January 6 could be the basis of a Hollywood blockbuster on a Shakespearian scale with plots involving the would-be king, the presence of his daughter and her husband, plus thousands of extras—devoted followers struggling to carry out a coup d'état.

The lesson, according to Popov, is that no country is safe from the appearance of authoritarian leaders like Hitler, Stalin, or Slobodan *Milošević* striving to make their country great again at any cost and seizing its "Winter Palace."

To understand these events, the House of Representatives established a Select Committee to Investigate the January 6th Attack on the United States Capitol. It consisted of thirteen members, most of them Democrats. Only two Republicans chose to take part—Adam Kinziger (Illinois) and Liz Chaney (Wyoming), daughter of former Vic President Dick Cheney. She became Vice Chair of the Committee chaired by Mississippi Democrat. Bennie Thompson. Cheney and Kinziger were condemned as traitors by Republicans, but Cheney put country above her own political future. Kinziger did so too but planned not to run again.

Why was the committee created? The January 6 attack emerged from a widespread social malaise. Two months before the 2020 elections, On September 24, 2020, FBI Director Christopher

---

gazeta, July 26, 2022.

10 The Socialist Revolutionary Party, receiving a plurality of the vote (37.6 percent), won the most seats. When the Constituent Assembly convened in January 1918, troops loyal to the Soviet government dispersed representatives of the non-Bolshevik parties, and the government officially dissolved the Assembly.

Wray (appointed by Trump) warned the House Committee on Homeland Security that (1) "[T]he underlying drivers for domestic violent extremism—such as perceptions of government or law enforcement overreach, sociopolitical conditions, racism, anti-Semitism, Islamophobia, misogyny, and reactions to legislative actions—remain constant." (2) "[W]ithin the domestic terrorism bucket category as a whole, racially-motivated violent extremism is, I think, the biggest bucket . . . . And within the racially-motivated violent extremists bucket, people subscribing to some kind of white supremacist-type ideology is certainly the biggest chunk of that . . . . (3) "More deaths were caused by DVEs [domestic violence extremists] than international terrorists in recent years. In fact, 2019 was the deadliest year for domestic extremist violence since the Oklahoma City bombing in 1995."

Shortly after President Biden's inauguration, the Department of Homeland Security (DHS) on January 27, 2021, issued a National Terrorism Advisory System Bulletin that due to the "heightened threat environment across the United States," in which "[s]ome ideologically-motivated violent extremists with objections to the exercise of governmental authority and the presidential transition, as well as other perceived grievances fueled by false narratives, could continue to mobilize to incite or commit violence."

The DHS "is concerned these same drivers to violence will remain through early 2021 and some DVEs (domestic violent extremists) may be emboldened by the January 6, 2021, breach of the U.S. Capitol Building in Washington, D.C. to target elected officials and government facilities." The DHS opined that "threats of violence against critical infrastructure, including the electric, telecommunications and healthcare sectors, increased in 2020 with violent extremists citing misinformation and conspiracy theories about Covid-19 for their actions...."

As the hearings began, Chairman Thompson outlined the "charges." He said that Trump was at the center of a "sprawling, multi-step conspiracy aimed at overturning the presidential election," and that he "spurred a mob of domestic enemies of the Constitution to march down to the Capitol and subvert American democracy."

The committee then outlined the classic elements of a criminal case—that the president had the means, motive, and opportunity to commit unlawful acts. The committee presented testimony from Trump's own aides and advisers that he knew the claims he was making of election fraud were untrue and that steps he was taking to overturn the results were illegal.

No defense was presented because the president's allies in Congress chose not to participate.

Vice Chair Liz Cheney reported in April 2022 that the committee had already gathered enough material to build a criminal case against the former president. "It's absolutely clear that what President Trump was doing--what a number of people around him were doing--that they knew it was unlawful. They did it anyway."

Some of the most powerful testimony came from witnesses who appeared in person to describe the toll that Trump's attempts to overturn his electoral defeat inflicted on them. Police officer Caroline Edwards spoke of the injuries she sustained as protesters stormed the Capitol. She witnessed "carnage" and "chaos" reminiscent of a war movie as her fellow officers bled and vomited on the grounds of the Capitol.

Former Attorney General William Barr testified to the committee that he had "three discussions with the president" from late November to early December 2020 in which he told Trump that the stolen-election claims were "bullshit." Ivanka Trump and her husband, Jared Kushner, also made attention-grabbing appearances. Ivanka said she believed Barr's conclusions about a lack of fraud evidence. Jason Miller, a senior figure in Trump's two presidential campaigns, also recounted in recorded testimony that several days after the election, the campaign's lead data expert, Matt Oczkowski, conveyed to the former president in "pretty blunt terms" that Trump was bound for defeat.[11]

Testimony and material evidence presented at the hearings revealed that Republican members of Congress took part in the

---

11 For the full text, see *The January 6th Report*, Preface by David Remnick and Epilogue by Jamie Raskin (New York: Celadon Books and *The New Yorker*, 2022).

scheme to overthrow the election. Witness testimony illustrated how the ceaseless stream of false claims spouted from every echelon of the Republican Party turned formerly sleepy elected offices and election-administration positions into lightning rods of scrutiny and abuse--even death threats. The evidence and testimony offered by the committee exhibited how perilously close American democracy came to a constitutional freefall. Many of the witnesses called were the individuals whose dedication to their constitutional oath and the rule of law walked the nation back from that precipice.

Panel members noted that the hearings were both an excavation of the past and a warning for the future. In the words of Chairman Bennie Thompson, "The conspiracy to thwart the will of the people is not over." Polls showed, however, that most Republican voters ignored the hearings. Still, Republicans they showed evidence of Trump-fatigue and looked for a fresh face to support in the future, another Trumpist.

Republican officeholders who refused to go along with the president's plans described threats to themselves and their families. Rusty Bowers, the Arizona Senate Majority Leader, said protesters gathered outside his house and used loudspeakers to call him a pedophile and a pervert. Two Atlanta election workers, Shaye Moss and her mother, Ruby Freeman, spoke of facing death threats and being forced to leave their home after Trump's lawyer Rudy Giuliani mentioned them by name, claiming they were "trying to steal the election."

"There is nowhere I feel safe," Ms. Freeman said.

The committee also made use of the hundreds of hours of recorded testimony from more than a thousand interviews it conducted. The committee aired tape of senior White House staff recounting how members of Congress had requested presidential pardons for their involvement in attempts to overturn the 2020 presidential results. The list included Matt Gaetz of Florida and Marjorie Taylor Greene of Georgia.

On July 21, 2022, Vice Chair Cheney noted the bravery of witnesses such as 26-year-old Cassidy Hutchinson, aide to Trump's chief-of-staff Mark Meadows. She sat alone, took the oath and testified before millions of Americans. She knew all along that she would be attacked by the ex-president and by the 50-, 60- and 70-year-old men who hide themselves behind executive privilege. But like other witnesses, she testified anyway.[12]

Cheney noted that the case against Donald Trump in these hearings was not made by witnesses who were his political enemies. The case was made by Trump's own appointees, his own friends, his own campaign officials, people who worked for him for years, and his own family. They came forward and told the American people the truth. President Trump declared victory when his own campaign advisors told him he had absolutely no basis to do so. A recording by Steve Bannon demonstrated Trump's plan to falsely claim victory in 2020--no matter the facts--was premeditated. Worse, Donald Trump believed he could convince his voters to buy it, whether he had any actual evidence of fraud or not. And this same thing continued to occur from Election Day onward through January 6th and beyond.

Trump was confident he could convince his supporters that the election was stolen no matter how many lawsuits he lost, and he lost scores of them. He was told repeatedly that the election was not stolen, there was no evidence of widespread fraud. It didn't matter. Trump was confident he could persuade his supporters to believe whatever he said, no matter how outlandish, and ultimately that they could be summoned to Washington to help him remain president for another term. President Trump's legal team, led by Rudy Giuliani, knew they had no actual evidence to demonstrate the election was stolen. Again, it didn't matter.

On January 6th, Cheney continued, Trump turned his supporters' love of country into a weapon against the Capitol and Constitution. He purposely created the false impression that America is threatened by a foreign force controlling voting machines, or that a wave of tens of millions of false ballots were secretly injected into our election system, or that ballot workers have secret thumb drives and are stealing elections with them. All complete nonsense. We must remember that we cannot abandon the truth and remain a free

---

12 Most of the following is a direct quote from Cheney's July 21, 2022, statement with a few sentences omitted and a few with italics added for emphasis.

nation. In late November of 2020, while President Trump was still pursuing lawsuits, many of us were urging him to put any genuine evidence of fraud forward in the courts and to accept the outcome of those cases. As January 6th approached, I circulated a memo to my Republican colleagues explaining why our congressional proceedings to count electoral votes could not be used to change the outcome of the election. But what [Cheney] I did not know at the time was that President Trump's own advisers, also Republicans, also conservatives, including his White House counsel, his Justice Department, his campaign officials, they were all telling him almost exactly the same thing [she] was telling [her] colleagues: There was no evidence of fraud or irregularities sufficient to change the election outcome. Our courts had ruled. It was over. Now we know that it didn't matter what any of us said because *Donald Trump wasn't looking for the right answer legally or the right answer factually. He was looking for a way to remain in office.*

Public Opinion

The hearings showed an American president faced with a stark, unmistakable choice between right and wrong. There was no ambiguity, no nuance. *Donald Trump made a purposeful choice to violate his oath of office,* to ignore the ongoing violence against law enforcement, to threaten our Constitutional order. There is no way to excuse that behavior. It was indefensible. And every American must consider this: Can a president who is willing to make the choices Donald Trump made during the violence of January 6th ever be trusted with any position of authority in our great nation again? Citizens could ask: Could today's leaders of a GOP that stood by such a reprobate anti-patriot ever be trusted?

One year after the deadly attack on the U.S. Capitol, Republicans and Democrats were deeply divided over what happened that day and the degree to which former president Donald Trump bears responsibility for the assault. Some 60 percent of Americans said that Trump bears either a "great deal" or a "good amount" of responsibility for the insurrection, but 72 percent of Republicans and 83 percent of Trump voters said he bears "just some" responsibility or "none at all." About 7 in 10 Americans said

Biden's election as president was legitimate, but that left almost 3 in 10 who said it was not, including 58 percent of Republicans and 27 percent of independents.

The survey found that 40 percent of Republicans, 41 percent of independents and 23 percent of Democrats said violent action against the government is sometimes justified.[13] In May 2022, a majority of Americans said the U.S. government is corrupt and almost a third said it might soon be necessary to take up arms against it, according to a poll by the University of Chicago's Institute of Politics. Two-thirds of Republicans and independents said the government is "corrupt and rigged against everyday people like me," compared to 51 percent of liberal voters (still a very dour view of politics).

Some 28 percent of all voters, including 37 percent of gun owners, agreed "it may be necessary at some point soon for citizens to take up arms against the government," a view held by around 35 percent of Republicans and Independents. One in five Democrats concurred.

Those polled said Trump readily accepted and even encouraged the attack from his supporters and watched violence play out on television for nearly three hours before finally making a statement telling them to go home. Despite all this, Trump still enjoyed broad support among Republicans, most of whom were more concerned about inflation, education, and crime than about January 6. About 56 percent of Americans said the 2020 elections had been fair and accurate, but that number fell to 33 percent among Republicans.

The division between conservatives and liberals continued to grow, the May 2022 poll showed. A quarter of Americans said they have lost friends over politics. More than 70 percent of Republicans and Democrats agreed that people on the other side "are generally bullies who want to impose their political beliefs on those who disagree." And half of all Americans believe the other side is misinformed about politics because of where they get their information and news, the poll found.

---

13 https://uchicagopolitics.opalstacked.com/uploads/homepage/Polarization-Poll.
 pdf.

Trump and the Espionage Act

Armed with a search warrant, the FBI raided Trump's Mar-a-Lago estate on August 7, 2022, while he was away. This event triggered a defiant response by the ex-president and his backers.

The U.S. Department of Justice investigated the former president for possible violations of the Espionage Act of 1917 and other laws meant to protect sensitive materials. The Espionage Act prohibits obtaining information, recording pictures or copying descriptions of any information relating to national defense with intent or reason to believe that the information may be used for injury of the United States or to the advantage of any foreign nation. The act goes beyond "spying" activities to include offenses involving mishandling of classified material. Under a heading that reads "Property to be seized," the warrant refers to: "All physical documents and records constituting evidence, contraband, fruits of crime, or other items illegally possessed in violation of 18 U.S.C. §§ 793, 2071, or 1519." Here is what these laws forbid:

- 18 U.S.C. §§ 793: Gathering, transmitting, or losing defense information, which carries a penalty of up to 10 years in prison.

- 18 U.S.C. §§ 2071: Concealment, removal, or mutilation generally, which carries a penalty of up to three years in prison and disqualification from holding office.

- 18 U.S.C. §§ 1519: Destruction, alteration, or falsification of records in Federal investigations and bankruptcy, which carries a penalty of up to 20 years in prison.

The Federal Bureau of Investigation recovered boxes of classified documents from Trump's Florida home. The U.S. District Court for the Southern District of Florida unsealed the warrant authorizing the search, which identifies three federal crimes that the Justice Department is looking at as part of its investigation of Trump: violations of the Espionage Act, obstruction of justice, and criminal handling of government records.

The property receipt from the search revealed that FBI agents recovered more than 20 boxes of documents some labeled top secret, secret and confidential, as well as items marked "Potential Presidential Record," "Miscellaneous Secret Documents," photos, and handwritten notes. The search locations included Trump's office, "all storage rooms, and all other rooms or areas within the premises used or available to be used" by Trump and his staff and "in which boxes or documents could be stored, including all structures or buildings on the estate."

The search was personally approved by Attorney General Merrick Garland, who said that the Department of Justice "does not take such a decision lightly" and where possible would "seek less intrusive means as an alternative to a search and to narrowly scope any search that is undertaken."[14]

Whether or not Trump ends up in criminal jeopardy, the case is already damaging to national security, said Georgetown University fellow Paul R. Pillar, who spent 28 years with the Central Intelligence Agency. Even now that the documents are in the FBI's possession, Pillar said, there may be individuals who have had access to them and now become potential targets of recruitment for foreign intelligence sources. U.S. intelligence agencies will have to mitigate the "possible damage to the sources and methods of intelligence," particularly human intelligence sources such as informants. Other governments will want to know whether any of the material might be embarrassing or damaging to them. One of the items retrieved from Trump's home was labeled "Info re: President of France."

Defiant Trump and Trumpists

A defiant Trump responded by making the baseless accusation that former President Barack Obama kept classified documents after leaving office. "President Barack Hussein Obama kept 33 million pages of documents, much of them classified," Trump wrote in a statement. "How many of them pertained to nuclear? Word is, lots!" The National Archives immediately replied that it had "assumed exclusive legal and physical custody" of Obama's presidential records after he left office. Trump claimed that, as president, he

---

14 Patsy Widakuswara, "Trump Investigated for Possible Violation of Espionage Act," *Global Security*, August 12, 2022, at https://www.globalsecurity.org/intell/library/news/2022/intell-220812-voa01.htm?

had declassified all the documents taken to Mar-a-Lago. But former Trump officials said his claim of a "standing order" to declassify documents was nonsense—"ludicrous," "ridiculous," "a complete fiction."

Some Republicans used the FBI raid to criticize the Biden administration. Elise Stefanik, a U.S. representative from New York, demanded "answers to the American people regarding Joe Biden and his administration's weaponization of the Department of Justice and FBI against Joe Biden's political opponent." Some Trumpists threatened violence against Garland, the Florida judge, and FBI people anywhere. One armed Trumpist, Ricky Walter Shiffer, attacked the FBI office in Cincinnati and engaged in a prolonged gun fight until he was shot.

Why would Republicans immediately rally around Trump after the FBI search? David French answers: "Because their entire story of the past six years teaches them that Trump is persecuted, he's God's instrument, and the Democrats (and 'deep state') are thwarting God's divine plan."[15]

The Department of Homeland Security identified "multiple articulated threats and calls for the targeted killing of judicial, law enforcement, and government officials associated with the Palm Beach search, including the federal judge who approved the Palm Beach search warrant." It also warned that certain personal information such as addresses and the identification of family members of agents had been shared online.

Complementing the poll results, other studies found a growing acceptance of violent ideologies that historically were confined to fringe elements. Extremist ideas have been laundered into the mainstream right over decades, creating an "increasing undertone of violence simmering since the early 1990s.

---

15 David French, "The case for Trump is getting more radical every year. It's not 2016 anymore," *The Atlantic*, August 19, 2022.

How Did the GOP Establishment Become an Extremist Fringe?

Donald Trump transformed the GOP from a party of law and order and anti-Evil Empire into a party that trashes the FBI and whose boss embraced a Russian dictator. "It is the greatest con of the century's greatest con man: hijacking his own party." Their fundraising e-mails ranting about the FBI search at Mar-a-Lago should be headlined: "Let's Ruin America So We Can Make Some Money Off It."[16]

But Donald Trump didn't create this noxious environment. A brilliant opportunist, he saw the direction the Republican Party was taking, spurred by Newt Gingrich since the early 1990s, and the appetites it nurtured. The onetime pro-choice advocate of universal health care reinvented himself to give Republicans what they wanted.

What we are living through today is a continuation of the GOP's direction for the past 30 years—appeals to white nationalism, sabotage of government functions, the routine embrace of disinformation, stoking the fiction of election fraud and the "big lie," and the steady degradation of democracy.[17]

Republicans and their allied donors, media outlets, interest groups, and fellow travelers have been yanking on the threads of democracy and civil society for decades. We see it in the triumph of lies and disinformation, in the mainstreaming of racism and white supremacy, in the erosion of institutions and norms of government, and in the dehumanizing of opponents and stoking of violence. Republicans have destroyed truth, decency, real patriotism, national unity, racial progress, their own party, and subverted U.S democracy. It was Newt who in 1990 poisoned the well by issuing a manual with 65 insults and abusive phrases for Republicans to deploy against Democrats: "traitors," "sick," "corrupt," "betray,"

---

16 Maureen Dowd, "Trump Sics the GOP on the FBI," *The New York Times*, August 14, 2022.

17 Dana Milbank, "In the GOP, the paranoid fringe is becoming the establishment," *The Washington Post*, August 3, 2022. For more, see Milbank, *The Destructionists: The Twenty-Five Year Crack-Up of the Republican Party* (New York: Doubleday, 2022).

"bizarre," "pathetic," "abuse of power," "anti-flag," "anti-family," "anti-child," etc. To a group of College Republicans he mused, "I think that one of the great problems we have in the Republican Party is that we don't encourage you to be nasty." Problem solved.

"The purpose of his Devil's Dictionary and his sermon on civility to peach-fuzzed Republicans was to inculcate demonization and weaponize paranoia. And so here we are, in the era of 'alternative facts', QAnon, Jewish space lasers, anti-vaxxing, birthers and Alex Jones conspiracies about the dead children of Sandy Hook being ketchup-smeared actors in a government plot to seize our AR-15s." Two decades before Trump's "big lie" about election fraud, Republican operatives intimidated the Miami-Dade County Elections Department into stopping the recount of the 2000 election results. John Ashcroft, who became attorney general after the Supreme Court's 5-4 decision in *Bush v. Gore* handed the presidency to George W. Bush, falsely claimed in 2001 that dead people had voted and that "votes have been bought, voters intimidated, and ballot boxes stuffed."

Conservative radio giant Rush Limbaugh aired the song "Barack the Magic Negro," Fox News's Glenn Beck claimed President Obama had a "deep-seated hatred for white people," and Tea Party activists chanted the n-word at black members of Congress outside the Capitol.

The Supreme Court's conservative majority stacked the deck for Republicans with its 2010 *Citizens United* decision, which made it possible for wealthy interests to flood elections with unlimited, unregulated "dark money," and its 2013 gutting of the 1965 Voting Rights Act, which invited GOP-led states to restrict voting in ways that disproportionately affect voters of color.

Thousands of Tea Party activists, on the eve of final passage of Obamacare in the House in 2010, got to within 50 feet of the Capitol. GOP lawmakers inflamed the crowd, waving signs and leading chants of "Kill the bill."

Fox News in 2011 served as the forum for Trump and others to perpetrate the "birther" libel asserting that Obama, the first black president, was not U.S.-born.

Degradation is accelerating. We see this in the determined efforts by Republican leaders to ignore, or discredit, the truths revealed by the House January 6 select committee: and to the elementary fact that the ex-president illegally took huge quantities of classified documents to Mar-a-Lago where they were stored in a slipshod fashion. Averting their gaze from these revelations, Republicans are instead looking to a familiar guide: Newt Gingrich. The former speaker, in 2022 served as a board member of the pro-Trump America First Policy Institute and as a consultant to House GOP leader Kevin McCarthy and his team.

The root problem in U.S. politics is not polarization but that one of our two major political parties has ceased good-faith participation in the democratic process. Democrats have their share of failings and misdeeds, but the scale isn't at all comparable. Only one party fomented a bloody insurrection and even after that voted in large numbers (139 House Republicans, a two-thirds majority) to overturn the will of the voters in the 2020 election. Only one party promotes a web of conspiracy theories in place of facts. Only one party is trying to restrict voting and discredit elections. Only one party is stoking fear of minorities and immigrants.

Why have Republicans become an authoritarian faction fighting democracy? Democracy is working against Republicans. In the eight presidential contests since 1988, the GOP candidate has won a majority of the popular vote only once--in 2004. As whites become a minority (less than half the U.S. population by 2045), Republicans have become the voice of white people, particularly those without college degrees who fear the loss of their way of life in a multicultural America. Whipped along by talk radio and Fox News, white grievance and white fear reinforce the tribalism and dysfunction in the U.S. political system.

When a right-wing fanatic broke into House Speaker Democrat Nancy Pelosi's home in San Francisco in October 2022, planning to kidnap and break her knee-caps, she was not there. So the intruder bashed the skull of her 82-year old husband. Did any top Republicans express their condolences? No, but a number of them, abetted by

Elon Musk on Twitter, made fun of the incident.[18]

A former professor at the Naval War College observed: "One might think that it would be easy for America, as one nation, to condemn an attempt to kidnap the woman second in line to the presidency that resulted in the beating of her husband with a hammer. As Ernest Hemingway would say: Pretty to think so. Instead, we have seen the dark heart of the Republican Party, with a reaction so callous, so flippantly sadistic, so hateful, that it all feels *irredeemable*."[19]

THE 2022 ELECTION AND THE FUTURE OF THE GOP

The 2024 midterm elections produced a repudiation of Trump-backed candidates who denied the legitimacy of the 2020 presidential election. For Trump and many Trumpists, however, these defeats were mere skirmishes in a larger war that continued.

A majority of Republican nominees on the 2022 ballot for the House, Senate and key statewide offices—291 in all—denied or questioned the outcome of the 2020 presidential election, according to a *Washington Post* analysis. But almost every Republican competing for a position that would have given them oversight of the 2024 elections and who were also "election deniers" lost their races. These included deniers running for secretary of state and governor positions in battleground states Nevada, Arizona, Pennsylvania, Wisconsin, and Michigan. One of the most extreme deniers, Kari Lake, running for governor of Arizona fell to the incumbent, Democrat Katie Hobbs.

Still, many election deniers were elected, for example, Marjorie Taylor Greene in the House of Representatives and JD Vance in the Senate. A BBC analysis found that out of 178 candidates for Congress or governor who "fully and publicly" denied that the 2020 election was legitimate, a majority—126—won, while only 48 lost.[20]

---

18 In November 2022 they included the Arizona gubernatorial contender Kari Lake, Virginia Governor Glenn Youngkin, and sitting Representative Clay Higgins. Senator John Cornyn of Texas tried to raise immigration as an issue.

19 Tom Nichols, The *Atlantic,* November 1, 2022, *at* https://www.theatlantic.com/newsletters/archive/2022/11/the-dark-heart-of-the-gop/671965/

20 Sarah Smith, "Did democracy win in US midterms?" (11/15/22) at https://www.

Voters rejected individual candidates rather than their party. Plenty of Republican candidates who accepted the 2020 election result were elected. In Georgia, Brian Kemp and Brad Raffensperger, both of whom resisted pressure from Donald Trump to overturn the 2020 result in Georgia, were easily re-elected as governor and secretary of state. They got hundreds of thousands more votes than the Republican Senate candidate in Georgia, the election denier Herschel Walker, who lost to Democrat Raphael Warnock.

CNN found that no state expected to be a presidential battleground state in 2024 will have a 2020 denier as its elections chief. Among the losers was Pennsylvania gubernatorial candidate Doug Mastriano, who would have had the power to choose his state's election chief, also lost.

Not long after many his recommended candidates lost in the 2022 midterms, Trump announced he would run again for the presidency in 2024. As Timothy L. O'Brien summed up the situation; 'Trump has a firm grip on the hearts and minds of about a third of Republican voters. A majority of Republicans identify as MAGA, and an abundance of GOP voters want Trump to run for president again. Trump will swing that loyalty like a cudgel against party elders who are considering abandoning him. They may sincerely want to court moderate Republicans and independent voters to avoid repeating the midterm debacle when the 2024 election rolls around, but Trump will start to attack them for it soon enough. It's also not clear that Republicans truly have the courage to take on Trump in a full-blooded way anyhow. After all, Senator Mitch McConnell and Representative Kevin McCarthy have been here before. They briefly decried Trump after the Jan. 6 insurrection in 2021, and then, in due time, got out of his way or went to work accommodating him once he went on the attack by propagandizing the Big Lie. McCarthy, in particular, has since become so craven about wooing MAGA-teers that he's empowered the likes of Representative Marjorie Taylor Greene."[21]

A Trumpian vise still encumbers GOP discussions about 2024 presidential contenders, Some Republicans may prefer a different

---

bbc.com/news/world-us-canada

21 "Trump Reminds Republicans He's Not Going Away," Bloomberg Opinion, November 15, 2022

candidate with a broader appeal. But if they do not back him, they risk that he will turn on them, as. Frankenstein's monster did to his enabler. Appeals to Trump based on a sense of duty or responsibility will be nonstarters. He isn't in politics for anyone other than himself —and especially not for the legions of working-class voters for whom he always says he's battling—as when he crafted a federal tax cut for the affluent and did little for working Americans. Trump's entry into the 2024 contest promises prolonged internecine warfare within the Republican Party.[22]

The upshot: Most Americans reject political extremism left or right, but Trump and Trumpists continue to divide the country and undercut democratic institutions.

---

22 Ibid.

You who are strong,

Rebuild the shattered world and beauty undone

Build it again, from within!

Begin a new life, a new way

With clear minds and bright sounds

Create and celebrate with new songs—

—CHOIR OF SPIRITS in *Faust* I, lines 1621-1626

9

REBOOTING AMERICA

To reboot a large and complex country is a difficult task that will take years. The word "reboot" implies that Americans must not merely "recover" but reinvent and orient their society toward higher levels of human development. How can Americans shift from a me-first, zero-sum orientation to one that fosters mutual gain?

Raising "human development" means helping people enjoy and utilize a greater potential to be all they can and want to be. For starters, this means good health. The U.S. system of health care needs to be revamped and upgraded so that all Americans can access good preventive, curative, and restorative treatment. The quality of life, as well as years of life, can be increased. A flurry of new laws enacted in the summer of 2022 advanced these goals. They are summarized in this chapter.

A comparison of global perceptions in 85 countries by *U.S. News & World Report* (September 27, 2022) ranked the United States the fourth "best country" in the world —below Switzerland, Germany, and Canada but just above Sweden, Japan, and Australia.[1] The United States climbed two places since 2021.

The USA ranked tops in *power* and in *agility* (the ability to adapt and respond efficiently to problems); second in *entrepreneurship*; and third in cultural influence. But it placed only 18th in social

---

1 https://www.usnews.com/news/best-countries/rankings

purpose and 21st in quality of life. With regard to social purpose, the survey found that Americans are most devoted to religious freedom; second, to property rights; third, to gender equity; They are somewhat concerned for human rights and animal rights; little concerned about the environment and climate goals; and nearly indifferent to issues of trustworthiness and racial equity.

America's improving perception abroad was linked to its changing leadership. A report from the nonpartisan Pew Research Center in June 2021 showed that a median 75% of respondents in twelve surveyed nations had confidence in President Biden to do the right thing in global affairs. That number had been only 17% for former President Trump during his last year in office. Richard Wike, director of global attitudes research at Pew, explained that "Biden is much more popular than Trump was…. there's just more confidence in his leadership, and more approval of how he approaches world affairs."

After invading Ukraine in February 2022, Russia fell 12 spots from 2021 to No. 36. Putin's ally Belarus plummeted to No. 85—the lowest-ranked country in the analysis. Former Russian vassal states Uzbekistan and Kazakhstan along with Iran and Serbia ranked in the low 80s. Ukraine moved up nine spots to No. 62, and three of its regional partners--Lithuania, Poland, and Romania--jumped at least nine spots each as well. Poland, a safe haven for Ukrainian refugees, rose from No. 43 in 2021 to No. 32 in 2022.

MEETING WORKER, CONSUMER, AND CORPORATE NEEDS

When future generations look back on how Americans responded to the worst public health crisis and the largest economic shock in nearly a century, what will they see? Will they see leaders who were stuck in old ways of thinking and tried to save the declining technologies of the past? Or will they see leaders who recognized the opportunities to build a better a smarter future—and converted a devastating crisis into a turning point? A Bloomberg analysis called on Congress to turn away from fossil fuel lobbyists and listen to mayors and business leaders close to consumer and commercial markets. Both groups for years pleaded for a major federal investment in clean energy production and delivery. The choice is clear: either invest heavily in clean energy infrastructure to create jobs and improve public health—or keep protecting polluting industries. The Trump administration consistently chose the latter, bailing out oil and gas companies.[2]

The coronavirus pandemic sharpened America's fiscal challenges, but the country was already on an unsustainable path, with structural drivers that existed long before Covid. The economic meltdown caused by the Covid-19 crisis led the Federal Reserve to flood the economy with new credit. This "whatever-it-takes" paradigm multiplied Federal government borrowing. Government debt rose from $14.6 trillion in 2017 to over $21 trillion in 2020 to more than $30 trillion in 2022. This sum exceeded the GDP of the USA ($22 trillion). It also exceeded the combined GDP of China, Japan, Germany, and the United Kingdom. There was some good news in 2022. The cumulative deficit for the first nine months of FY22 was 75 percent lower than it was through the first nine months of FY21, reflecting a large increase in revenues and an even larger decrease in outlays.[3]

Corporate debt in the United States rose from $20 trillion in early 2018 to some $23 trillion by late 2021. The unprecedented deluge of corporate credit to make up for revenue shortfalls could be used to "ensure a stronger foundation for high and durable growth that benefits more than the well-off," the economist Mohamed A. El-Erian wrote in the *Financial Times*. The other choice would be to allow companies to use the money to pad executive pay while indulging in more financial engineering.[4] One path leads to greater prosperity for all—a New Deal for the "essential workers," gig employees, and internal migrants who have taken the brunt of the Covid-19 onslaught. The other path, to crippling debt and bankruptcies.

---

2   *Turning Points*, June 13, 2020 at https://www.bloomberg.com/news/ newsletters/2020-06-13/bloomberg-new-economy-the-inevitable-chinese-superpower (accessed 6/13/20).

3   https://www.pgpf.org/the-current-federal-budget-deficit

4   Mohamed A. El-Erian," Bad things happen when finance front-ends the economy," *Financial Times*, June 11, 2020.

Zach Conine, state treasurer of Nevada, wrote in 2020: "America was built on a simple idea—that economic opportunity was the key to getting ahead." The United States and its workforce have survived in the face of downturns and recessions, always coming back stronger. In 2020, however, stagnant wages forced many workers to live paycheck-to-paycheck with minimal access to affordable health care. Conine and other state treasurers pressed for:

- A wage that workers can live on without public assistance;

- Risk-appropriate hazard pay;

- Affordable and sufficient health insurance;

- Paid time off that removes penalties for staying home if workers' presence on the job would be a risk to customers, co-workers, or themselves;

- Appropriate protective gear;

- Disability and life insurance for these workers' dependents if their ability to earn is disrupted by Covid-19;

- A contribution to retirement savings.[5]

Covid aggravated other problems at work. Surveys of workers in Massachusetts in 2020 showed that 86 percent of workers were experiencing serious stress. Many employers did not provide proper safety gear. Most essential workers did not feel safe at work. Negative patterns were worse for African-American and Latino workers.[6]

Law professor Mehrsa Baradaran suggested that we fix the big flaws propagated over the last half century by taxing the largest fortunes, breaking up large banks, and imposing market rules that prohibit the predatory behaviors of private equity firms. Government

---

5　Zach Codine in *Reno Gazette Journal*, May 4, 2020 at https://www.rgj.com/story/opinion/voices/2020/05/04/nevada-treasurer-zach-conine-new-deal-essential-workers-livable-wage-paid-time-off-health-insurance/3069358001/

6　Clare Hammonds, et al. "Stressed, Unsafe, and Insecure: Essential Workers Need a New, New Deal," Center for Employment Equity, University of Massachusetts, June 5, 2020 at https://www.umass.edu/employmentequity/stressed-unsafe-and-insecure-essential-workers-need-new-new-deal (accessed 6/20/20).

must continue to provide good roads, mail delivery, police, and other services. Private enterprise such as UPS still compete but the government needs to assure basic services to everyone. "We can move beyond the myths of neoliberalism that have led us here. We can have competitive and prosperous markets, but our focus should be on ensuring human dignity, thriving families, and healthy communities. When those goals conflict, we should choose flourishing communities over profits."[7]

Despite partisan differences, Republicans voted with Democrats for the *Infrastructure Investment and Jobs Act* signed into law by President Biden on November 15, 2021. It called for investing $110 billion of new funds for roads, bridges, and other major projects. The law aimed to rebuild America's roads, bridges, and rails, expand access to clean drinking water, ensure every American has access to high-speed internet, tackle the climate crisis, advance environmental justice, and invest in communities too often been left behind. The legislation aimed to ease inflationary pressures and strengthen supply chains by making long overdue improvements for ports, airports, rail, and roads. It sought to foster the creation of good-paying union jobs and grow the economy sustainably and equitably so that everyone gets ahead for decades to come. It aspired to add 1.5 million jobs per year during the next 10 years.

Health, Climate, Inflation

A flurry of legislation in August 2022 tried to ameliorate many of these problems. For starters, *The Inflation Reduction Act* addressed health as well as climate issues and social-economic inequality. It included record spending on clean energy initiatives, measures to reduce prescription drug prices, and a tax overhaul to ensure that large corporations pay some income taxes. Every Democrat voted in support and every Republican against the measure. The White House's loftier ambitions to expand the social safety net in the 2021 Build Back Better bill were scrapped during a roller-coaster year of negotiations among Democrats. The bill allows Medicare to

---

7   Mehrsa Baradaran, "The Neoliberal Looting of America," *The New York Times*, July 2, 2020.

negotiate prices for some but not all prescription drugs, a practice long opposed by the pharmaceutical industry. The bill extends Affordable Care Act subsidies for three years through 2025. Thus, the bill seeks to use the health care system to reduce economic inequality. The bill sets a $2,000 annual cap on the amount of money that any senior pays for drugs. After somebody hits that cap, a combination of the federal government, private insurers, and drug companies will pay the remaining bills.

The bill's benefits will flow overwhelmingly to poor, working-class and middle-class families. Its costs will be borne by increases in corporate taxes (which ultimately fall on shareholders, who tend to be wealthy) and reductions in the profits of Big Pharma. However, the pharmaceutical industry will remain profitable and continue to develop new drugs. The Congressional Budget Office estimated that the law will reduce the number of new drugs introduced over the next 30 years by a mere 1 percent.

The bill would raise about $739 billion in tax revenue, more than offsetting the $433 billion increase in proposed spending. To pay for these and other measures, the bill would establish a 15% corporate minimum tax. To reduce tax cheating the bill called for an $80 billion boost to the I.R.S. budget. The aim was to enable the agency to go after wealthy tax dodgers and to tax stock buybacks, thereby motivating corporations to invest in capital equipment and research rather than elevating their stock prices. The Congressional Budget Office estimated that the legislation package legislation would decrease the federal deficit by $102 billion over the next decade.

In spending nearly $370 billion to reduce emissions that contribute to climate change, the bill advanced efforts to create a clean energy economy. The bill could also help revive U.S. global leadership in the quest to save the planet by prodding other nations to follow suit. Two rogue Democrats, West Virginia's Joe Manchin and Arizona's Kyrsten Sinema, eked out concessions to appease their rich clients—changes that progressives felt they had to accept in order to save the bill.

The bill included $10 billion in tax credits to build electric vehicles, solar panels, and wind turbines; not all EVs would qualify, but the law provided a $7,500 tax credit for consumers to buy electric vehicles; and $9 billion for energy-efficient home retrofits for low-income Americans.

The bill offered up to $20 billion for loans to support electric vehicle plants, $20 billion to assist farmers and ranchers with climate change, and $30 billion for cities and states to transition utilities to clean electricity.

In addition, the bill aimed to boost employment in the clean-energy and clean-manufacturing sectors. How big a boost? The Political Economy Research Institute at the University of Massachusetts, Amherst estimated that the bill would create more than nine million jobs in this sector over the next ten years.

The bill did not pass unscathed: Republicans stripped a $35 monthly cap on insulin co-pays. Many features of Biden's 2001 agenda were omitted. They included the enhanced child income-tax credit to reduce child poverty; paid leave; guaranteed pre-school for four-year olds; expanded child care; a reversal of the high-income tax cuts in Trump's 2017 tax bill; and an end to the carried-interest loophole for private equity and hedge funds.

Americans must someday pay for the 2017 package of tax cuts that enriched an already wealthy minority. Republicans claimed that the 2017 package would "pay for itself," but it did not. Corporate-tax collections soon fell by one-third and trillion-dollar deficits ensued--with no ramp-up in social spending. Trump diverted the attentions of his less affluent followers to immigration and border walls.[8]

Biden accepted a final result that fell far short of his original aspirations for a Franklin Roosevelt-style transformation. Senator Bernie Sanders, the Vermont Independent, complained that the Inflation Reduction Act did not transform home health care, increase education funding, or offer dental and vision plans under Medicare. In spite of his reservations, Sanders joined the 49 Democratic Senators and tie-breaker Vice President Kamala Harris in approving the bill.

Mitch McConnell, the GOP leader in the Senate, denounced the

---

8   Indrees Kahloon, "The Leveller," *The New Yorker*, March 9, 2020.

bill, saying it would aggravate inflation; kill jobs with tax hikes; and make "war on American fossil fuel" at a time of high energy prices. All 50 Republican Senators voted against the bill.

Congress in August 2022 passed the *Promise to Address Comprehensive Toxics (PACT)* Act--probably the most significant expansion of benefits and services for toxic exposed veterans in more than 30 years. The bill created an entitlement program for veterans who may have been exposed to toxic waste from fires on military bases known as "burn pits." The bill expanded medical care eligibility to an estimated 3.5 million people. It projected $280 billion over the next decade for ailments tied to those exposures. It also streamlined veterans' access to such care. Republicans withdrew their support just before the Senate vote. Senator Patrick J. Toomey, Republican of Pennsylvania, tried and failed to cap the amount of money that could be put into the fund every year, a move that Denis McDonough, the Secretary of Veterans Affairs, warned could lead to "rationing of care for vets." Most GOP Senators finally approved the bill. "Before signing the PACT Act, President Joe Biden took a moment to honor comedian Jon Stewart's tireless advocacy of veterans; "We owe you big," Biden said.

Better health care could not only save money but energize the country's productive capacities, but the legislation did nothing to encourage changes in lifestyle--nothing to foster better eating habits and exercise. Fewer calories and less meat would be good for health, the pocketbook, and the environment. An aging population needs to know how to move gracefully and without injury.

Homicide is also a health risk. The United States leads industrialized countries in gun deaths. Even as the Supreme Court and some state legislatures loosened restrictions on possessing and carrying guns, Congress in June 2022 passed the first gun-control bill in thirty years. Pitifully short of the controls many critics wanted, the bill tightened background checks for young buyers and provided incentives for states to expand "red flag" laws that allow the authorities, with the approval of a judge, to disarm dangerous individuals.

All this was progress, but Congress did little to tackle racism and inequality. Unlike private-equity tycoons, poor and working-class families don't have the entire Republican Party, platoons of highly-paid lobbyists, and a certain Democratic senator from Arizona looking out for their interests. Unlike green-energy producers and manufacturers of electric vehicles, most Americans are not making hefty investments that need tax breaks to push the economy away from fossil fuels. So their needs must wait.

INEQUALITY AND EDUCATION

Education must be improved for people of all ages--from pre-school to middle-aged and older Americans. We must see and treat teachers as no less valuable than engineers and lawyers. To improve education costs money—teachers' salaries, school buildings, equipment, clean streets, and public safety. The United States already pays handsomely for education but even greater—and much wiser—investment is needed. Gaps in educational opportunities must be narrowed between affluent and other communities. Paying for schools from the local tax base gets you nowhere, because some communities operate with much higher property taxes than others. Subsidies from other sources, public and private, are needed to help schools in poorer districts achieve a better learning environment. Funds saved from exorbitant medical and military outlays could go to instead to narrowing these gaps.

Technology must be developed to enhance life and not just divert us from boredom. Not everyone wants or needs a degree in liberal arts or science, but nearly everyone needs training for the skills required to function in a technologically sophisticated economy. The Department of Education needs to make sure that every student has his or her own computer. Unless America's schools generate more students who pursue technical training or college, inequalities in education, housing, and even in aspiration will continue.

JUMP-STARTING AMERICA

Americans have the knowledge and the means to raise human development, but they lack the vision that guided the country under Thomas Jefferson and some other presidents.[9]

---

9   After the Louisiana Purchase in 1803, Jefferson commissioned the Louis and

A major biggest gap in U.S. politics is trust in science and its capacity to elevate the human condition, as fostered by the 18[10] century Enlightenment.[10] We know that Benjamin Franklin and Thomas Jefferson shared this vision. So, in his way, did Theodore Roosevelt. Franklin Roosevelt and Harry Truman were not men of science, but they were open to the wisdom and practical suggestions of the best minds. FDR and then Harry Truman came to trust Vannevar Bush, whom Robert Zoellick calls "Inventor of the Future."[11] Confident in this MIT scientist and holder of many patents, Roosevelt let him supervise not only the Manhattan Project but the labs that enhanced radar and cryptography. In 1944, FDR asked Bush, "What's going to happen to science after the war?" Bush replied with a paper entitled, "Science, the Endless Frontier," It called for governmental funding of basic research in peacetime—in partnership with universities and industry—to discover the "largely unexplored hinterland" of science. Bush wrote that "scientific progress is one essential key to our security as a nation, to our better health, to more jobs, to a higher standard of living, and our cultural progress." His views led to creation of a military-industrial-academic network that gave the United States an unmatched technological edge in world affairs. Bush also launched programs that led to the National Science Foundation and National Institutes of Health. More generally, Bush persuaded FDR and then Truman to create a synergy fusing the best of government, universities, and industry.

Contrast the Enlightenment outlook of earlier times with the "what's in it for me" outlook of former president Trump and the Republican politicians who embraced him. Trump had little interest in any idea or fact except as it could bolster his political or financial interests. His "know-nothing" perspective is shared by a large segment of the voting public. Trump's rejection of serious

---

Clark expedition to explore and map the newly acquired territory. He wanted to establish an American presence in this territory before European powers claimed it. The campaign also surveyed the area's flora, fauna, and geography and sought to establish trade with Native American tribes.

10 Steven Pinker, *Enlightenment Now: The Case for Reason, Science, Humanism, and Progress* (New York: Viking, 2018).

11 Robert B. Zoellick, *America and the World: A History of U.S. Diplomacy and Foreign Policy* (New York: Twelve, Hachette Book Group, 2020), pp, 291-314.

science weakened America's response to Covid-19. Trump and GOP defunded all science and culture except for military R&D, even as they offered more subsidies to polluters.

Thanks to Vannevar Bush and others, the United States in the decades that followed World War II, led the world in innovation, creating new sectors such as jet aircraft, life-saving drugs and vaccines, microelectronics, satellites, and digital computers. Widespread innovation boosted productivity. Household income increased faster than ever before, while inequality declined.

Since the 1970s, however, U.S. productivity growth has slowed. Total GDP growth slowed from 4% in the postwar years, to under 3% from the mid-1970s, to under 2% since 2000. Some estimates projected growth in the mid-2020s of only 1.7%. The best jobs are still in a small number of superstar cities. Many people elsewhere feel left behind.

The innovation that led to rapid growth after World War II was the direct result of a fruitful partnership between the private sector, federal government, and universities that allowed Americans to generate and benefit from these spillovers as a country. Almost every major innovation in this era relied on federal support, provided by both Democratic and Republican administrations. Public spending on research and development peaked at nearly 2% of GDP in 1964. Today, however, public funding for R&D amounts to no more than 0.7 percent of total economic output. Lower public investment in science has contributed to the slowdown in productivity growth.

America faces the imminent prospect of falling behind other nations in science and technology. Around the world, including in China, government-supported research initiatives are helping to create the technologies of tomorrow. The great minds and great universities are still great but need to be mobilized—not ostracized. There may be another Vannevar Bush out there, perhaps in Seattle, in Silicon Valley, in North Carolina's Research Triangle, or inside Interstate 95 encircling Boston.

To change the trajectory of social and economic inequality will require major changes in education, technological training, and access to capital. What to do? Here are some guidelines proposed by two economists at MIT:

- First, expand federal funding for basic science, as well as for the technology development that creates jobs through commercialization.

- Spread the benefits much more broadly across the country. There are more than 100 urban communities that could become next-generation tech hubs—all with large populations, highly educated workforces, and a low cost of living. They include Albuquerque, NM; Baton-Rouge, LA; Columbia, SC; Wichita, KS, Dayton, OH; and Idaho Falls/Pocatello, ID.

- Create a national competition for municipalities to become new technology hubs. Potential hubs should increase the supply of skilled workers, make higher education more affordable, and provide technical training for those with only a high school-level education. Create an Innovation Dividend so that capital appreciation and rents from these hubs would flow to all Americans—something like the Alaskan fund that redistributes oil royalty revenue.[12]

Many of these proposals were addressed by the *CHIPS and Science Act of 2022,* enacted in August with wide bipartisan support. The act sets aside $52.7 billion for the research, development and domestic manufacturing of semiconductors; $39 billion of which goes toward incentivizing manufacturers, with $2 billion being used to create existing/legacy chips for automotive and defense industries. Another $13.2 billion will be invested in R&D and workforce development.

"CHIPS" stands for "Creating Helpful Incentives to Produce Semiconductors." The act provides major funding increases for the Department of Energy's Office of Science, the National Science Foundation and the National Institute of Standards and Technology. It also sets out new policies for NASA, including extending support

---

12 Jonathan Gruber and Simon Johnson, *Jump-Starting America; How Breakthrough Science Can Revive Economic Growth and the American Dream* (New York: Public Affairs, 2020).

for the International Space Station through 2030 and reorganizing a program for sending humans back to the moon and eventually to Mars.

Because so many fields rely on computer chips, the new law's effects will go well beyond the semiconductor industry, according to Russell Harrison at the Institute of Electrical and Electronics Engineers.[13] The bill funds worker training at all levels. Large chunks of this country are not yet involved in the 21st-century economy. The CHIPS Act deliberately tries to change that through regional technology hubs and investments in underserved communities. Investments in workforce development go beyond graduate students to include undergrad research and vocational/ professional training, certification programs, and community colleges. Sixty percent of expected jobs in this field do not need a college degree, but they do require training to build robots, repair robots, run cybersecurity systems. These are well-paying jobs and are essential for this entire operation. The CHIPS Act tries to pull in parts of the country not yet engaged in this work. It should raise prosperity across the United States in the long run and give a boost to diversity, To bring in populations that are not currently engaged in the STEM fields, it aims to bring the industry to them.

In August 2022 Michigan Governor Gretchen Whitmer signed an executive order focused on the act. "It's important for us to make things in America," the governor said. "We're making a once in a century investment in industry and bringing the supply chain from China to Michigan." The choice of location was clear, given Michigan has come to represent both the rise—and decline —of U.S.-based manufacturing in the auto industry.

CAN WE REINVENT POLITICS?

Trump, like George W. Bush, was voted president by the Electoral College even though he garnered fewer popular votes than his Democratic rival. The system is stacked so that states with smaller populations, such as Nevada, have more clout, per capita, than those

---

13 https://www.scientificamerican.com/article/nearly-53-billion-in-federal-funding-could-revive-the-u-s-computer-chip-industry/

with larger populations, such as California. This unfairness has been multiplied by gerrymandering. District maps in many states have been redrawn to concentrate likely Democratic voters in a few districts.

The impact of gerrymandering is heightened by repression of minority voting by Republican-controlled legislatures and Republican secretaries of state responsible for voting procedures and vote counts.

"How to help a nation in crisis emerge with a more resilient democracy? Our ties to one another are fragile. The very institutions that should be the instrument of our freedom and the source of our protection appear to fail us. We do not trust them; we do not trust one another. In fear for and anxiety about our own prospects, we turn on one another. We starve our constitutional democracy of the nourishment it needs, closing our hearts to our fellow citizens." This the challenge as seen by a bipartisan commission convened by the American Academy of Arts & Sciences to remold America's body politic. After two years of study, the commission proposed a broad program with six major goals and many ways to advance them. Its report is entitled *Our Common Purpose: Reinventing American Democracy for the 21st Century.*[14] Here are its major goals:

Strengthen Equality of Voice and Representation

Expand the House of Representatives (and therefore the Electoral College) by at least fifty members. Institute universal voting and instant voter registration for all eligible Americans. Support adoption, through state legislation, of independent citizen-redistricting commissions in all fifty states. Amend the Constitution to regulate election contributions and eliminate undue influence of money in our political system. Pass clean election laws for federal, state, and local elections through public matching donation systems and democracy vouchers to amplify the power of small donors.

---

14 For details, see the 73-page report at https://www.amacad.org/sites/default/ files/publication/downloads/2020-Democratic-Citizenship_Our-Common- Purpose_0.pdf (accessed 6/12/20). The commission was headed by Danielle Allen, Harvard University; Stephen Heintz, Rockefeller Brothers Fund; and Eric Liu, Citizen University. Most of the commission's s thirty-two members were university professors, foundation executives, or journalists.

Empower Voters

Make voting in federal elections a requirement, like jury duty, for all citizens. Introduce ranked-choice voting in presidential, congressional, and state elections. Give people more choices about where and when they vote and implement convenient vote centers and early voting. Change federal election day to Veterans Day and ensure that voting can occur on a day when many people have off from work. Establish same-day registration and universal automatic voter registration. Establish the preregistration of sixteen- and seventeen-year-olds and provide education to practice voting.

Restore federal and state voting rights to citizens with felony convictions upon their release from prison. Promote electoral reforms to increase representation and decrease hyper-partisanship. Increase resources and resolve for community leadership, civic education, and an American culture of shared commitment to constitutional democracy and one another.

Bolster Responsiveness of Government Institutions

Encourage widespread participation in official public hearings and meetings at local and state levels. Promote experimentation with citizens' assemblies to enable the public to interact directly with Congress. Establish eighteen-year terms for Supreme Court justices with appointments staggered such that one nomination comes up during each term of Congress.

Expand Civic Bridging Capacity

Establish a National Trust for Civic Infrastructure to scale up democratic infrastructure. Fund the Trust with a major nationwide investment campaign that bridges private enterprise and philanthropic seed funding. Persuade funders to invest in the leadership capacity of the so-called civic one million: the catalytic leaders who drive civic renewal.

Build a Civic Information Architecture that Supports Common Purpose

Establish a Democratic Engagement Project—a new data source and clearinghouse for research on civic infrastructure and democratic engagement in digital contexts. Subsidize innovation to reinvent the public functions that social media have displaced. Tax digital advertising to support public social media platforms as well as local investigative journalism. Establish for-profit social media platforms to support public-friendly digital spaces.

Establish an expectation of national service by all Americans. Create a "Telling Our Nation's Story" initiative to engage communities in open-ended conversations about the evolving American story. Launch a philanthropic initiative to support a civil society ecosystem to foster civic values. Increase public and private funding for media campaigns and grassroots narratives about how to revitalize constitutional democracy. Invest in civic education for all ages and all communities through curricula, program evaluations, professional development for teachers, and a federal award program that recognizes civic-learning achievements.

AMERICA'S VALUES

The main problem with America's democracy is a political culture that has spawned a cult of selfishness. The Economist Intelligence Unit reports that U.S. political culture has deteriorated. The country lacks a sufficient degree of societal consensus and cohesion to underpin a stable, functioning democracy. Too many Americans favor a strong leader who bypasses parliament and elections. Too few want a government that listens to experts and bases its policies on science. Too few believe that democracies are good at maintaining order. Too many trust in punishing criminals instead of rehabilitating them. Too few believe that democracy benefits economic performance. Too few accept that democracy is better than any other form of government. Too few believe in separation of Church and State.

Trump and his allies have fostered a belief that "greed is good, that we're all better off when individuals engage in the untrammeled pursuit of self-interest" and that, as Ayn Rand argued, "unrestricted profit maximization by businesses and unregulated consumer choice is the recipe for a good society."[15] This outlook

---

15 Paul Krugman, "A Cult of Selfishness Is Killing America," *The New York Times*,

supports wealthy whites at the expense of middle- and low-income whites and most non-whites. As Karl Marx predicted, the wealthy minority has shaped both the political culture and the political-economic system to perpetuate its advantages. This have-got culture and political system permitted the Trump/Republican coalition to take power and dominate American life. The Trump virus has infected our bodies, minds, and souls. It is a hydra-headed monster that must be attacked on many fronts. Reorienting the economy and reinventing the political system will help—but curtailing sheer greed and deeply rooted racism is a long-term challenge for the entire body politic.

Chris Hedges doubts that the narrow mind-sets fostered by the Alt-Right and Christian Right can be changed just by the advent of a new president. Hedges believes these attitudes are supported by billionaires and corporations that profit from ultra-conservative politicians and publics.[16] The decline the U.S. democracy will not be solved by elections. "The political rot and depravity will continue to eat away at the soul of the nation, spawning crisis cults—movements led by demagogues that prey on an unbearable psychological and financial distress."[17]

Hedges supports the concerns raised above in Chapter 2. Followers of Christian fascists "see themselves as eternal victims, oppressed by dark and sinister groups." Their leaders claim that they alone know the will of God. Accordingly, they seek total cultural and political domination. For their followers, the secular, reality-based world--where Satan, miracles, destiny, angels, and magic do not exist—destroyed their lives and communities. "The only thing that saved them was their ... realization that God had a plan for them."[18]

July 27, 2020.

16 Hedges is an anarchistic-vegan-Presbyterian minister living with his wife and children in Princeton, NJ.

17 These crisis cults of the Christian Right and Donald Trump peddle magical thinking and an infantilism that promise prosperity, a return to a mythical past, with order and security.

18 Chris Hedges, "Onward, Christian Fascists," *Truthdig*, December 30, 2020, at https://www.truthdig.com/articles/onward-christian-fascists/ (accessed 8/20/20).

Reason, facts, and verifiable truth are impotent against this belief system, says Hedges. We can blunt the rise of Christian fascism "only by reintegrating exploited and abused Americans into society, giving them jobs with stable, sustainable incomes, relieving their crushing personal debts, rebuilding their communities, and transforming our failed democracy into one in which everyone has agency and a voice."

These tasks must be integral to any effort to reboot America.

Despite the many challenges facing America and the world, the director of the Smithsonian Institution, Lonnie O. Bunch III, found reasons for hope. "There's no doubt that this is a partisan time. But you can't be a historian of black America [as Bunch is] without being hopeful. Because this is a group of people who, in many ways, believed in a country that didn't believe in them. So for me, there is always hope. There is always resilience. That also is what inspires me to always tell the unvarnished truth. And I would argue that in a partisan time what you need more than anything else is clarity based on scholarship, understanding, and trying to find reconciliation and truth." His advice: "The work you do shouldn't be about you. It should be about the greater good. It should help people understand themselves better."[19]

To reboot America will be an uphill struggle. The long-term answer to forming a constructive political culture lies in education and, more generally, the upbringing shaped by family, the media, and institutions such as schools, churches, and civic organizations. To reboot America is a job for every citizen.

WHY ALL AMERICANS SHOULD VOTE AGAINST TRUMPISTS

Think About Your Kids

Trump Republicans set a bad example for our children—not just their boundless greed and intolerance but also their indifference to truth and science. You don't want your kids to become like Trumpist Republicans—

---

19 Lonnie G. Bunch III interviewed by KK Ottesen in *The Washington Post*, June 23, 2020.

- professional liars, frauds, con artists;

- sexist—abusive or condescending to women and transsexuals;

- misinformed about political and social realities;

- dumb—indifferent to knowledge, truth, and the arts;

- racist—abusive or condescending to anyone because of skin color;

- bigoted—intolerant of others' religious and other beliefs;

- crude—with vulgar speech or manners;

- blindly self-centered and thinking only of themselves.

Trump Republicans stiffed public education and defunded science. They ignore that our way of life depends on educated people who create and sustain advances in science, technology, and medicine; an infrastructure of roads, bridges, cars, trains, and airplanes for safe travel; vibrant media, arts, and entertainment for mental and emotional wealth. If you have become rich (and even you attended a private school), public education has made your wealth possible. We need to make it better.

Think About Health

You want good health not only for your family and friends but for everyone. Your own well-being requires the well-being of all Americans. Prevention is the best medicine. Good health begins with how each of us lives. But if anyone needs medical advice or treatment, a strong health care system must be there and be accessible. There is no need for a costly layer of intermediaries— insurance companies and accountants. Support universal health care.

Think About Wealth

Despite claims to be the party of business, Republicans have usually been bad for the economy. Their cupidity and myopia helped bring on the Panic of 1873, the Great Depression of 1929, and the Great Recession of 2008. Thanks in large part to President Trump's mishandling of Covid-19, the U.S. economy contracted at 5% in the first quarter of 2020 and nearly 10% in the second quarter; at 3.5% for the year. The United States economy lost 9.4 million jobs in 2020, and the unemployment rate was at 6.7% at the end of December. The largest *yearly* drop in GDP between the 1930s and 2020 was 10% in 1958—under another Republican president, Dwight D. Eisenhower.[20]

Economic booms under Democrats have been broader and deeper than under Republicans. Economic growth under Democrats has involved technology, media, bio-sciences, pharmaceuticals, construction and infrastructure, green economy, finance, and housing. Republican booms, as under Ronald Reagan, have centered on defense, security, prisons, and fossil fuels. Republican tax cuts have ballooned deficits to dangerous levels. With have-gots writing the laws, many large corporations pay little or nothing in taxes. Many exploited tax havens such as Grand Cayman and Ireland.

Wall Street growth does not mean greater well-being for Main Street. But investors should know that stock markets have done better under Democrats than under Republicans. From 1926 to 2019, we have had a Republican president for 46 years, and a Democratic president for 48 years. The average annual return for the S&P 500 index under Republican presidents was 9.12%. Under Democratic presidents, the S&P 500 grew at an average 14.94% per year—a premium of a better than 5.8% per year on average.[21] A comparison of economic performance under Democratic and Republican presidents from 1945 to 2012 showed that the most successful were three Democrats—Harry S. Truman, John F. Kennedy, and Lyndon B. Johnson. The bottom three were George H. W. Bush, Jimmy Carter, and George W. Bush. Bill Clinton placed sixth and Richard

---

20 This was the worst quarter since at least 1875. The runners-up were the third quarter of 1893 and the fourth quarter of 1937—with declines of 8.4 percent and 7.2 percent respectively. Since 1947, when GDP measurement began, no quarter had seen a decline of even 3 percent. The worst was 2.6 percent in 1958. Rachel Siegel and Andrew Van Dam, "U.S. economy contracted at fastest quarterly rate on record from April to June [2020] as coronavirus walloped workers, businesses," *The Washington Post*, July 30, 2020.

21 Rhymer Rigby, "The super-rich have a history of doing well out of a global crisis," *Financial Times,* June 14, 2020.

Nixon seventh.[22] As of 2012, Ronald Reagan ranked eighth and Barack Obama ninth. By the end of Obama's second term, however, his record improved. The DJ index stood at 6,627 at the beginning of Obama's first term (March 6, 2009) and had tripled by the end of his second term—to 19,763 by January 20, 2017. If Trump's stock market were to achieve the same percentage increase, it needed to reach 39,349 by January 20, 2021.[23] As of late summer 2020, however, the DJ was about 28,000. The economy under Trump resembled the pattern under George W. Bush—an upward spurt thanks to tax cuts followed by a slump and larger deficits.[24]

How wealth is distributed is no less important than the size of the "pie." The more that all people benefit from the country's wealth, the more the economy can grow. The real wealth of working and middle-class Americans has not improved much for fifty years. Republican policies have enriched the rich and widened the wealth gaps. Republicans have thwarted Democrat efforts to better the material conditions of all Americans. Wealth gaps have become extreme. More poverty means less consumption, less productivity, larger emergency room bills, fewer taxes collected, more deficit, more crime, less security, more social unrest—and higher prospects of revolutionary chaos.

Think About Politics

If a country is run by corrupt, incompetent leaders who believe they are above the law, eventually everyone will lose. If you believe that every vote should have equal value, you must work to

---

22 Richard J. Carroll compared the twelve presidents using seventeen economic indicators including growth in GDP, unemployment, inflation, population below the poverty line, increase in the DJ Industrial Average, savings and investment rates, exports and trade balances, federal budget growth, and debt and federal taxes as a share of GDP. See his *The President as Economist: Scoring Economic Performance from Harry Truman to Barack Obama* (Santa Barbara, CA: Praeger, 2012).

23 Richard. J. Carroll, "Setting the Baseline for Trump's Economy," March 3, 2017 at https://www.bloomberg.com/opinion/articles/2017-03-03/setting-the-baseline-for-trump-s-economy (accessed 6/30/20).

24 Richard J. Carroll, May 3, 2019 at https://www.bloombergquint.com/opinion/trump-s-economy-could-mimic-george-w-bush-s (accessed 8/2/20).

stop gerrymandering and other tricks that minimize the weight of minorities. If you don't like rule-of-thieves kleptocracy, indifference to foreign election meddling, ousters of inspectors general and whistle-blowers, and other White House grabs for absolute power, you must vote against Trumpist Republicans.

Think About the Weather

You and everyone else needs clean air, water, soil, and a stable climate. But Republicans are gutting environmental protection and ignoring the potential of clean energy. They deny what is there for all to see and feel and suffer. Everybody needs a Green New Deal.

Think About the World

Peace and prosperity benefit from a strong United States that supports world order and development. Democrats and Republicans have contributed to these goals, but leaders in both parties have also made serious mistakes in foreign affairs. Our greatest foreign policy achievements such as Europe's reconstruction took place under Democrat Harry Truman. That darling of the GOP George W. Bush initiated our greatest foreign blunder, the Middle East wars that continued under Donald Trump. Republican presidents Reagan, George W. Bush, and Trump bloated Pentagon budgets, enriching a few but harming most Americans—as well as destroying a balanced budget.

Many Republicans in times past (such as Teddy Roosevelt) were open to the world. They saw global interdependence as a reality—one that, if managed well, could benefit all parties. Trump has treated trade and other dimensions of foreign policy as tools to enhance his own wealth and political power. Nearly all Republicans have approved or acquiesced in his self-aggrandizement.

Trump alienated staunch allies and kowtowed to hostile dictators. Benefiting from Kremlin support, he ignored or downplayed Russian as well as Chinese violations of human rights and international law. Trump eviscerated the "city on the hill" ideal of virtue and freedom and replaced it with a model of venal greed mocked and despised by people of good will.

Conservatives and independents as well as progressives should reject today's Trump's GOP and vote to reboot America.[25]

---

25 A former lead speechwriter for President Reagan concedes that "the two-party system is a mess and a great daily frustration. But in the end, together and in spite of themselves, both parties still function as a force for unity." If Democrats win the White House and all of Congress, they will launch a runaway train of spending. "When the Trump experience is over, the Republican Party will have to be rebuilt....It won't be enough to repeat old mantras or formulations from 1970 to 2000." Peggy Noonan, "Burn the Republican Party Down?" *The Wall Street Journal, July 30, 2020.*

AFTERWORD

What Any Politician Could Learn from Our Shih-Tzu Eddie

Here is Eddie's advice—to dogs, humans, and even to politicians. It is nearly the opposite of the amoral code of Republican elites. For Eddie, size and prestige are not decisive: he weighs just 18 pounds, but he deals with other beings large and small as equals.

1. *Always tell the truth.* Eddie practices unflinching honesty. He lets you know exactly what he is feeling. When he likes some human or another dog, he wags his tail. When depressed or sad about something, he bends his head and tail downward. When the people around him are happy, he smiles. His eyes glisten and open wide. When happy and off-leash, he runs full steam in large loops around the yard. But if he has reason to distrust some other being, he withdraws or barks.

2. *You are not the center of the cosmos.* Some people may give you the idea that you are the center of everything, but you are not. We are all here for a short time. Do what you can to make the most of it.

3. *Be open to what each being has to offer.* You will find that most humans, dogs, and other beings are open to friendship. If you show them good will and warmth, many if not most will respond in kind.

4. *Be nice to others with no expectation of reward.* Do not demand something in exchange for whatever you offer or bring to the table.

5. *Respect each gender.* Treat females and males equally and respect their personal space.

6. *Look for mutual gain* Yes, some persons and dogs see everything as a contest. They act as though everything is winner-take-all—as though only one could get a bone or other valued object. Better to act as though sharing is better than grabbing. Less growling and more play.

7. *Keep a healthy balance between sitting, walking, running.* If you have been sedentary for some time, yawn and stretch fully. Do what yogis call upward-facing dog and downward-facing dog. Roll on your back and shake your limbs. Good exercise is free; medical attention and medicines are not.

8. *Be loyal to your master.* For the president, this means the people you have been elected to serve--not whoever gives you a treat.

9. *Don't pout.* If you feel bad, keep it to yourself or share your problem with a friend—not with the whole world.

10. *Try to make others happy.* Try to associate with beings you like and trust. If you can do a trick that amuses and the setting is right, smile, and perform the trick. But don't just be a show-off.

11. *Watch your manners.* Be a warm host and a courteous visitor or guest. Don't bully others or try to dominate a social event. Hold back most of the time and let others do their thing.

12. *Keep regular hours.* We all need sleep to be our best. Sleep-deprived, we become sluggish, cranky, and disjointed. Stay away from electronic devices. TV programs and telephones get in the way of clear thinking and effective action. If you stay up late one night, next day go to a quiet place and take a nap and refresh.

13. *Be tidy and neat.* Keep your hair neat and clean. Wash everywhere.

14. *Be content with you as you are.* Don't depend on praise to find satisfaction.

15. *Do what you can to fulfill your own potential and make the world a better place.* Win or lose, being good is its own reward.

16. *Still, do not let down your guard.* There are mean persons and mean dogs. If you have reason to fear or distrust another being, keep a safe distance. Observe them carefully but know that your first impressions can be wrong.

ACKNOWLEDGEMENTS

For their many suggestions and moral support, the author thanks Ronald H. Linden, Stephen Advocate, Christopher Miller, Mel Gurtov, Igor Lukes, and Tamer Balci. Daniel Gutierrez-Sandoval, Executive Director of the Policy Studies Organization, has supported this project in many ways. Ali Ho Clemens has vetted ideas and overcome many challenges of modern technology. Any errors are mine alone. The children, grandchildren, and great grandchildren mentioned in the dedication helped motivate many slogs through the detritus of Trump and Trumpism.

ABOUT THE AUTHOR

The author, his daughter, and their dog

WALTER CLEMENS has analyzed the United States and the world for over 50 years. He has taught at Iolani School, the University of California, M.I.T., Salzburg Seminar in American Studies, University of the West Indies, and Boston University, where he is Emeritus Professor of Political Science. Since 1963 he has been Associate, Harvard University Davis Center for Russian and Eurasian Studies. Supported by the Ford Foundation, Rockefeller Foundation, the Fulbright Program, and the U.S. Information Agency, he has lectured on world affairs across the United States, Asia, Europe, Latin America, North Africa, and the Soviet Union. He has conducted research at the University of Vienna, Moscow State University, Hoover Institution, UCLA, and the Wilson Center. Ph.D. and M.A, Columbia University; A, B., *Magna Cum Laude,* Notre Dame University.

Raised in Cincinnati, Ohio, where he voted Republican, Clemens lives near Boston with his wife, daughter, and Shih-Tzu Eddie, featured in the book's Afterword. He has been Book Review Editor, *Asian Perspective* and a regular contributor to *Global Asia* and *New York Journal of Books*. His essays have been published in *The New York Times*, *The Wall Street Journal*, *The Washington Post*, *Financial Times*, *Christian Science Monitor*, *Europe's Edge*, *The Hill*, *The Times* (London), *Der Standard* (Vienna), and *Sovetskaya Estoniya* (Tallinn).

For details, see https://en.wikipedia.org/wiki/Walter_Clemens or http://www.bu.edu/polisci/people/faculty/clemens/ His paintings are at waltclemens.art.

ALSO BY THE AUTHOR

North Korea and the World: Human Rights, Arms Control, and Strategies for Negotiation

Complexity Science and World Affairs, Foreword, Stuart A. Kauffman.

Ambushed! A Cartoon History of the George W. Bush Administration, with Jim Morin.

Dynamics of International Relations: Conflict and Mutual Gain in an Era of Global Interdependence

Bushed! What Passionate Conservatives Have Done to America and the World, with Jim Morin.

National Security and U.S.-Soviet Relations

The Baltic Transformed: Complexity Theory and European Security, Foreword, Jack F. Matlock, Jr.

America and the World, 1898-2025: Achievements, Failures, Alternative Futures

Baltic Independence and Russian Empire

Can Russia Change?

The USSR and Global Interdependence

The Superpowers and Arms Control

Die Tschechoslowakei unter Husak

The Arms Race and Sino-Soviet Relations

Outer Space and Arms Control

Co-author, *Khrushchev and the Arms Race*

Co-author and editor, *World Perspectives on International Politics*

Co-author and editor, *Toward a Strategy of Peace*, Foreword, Robert F. Kennedy.

Soviet Disarmament Policy, 1917-1963: An Annotated Bibliography of Soviet and Western Sources

INDEX

Related Titles from Westphalia Press

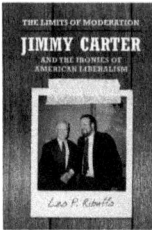

The Limits of Moderation: Jimmy Carter and the Ironies of American Liberalism
by Leo P. Ribuffo

The Limits of Moderation: Jimmy Carter and the Ironies of American Liberalism is not a finished product. Yet, this book is a close and careful history of a short yet transformative period in American political history, when big changes were afoot. and continue to shape our world.

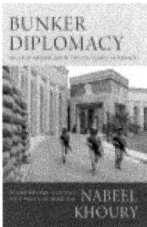

Bunker Diplomacy: An Arab-American in the U.S. Foreign Service
by Nabeel Khoury

After twenty-five years in the Foreign Service, Dr. Nabeel A. Khoury retired from the U.S. Department of State in 2013 with the rank of Minister Counselor. In his last overseas posting, Khoury served as deputy chief of mission at the U.S. embassy in Yemen (2004-2007).

Energy Law and Policy in a Climate-Constrained World
by Victor Byers Flatt, Alfonso López de la Osa Escribano, Aubin Nzaou-Kongo

This book presents reflections on concepts, foreign policy, regional and international cooperation, and the specific role the state is to play when it comes to such thing as energy law and policy.

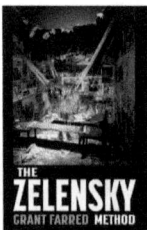

The Zelensky Method
by Grant Farred

Locating Russian's war within a global context, The Zelensky Method is unsparing in its critique of those nations, who have refused to condemn Russia's invasion and are doing everything they can to prevent economic sanctions from being imposed on the Kremlin.

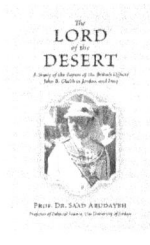

The Lord of the Desert: A Study of the Papers of the British Officer John B. Glubb in Jordan and Iraq
by Dr. Sa'ad Abudayeh

John Bajot Glubb, a British engineer officer, was sent to Iraq in 1920 to resolve the problems which erupted after the Iraqi revolt. He remained in the area for ten years, working with the Bedouins. In 1930, he moved to Jordan for twenty-six successful years. He invented what Dr. Abudayeh calls the Diplomacy of Desert.

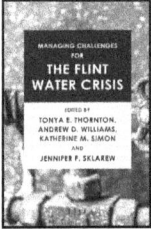

Managing Challenges for the Flint Water Crisis
Edited by Toyna E. Thornton, Andrew D. Williams, Katherine M. Simon, Jennifer F. Sklarew

This edited volume examines several public management and intergovernmental failures, with particular attention on social, political, and financial impacts. Understanding disaster meaning, even causality, is essential to the problem-solving process.

Resistance: Reflections on Survival, Hope and Love
Poetry by William Morris, Photography by Jackie Malden

Resistance is a book of poems with photographs or a book of photographs with poems depending on your perspective. The book is comprised of three sections titled respectively: On Survival, On Hope, and On Love.

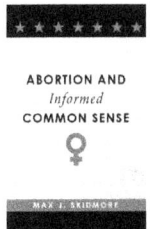

Abortion and Informed Common Sense
by Max J. Skidmore

The controversy over a woman's "right to choose," as opposed to the numerous "rights" that abortion opponents decide should be assumed to exist for "unborn children," has always struck me as incomplete. Two missing elements of the argument seems obvious, yet they remain almost completely overlooked.

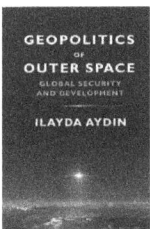

Geopolitics of Outer Space: Global Security and Development
by Ilayda Aydin

A desire for increased security and rapid development is driving nation-states to engage in an intensifying competition for the unique assets of space. This book analyses the Chinese-American space discourse from the lenses of international relations theory, history and political psychology to explore these questions.

The Athenian Year Primer: Attic Time-Reckoning and the Julian Calendar
by Christopher Planeaux

The ability to translate ancient Athenian calendar references into precise Julian-Gregorian dates will not only assist Ancient Historians and Classicists to date numerous historical events with much greater accuracy but also aid epigraphists in the restorations of numerous Attic inscriptions.

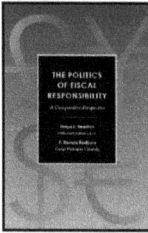

The Politics of Fiscal Responsibility: A Comparative Perspective
by Tonya E. Thornton and F. Stevens Redburn

Fiscal policy challenges following the Great Recession forced members of the Organisation for Economic Co-operation and Development (OECD) to implement a set of economic policies to manage public debt.

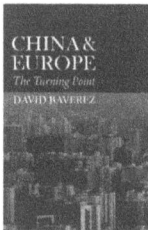

China & Europe: The Turning Point
by David Baverez

In creating five fictitious conversations between Xi Jinping and five European experts, David Baverez, who lives and works in Hong Kong, offers up a totally new vision of the relationship between China and Europe.

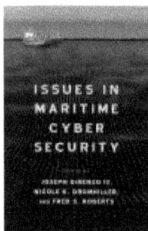

Issues in Maritime Cyber Security
Edited by Dr. Joe DiRenzo III, Dr. Nicole K. Drumhiller, and Dr. Fred S. Roberts

The complexity of making MTS safe from cyber attack is daunting and the need for all stakeholders in both government (at all levels) and private industry to be involved in cyber security is more significant than ever as the use of the MTS continues to grow.

Freemasonry, Heir to the Enlightenment
by Cécile Révauger

Modern Freemasonry may have mythical roots in Solomon's time but is really the heir to the Enlightenment. Ever since the early eighteenth century freemasons have endeavored to convey the values of the Enlightenment in the cultural, political and religious fields, in Europe, the American colonies and the emerging United States.

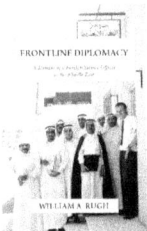

Policy Studies Organization

www.ingramcontent.com/pod-product-compliance
Lightning Source LLC
Chambersburg PA
CBHW062049270326
41931CB00013B/3003